ONE

HOMOGENEOUS

PEOPLE

ONE HOMOGENEOUS PEOPLE

Narratives of White
Southern Identity,
1890–1920

TRENT WATTS

THE UNIVERSITY OF TENNESSEE PRESS
KNOXVILLE

Library of Congress Cataloging-in-Publication Data

Watts, Trent, 1965–
One homogeneous people: narratives of white southern
identity, 1890–1920 / Trent Watts. — 1st ed.
      p. cm.
Includes bibliographical references and index.
ISBN-13: 978-1-57233-503-5 (hardcover)
ISBN-10: 1-57233-503-3 (hardcover)
1. Southern States—Civilization.
2. Whites—Race identity—Southern States—History.
3. Group identity—Southern States—History.
4. Race awareness—Southern States—History.
5. Southern States—Social conditions—1865–1945.
6. Whites—In literature.
7. American fiction—Southern States—History and criticism.
8. Page, Thomas Nelson, 1853–1922. Marse Chan.
9. Dixon, Thomas, 1864–1946. Leopard's spots.
I. Title.

F209.W37 2010
305.800975—dc22
2010016563

For my mother,
RITA SUE GIBSON

"What I have learned from my long affair with
Mississippi is that America's greatest strength,
and its greatest weakness, is our belief that we
can always start over, that things can be made
better, transcended."

—Anthony Walton, *Mississippi:
An American Journey*

CONTENTS

ACKNOWLEDGMENTS

It is a pleasure to acknowledge the assistance that I received in writing the dissertation on which this book is based and in revising that dissertation for publication. What follows in these pages is a story of narratives and their consequences. But at the same time, this manuscript has generated many stories of its own, and along the winding road to its completion, not a few consequences as well.

I owe a great debt to Scot Danforth, the director of the University of Tennessee Press. As an acquisitions editor, Scot contacted me several years ago about this project and remained interested in it as I worked to convert it into publishable form. I appreciate his faith in the value of this book. Thanks to my friend Katie Hannah for suggesting that Scot get in touch with me in the first place. And thanks also to current acquisitions editor Kerry Webb at the University of Tennessee Press for her enthusiastic help in seeing the project through its last stages. The two readers of this manuscript made thorough and valuable suggestions for revisions. I, of course, am solely responsible for the flaws that remain.

Years ago I made my first trip to the Mississippi Department of Archives and History in Jackson to examine James K. Vardaman's papers. Anne Webster, Hank Holmes, and many other people there were welcoming and helpful.

Vardaman's papers and the rest of the material from the MDAH have now moved to the superlative quarters of the William F. Winter Archives and History Building. I have returned to Jackson many times since that first trip, and have never failed to receive a warm Mississippi welcome and superb professional assistance.

The graduate work and research that produced this manuscript would not have been possible without generous financial assistance from the following sources: a University Unendowed Fellowship and a Century Fellowship from the University of Chicago, an Archie K. Davis Fellowship from the North Caroliniana Society of the University of North Carolina, a Travel-to-Collections Grant from the Newcomb College Center for Research on Women, a Summer Travel Grant from the Andrew W. Mellon Foundation, an Andrew W. Mellon Foundation–University of Chicago Dissertation Year Fellowship, and an Edna T. Schaeffer Humanist Award at James Madison University. It is my pleasure to thank them all.

My family, not at all obsessed with the South, oddly enough, watched patiently (well, mostly patiently) as this dissertation and book manuscript ran its long, strange course. My mother has consistently been generous, loving, and encouraging, and to her this book is dedicated. I owe a special debt to my grandparents, Roy and Marjorie Gibson, who read to me when I was young and provided for me to receive a college education. It was my great good fortune to spend my early years with them. I regret that my grandmother did not live to see this work completed. As a little boy growing up around her south Mississippi beauty shop, I heard many southern stories, of course.

Many teachers were gracious with their time and guidance. At Brookhaven High School, Don Paterson taught me to take books seriously; in our conversations over many years I learned much about the history and literature of the South, especially his beloved Mississippi Delta. At the University of Mississippi, Joan W. Hall and the late Joseph C. Kiger spent hours listening to my questions. At the University of Iowa, Ellis Hawley, an exemplary scholar, was always supportive, even as my interests began to turn toward the South. And at the University of Chicago, Barry Karl, Kathleen Conzen, and Thomas Holt were a patient dissertation committee.

Fellow graduate students, colleagues, and students of my own have been unselfish friends and sources of support in many dark hours, and a few light ones, too. In return, I am proud to say that I forced very few of them to read any of this manuscript. During a conversation about Walker Percy and golf, which I am sure he has long forgotten, Fred Beuttler encouraged me to take up a southern history dissertation topic. At James Madison University, Steve Reich and Kevin Borg were model colleagues. Thanks for the stimulating conversation and much else to Wade Shilts, Ron Granieri, Marc Kilmer, and especially my good friend Vance Poole.

Here at the Missouri University of Science and Technology, the late Larry Vonalt always provided encouragement and always had time for conversations about the South. My colleague and current department chair Kris Swenson read much of this manuscript in an early stage; it is my pleasure to acknowledge her help. Jack Morgan, Kate Drowne, John Lemmermann, Anne Cotterill, and Linda Sands have offered inspiration and not a few laughs.

Finally, I thank my wife, Jennifer, for insisting that I finish this project. She and my children, Jack and Ellie, have taught me much about what to value. This book explores questions of home and family. I am richly blessed to have found one that provides such love.

INTRODUCTION

"The State is only a home on a larger scale."

Southerners have a reputation as storytellers, as a people fond of telling about family, community, and the southern way of life. This is a book about some of those stories and their consequences. *One Homogeneous People: Narratives of White Southern Identity, 1890–1920* examines the forging and the embracing of southern pan-whiteness as an ideal during the volatile years surrounding the turn of the twentieth century. Despite real and significant divisions within the South along lines of religion, class, and ethnicity, white southerners, especially in moments of perceived danger, asserted that they were one people bound by a shared history, a love of family, home, and community, and an uncompromising belief in white supremacy. They explained their region and its people to themselves and other Americans through narratives of white southern identity found in a variety of forms and contexts: political oratory, fiction, historiography, literary criticism, and the built environment.[1] Dominant voices asserted that the South was essentially a well-ordered household whose integrity proceeded from natural, racialized imperatives. In "The Creed of the Old South" (1892), for instance, Basil L. Gildersleeve, a Johns Hopkins University classicist and Confederate veteran, explained that while the "Virginia farmer" and the "Creole planter of Louisiana were of different strains," the "community of views, of interest, of social order" in the South constituted a "true nationality." In Gildersleeve's estimation, the South was constituted not ideologically but organically, by "an extraordinary ramification of family and social ties. . . . a few minutes' conversation sufficed to place any member of the social organism from Virginia to Texas."[2] Such arguments that defined the South as a community of views and interests and as a social organism brushed away class, ethnic, and subregional distinctions within the South, and suggested that America's South was one homogeneous people.

This community, this family, argued turn-of-the-century white southerners, needed vigilant policing against a threatening outer chaos. White writers and orators usually explicitly, but always implicitly, represented the southern people and the community they constituted as white, and the threatening chaos as black.[3] Writing of the overthrow of Reconstruction, Hilary A. Herbert explained: "To avert ruin white men united. . . . The race against which the negro had allowed himself to be arrayed has never yet met its master."[4] White southerners after Reconstruction went looking for and invented a common past and a vision of contemporary common identity. In the name of defending home and community and those asserted common interests, white southerners Jim Crowed, lynched, and subjugated the region's African Americans. The safety of home and family, and the maintenance of the southern way of life, they often said, demanded no less.

White southerners' explanations of themselves and their society as a family and a community proceeded from two fundamental assumptions: that racial difference existed and mattered, and that it was imperative to uphold this distinction to preserve order from disorder. Narratives of white southern identity both grew out of and affirmed most white southerners' commitments to white supremacy and black oppression. Their stories were built of potent and intertwined narratives that treated race and gender as fixed and determining lodestones of identity, and that simply refused to see social class as evidence of any fundamental inequities in southern society or as a potential solvent of white common interest. Broadly shared late-Victorian notions of domesticity made white southerners' cautionary tales about racial danger persuasive and effective.[5]

The metaphor of community or state as a well-ordered household was not invented in the nineteenth-century South, of course. The assertion was a staple of Western political discourse from classical antiquity through the Renaissance and beyond. Nineteenth-century Americans placed particular emphasis on the morally regenerative powers of home and family, often saying that the order and virtue engendered at home were essential in nurturing the larger culture's vitality. The opposite was true, too, they believed. After the Civil War, white southerners were particularly concerned about the fruits of disordered households, specifically the connection between disordered public and disordered private life.[6] Characterizing the white South as a family seemed natural, as well, in the context of contemporary progressive reform rhetoric. Reform movements, both southern and national, were suffused with the rhetoric of middle-class domesticity, with reformers such as Frances Willard of the Women's Christian Temperance Union seeking "to make the whole world homelike."[7] And male southern progressives, like their northern counterparts, found the paternalistic, corrective rhetoric of the period easy and convincing, whether directed at uplifting mountain whites or ordering African Americans.[8]

As a study of southern culture, this book is fundamentally a study of power. More precisely, this is a study of the power of narrative to render certain cultural arrangements and forms legitimate, at least in the eyes of their beneficiaries. Southern narratives of pan-whiteness served more complex ends than simply helping a community to define itself; they sought as well to transmit that sense of legitimacy to people outside the rhetorical community and to a subsequent generation.[9] I use the word "narrative" in this book in ways that most readers will, I hope, find familiar.[10] White southerners, like other human beings, used stories to explain who they were and how things worked. Their stories, or narratives, had beginnings, middles, and endings, and offered rational frameworks for a particularly chaotic time in the South's history. Typically, narratives contain plots, characters, and usually a moral, implicit or explicit. I take narrative not only in the strict sense of tales or parables or published works of fiction or nonfiction, although those forms are some of the things I examine. One also finds narratives of pan-white southern identity, as I suggest below, in political oratory, in the arrangement of works of fiction in anthologies, and in the constructed landscape and folkways of a county fair. As Richard Gray writes: "Communities are constructed, changed, defended and resisted by language . . . by monuments . . . by maps and museums."[11] The white South used narratives to assert that they were a community, to tell stories about it, and to define threats to it.

Storytelling in the western tradition is fundamentally metaphorical. Though theoreticians of language disagree on the epistemological foundation and work of metaphor, most scholars agree that "metaphors take words out of their usual context and transfer their meaning to a new context."[12] Within rhetorical communities, metaphors carry associations that do not need to be explicitly explained, although not everyone may agree upon a symbol's meaning. Roses, flags, and doves all seem to mean something beyond the literal, even if we differ upon precisely what that something is. What is important rhetorically and culturally is that metaphors operate at an unarticulated level.[13] Southerners have argued about the meaning of flags and statues, and those arguments are often so heated because these symbols do not have absolute meanings.[14] More precisely, those meanings vary, not only from one interpretive community to another, but also from individual to individual within those communities. Further, there are no arbiters of absolute authority over metaphor and symbol, although there were and are wielders of other kinds of power in the South. This is far from saying that narratives of southern identity at the turn of the twentieth century were arbitrary or ultimately meaningless. Stories about southern flags, statues, and families, among other topics, shaped and continue to shape broader stories southerners tell themselves and others about who they are.

White southerners heard and told stories about themselves and their region that operated metaphorically to explain or describe themselves and the South. Those stories, built from culturally resonant symbols and characters, reminded them what to value and what to fear. In the post-Reconstruction South, certain metaphors gained particular resonance: the Confederate veteran, the Lost Cause, black Reconstruction, white womanhood, and the black man.[15] The stories white southerners told not only contained metaphors, they also worked metaphorically. Stories of black men and their desires drew upon and complemented stories of pure white womanhood; stories of Reconstruction suggested what to think of northern interest in black welfare. One story helped white southerners understand another. Knowledge of stories and stock characters helped them to shape and order the present, and to predict what might happen next. Another feature of the narrative imagination is that it lends itself to teleology. Having learned what to value, white southerners feared its destruction.

In the chapters that follow I examine narratives that asserted an ordered, homogeneous white South (and the threats to it) in the years between the 1890s and the 1920s.[16] By no means were these narratives of a white South the only stories southerners told about themselves in these years. Black southerners rejected the legitimacy of white supremacy and contemporary economic relationships. Some whites, such as George Washington Cable in his essays *The Silent South* (1885) or his novel *The Grandissimes* (1880), recognized the corrosive effects of racism on the South.[17] Yet black southerners were limited in their abilities to challenge the rhetoric of pan-white southern identity; writers such as Cable were conspicuously rare. Even those who doubted the emerging narratives of white southern identity were unable completely to escape their power. Narratives of race might have been "fictive," but nevertheless quite potent.[18]

While New South boosters and Lost Cause guardians, among others, praised the genius and mission of the Anglo-Saxon South, there was nothing racially or historically preordained about this first of several asserted New Souths.[19] Yet, as David Goldfield has pointed out, the sense of white southern community and assertions of a deeply satisfying southern way of life that emerged in these years exercised tenacious cultural power; it soon seemed to many white southerners "a divinely inspired vision that captured [their] soul."[20] Narratives of a homogeneous white South periodically threatened by black disorder dominated the region in the formative decades of the twentieth century. They continue to resonate in the twenty-first-century South.

For some time historians have noted white southerners' practice of characterizing themselves and their region as a family or community. Such habits served many ends: the assertion of democratic, egalitarian values, the justification of slavery, or the championing of progressive reform; such characterizations blur distinctions between the domestic and public/political realms, whether intentionally or not. Most scholarship examining this narrative habit of white southerners has focused on the antebellum period. One thinks, for instance, of the work of Eugene Genovese and Elizabeth Fox-Genovese on what they call the mind of the master class. Other work has examined more broadly white southerners and the rhetoric of patriarchy. In *Masters of Small*

Worlds (1995), her study of Low Country South Carolina, Stephanie McCurry argues that what united white southerners was not *Herrenvolk* democracy—the idea that all whites were bound in some essential way by race and blood—but rather the rhetoric of mastery over the family, their land, and enslaved blacks.[21] In the late-nineteenth- and early twentieth-century South as well, the rhetoric of white community and of mastery of African Americans was pervasive, and to most whites, persuasive. When white southerners spoke about their families and communities or about the dangers posed by unmastered black men, they moved easily into larger questions of politics and citizenship. Whether in the rhetoric of a novelist such as Thomas Dixon or a politician such as James Vardaman—both figures that I examine in the pages that follow—discussions of economic, political, and social stability and the threats to it all coalesced around narratives of embattled white families and the broader notion that white southerners constituted one community.

To suggest that race is central to white southerners' stories about themselves, as contested and complex as those stories have been, is not new. Scholars since W. E. B. Du Bois and Ulrich Bonnell Phillips have written on the centrality of ideas of race to southern history, especially white southerners' determination to maintain white supremacy.[22] Any examination of the law, literature, journalism, political rhetoric, labor, or public space of the turn-of-the-century South demonstrates clearly the race obsession of that society. This book does not ask whether race is indeed the central theme of southern history. Instead, it seems to me more fruitful to consider the growth and reasons for the tenacity of certain stories about white southerners, their communities, and their values.

Narratives of a white South provided an argument not only about racial identity, but about regional identity as well. One of the challenges for white southerners in the post-Reconstruction years was to explain what they talked about when they talked about the South, to borrow Edward Ayers's phrasing.[23] Under rhetorical assault in the years before the Civil War by abolitionists and others who saw their region as the hypocritical and pathological Slave Power, white southerners asserted that their region was organic and orderly, a patriarchal household writ large. Those stories had been sorely tested in the crucibles of war and Reconstruction. The fact of freed slaves claiming their rights could not easily be squared with older prescriptions and stereotypes. To those committed to white supremacy, the entry of black men into the formerly white male-only realm of politics—the public arena—was evidence of a chaotic state, one that in turn threatened the domestic sphere.[24] It is easy to find white southerners lamenting their disordered state governments during Reconstruction, when, according to popular and academic narratives, untutored freedmen turned southern statehouses into dens of vice and corruption—into unruly houses, that is.[25] Now discredited, those charges of wholesale black malfeasance were resonant and tenacious, for they drew upon deep cultural narratives of domesticity and white superiority and what was long recollected and told as a common white southern experience of defeat and humiliation.

What were the political consequences for the twentieth-century South of the ideology of white southernness that gained fresh cultural legitimacy in these years? "It is a puzzling characteristic of southern politics," wrote V. O. Key sixty years ago, "that candidates can at times get themselves elected by their skill in advocacy of something on which everyone is agreed."[26] But not "everyone" agreed on the vision of a white South that stump speakers from Ben Tillman to George Wallace articulated. Key understood that to outsiders, southern politics in the years between Redemption and the New Deal and beyond often seemed pointless exercises in race baiting. How could politics in such a one-party region with little substantive debate truly matter, they wondered? Far from meaningless, however, the spectacle of southern political campaigns and elections, such as the one that I discuss in the pages below, was an assertion that the white South stood united in its determination to retain racial segregation and to protect the larger "southern way of life." It is because of the work of narratives of a white South that observers, even ones so astute as Key, could feel that "everyone" in the South viewed certain fundamental matters in much the same way. It is precisely when narratives have developed such a deep cultural hold that they most merit study.

Why have racialist narratives proved so persistent in the southern political tradition? To blame the James Vardamans or, later, the George Wallaces of the South is to offer an incomplete answer. A recent study of Mississippi politics claims that after disfranchisement black Mississippians disappeared from state politics, except as "a scapegoat in cynical political games played by white politicians."[27] Black Mississippians were indeed scapegoated. But was this scapegoating cynical political manipulation of a gullible white audience? White southerners were not duped by racism; southern politics was not simply tied to racism in some mechanical way. The metaphor of "tying" is misleading, for it implies the possibility of untying; even Gordian knots have their solution. Instead, southern politics in the post-Reconstruction years emerged from as well as shaped a broader cultural context.

Central to white southern culture—central to whites' conceptions of themselves and their society—was a definition of community and family, of which a central tenet was white supremacy. Jane Tompkins's study of early European narratives of American Indians provides a most useful way to think about white southern rhetoric and narratives: "what [European explorers and colonists] saw was not an illusion, was not determined by selfish motives in any narrow sense, but was there by virtue of a *way* of seeing which they could no more consciously manipulate that they could choose not to have been born."[28] White southerners have had difficulty crafting a post–Jim Crow sense of community because racism was not simply a cancer in the body politic that could be easily excised. Turn-of-the-century definitions of the South became naturalized and were persuasive because they were built upon late-Victorian stories of domesticity that enjoyed broad currency across class (and to some extent racial) lines. Those stories, as I argue below, can be traced across the cultural landscape of the South in the decades around the beginning of the twentieth century.

Narratives of white southern identity were never as tidy as their spinners might have wished. Black southerners in particular resisted becoming the caricatures that Jim Crow seemed to require.[29] But acts of resistance were often furtive and little publicized by southern whites eager to assure themselves and others that the foundations of their society were solid—in other words, that blacks knew and accepted their place as subordinates. Black southerners were given good reason to be guarded in their public statements, especially on race or politics. And women—black and white—had to negotiate a patriarchal New South as they set about defining who they ought to be and what they ought to do. There was tremendous pressure throughout the white South to conform in one's public statements and acts, especially on what was called the "race question." So the narratives of a pan-white southern identity held, and have not completely lost their power to explain and to divide.

The years from the end of Reconstruction through the turn of the twentieth century were volatile and unsettling ones for the South and the nation. The South experienced agrarian revolt, progressive reform battles, the hardening of Jim Crow, and the migration of southerners, especially African Americans, within and out of the region.[30] The nation as a whole witnessed wrenching conflict involving class, race, and ethnicity and the contestation of traditional ideas about gender and family during America's uneasy emergence as a modern, industrialized, imperial power.[31] These unsettling end-of-the-century changes prompted many white southerners, like other Americans, to consider the health and direction of their society, to rethink basic assumptions about common goals and purposes, and to engage in overt tasks of self-assessment and definition. Addressing the University of Tennessee's graduating class of 1899, Charles W. Kent, a professor of literature at the University of Virginia, spoke as one who had "lived through the period since Sixty-Five, who . . . belonged to the generation that coincides with this significant third of our closing century." "The South," Kent instructed his audience, "is proud of its past."[32]

But categories such as "the South," "southerner," and even "white southerner" were neither homogeneous nor uncontested terms, of course. Kent's contemporaries recognized variations and possible tensions among white southerners. Noting the divisive effects of the recent Populist challenge, Alabama Democrats in 1898 "deplored the past 'turmoil, strife and dissension among the white people of our county.'"[33] In 1919 historian Holland Thompson cautioned that "one must be careful not to write of the South as if it were a single country, inhabited by a homogeneous people. . . . No one who really knows the whole South could be guilty of such a mistake."[34] Divided by class, ethnicity, and religion, white southerners sometimes recognized the potential for significant differences among themselves, with dissent over secession and Confederate government policies and the high-stakes political battles of the agrarian movement of the 1880s and 1890s standing as two conspicuous examples.

Yet in other contexts, such as the aggressive defense of slavery in the decade before the Civil War or the overthrow of Reconstruction, the idea and practice of pan-white southernness proved useful, meaningful, persuasive, and cohesive.[35] The turn-of-the-century South was another such period of potent assertions of white common interest, especially expressed in narratives about the defense of home and family, and white supremacy over African Americans. In the same survey of the New South in which Holland Thompson cautioned against generalizations about the region's peoples, he wrote: "the white man has made certain decisions regarding the relation of blacks and whites and is enforcing them without regard to the negro's wishes. The Southerner is convinced that the negro is inferior and acts upon that conviction." Thompson's certainty that white southerners spoke with one voice on matters of race is as sure as his assumption that "the southerner" is white, and a man.

In fact, the fruits, psychological or material, of practicing white supremacy meant that in the New South white southernness, by which I mean a commitment to Jim Crow, white supremacy, and at least an implicit claim that white people were in essential ways one folk, was always a latently powerful category of identity. In a period rife with economic tensions and cultural unease, politicians, newspaper editors, and other public figures found audiences prepared to hear narratives of racial difference and white superiority. This conjuring of white community was, of course, more than a linguistic feat. White southernness manifested itself concretely and sometimes brutally: "You don't know how we feel down here," a white southerner told a northern visitor in 1908, "when there is a row, we feel like killing a nigger whether he has done anything or not."[36] However, invoking "white supremacy" does not completely or sufficiently explain southern culture at the turn of the twentieth century. White southerners did not share a universal ideology; no group of people ever thinks and acts with perfect uniformity.[37] But if one studies white southerners and their assertions about race and difference in the period's dominant cultural narratives—the mainstream of politics, the press, fiction and scholarship, and public space—one might well be excused for thinking so.

In the wake of Reconstruction and Populism, the ideology and practice of white southernness in the 1890s fed upon and supported narratives that worked to minimize class and other divisions among white southerners, emphasizing instead a homogeneous white South, and asserting one extended white southern community. Even Progressive era critics of southern pathologies easily fell into such language. In *The Rebuilding of Old Commonwealths*

(1902), Walter Hines Page wrote: "The Southern [white] people . . . are the purest stock we have."[38] In his influential study of South Carolinian "Pitchfork" Ben Tillman, Stephen Kantrowitz argues that asserting and practicing white community in the fractious, factionalized New South required nothing less than an act of "reconstruction." "It was one thing to posit white male unity and another thing entirely to create and enforce it. . . . White supremacy was hard work." Kantrowitz is surely right that white supremacists such as Tillman succeeded at their task because they "built on words and ideas with deep histories."[39] However, it is precisely because politicians like Tillman could work with commonly understood and racially charged words and ideas such as family, community, and the southern way of life that asserting white supremacy was not such hard work after all.[40]

The idea of whites as a community whose interests were all served by black oppression did in fact obscure class lines precisely because ideas of black and white were so viscerally resonant; the "deep histories" of those ideas served Tillman and other narrators of a white South quite effectively. Questions of debt and currency, land and commodity prices, or which candidate in the Democratic primary best spoke for the common (white) man, might have divided white southerners. But the evocation of racial difference—particularly when assertions of a black threat to white women or the white home activated turn-of-the-century anxieties over gender—caused seemingly substantive differences among white southerners to melt into air. Indeed, the reality and significance of the racial categories of blackness and whiteness seemed to white southerners one of the few matters that were obvious and not open to question. In the 1890s and beyond, it was often quite easy for white southerners to believe that they were essentially one people, especially when compared with black southerners.

Culturally dominant and broadly accepted southern narratives represented the region as white, democratic (and Democratic), and essentially stable.[41] The South, they asserted, held no social or economic flaws that could not be redressed by white southerners themselves. The agrarian revolt of the 1880s and 1890s, to take one awkward instance of white disagreement, disappeared beneath a chorus of New South rhetoric boasting of white solidarity, as well as the tractability of Anglo-Saxon labor. From the schools, pulpits, and political forums of the white South, southerners spun and heard narratives of white identity that represented them not only as members of families, churches, and local communities, but as members of a regionwide community as well—a community whose members were all threatened by African Americans who were "uppity," or worse, savage.[42] Long after the idea of political separatism seemed quixotic or quaint, white southerners lived day to day in an ideological landscape that stressed their common aims and interest in maintaining domination over blacks, and downplayed economic and class strife, all in the name of a common white identity.

Historians from C. Vann Woodward through Edward Ayers have explored the economic and social upheaval of the South in the decades surrounding the turn of the twentieth century. Contemporary civic boosters would have agreed—that the South was on the move, at least—as they seemingly proclaimed every hamlet in the New South to be progressive and thriving. In 1907, Dunbar Rowland, director of the Mississippi Department of Archives and History, boasted in characteristic New South rhetoric that Hattiesburg, "Queen of the Pine Belt" and a thriving railroad town, was "the envy of her rivals, the pride of the state, and the glory of her citizens." But the simultaneous emphasis by men such as Rowland on the past, on building Confederate memorials in courthouse squares, for instance, or gathering archival materials, or writing textbooks and histories, were all assertions that the passage of time need not bring loss of order.[43] Turn-of-the-century memorializations of the Lost Cause complemented larger New South racial imperatives and became a central component of the emerging narratives of pan-whiteness.[44]

To outsiders, white southerners were stereotypically, even charmingly, fixated on the past. But at the turn of the twentieth century this careful attention to a particular vision of the past was, in fact, very present-minded, backed by claims of legitimate authority and assertions of a permanent right to power. "The South of today thrills with filial love for the South that was," wrote Mississippian Edward Mayes in 1896, "and in her innermost heart sits enshrined an unwavering faith in the purity, the nobility, and the patriotism of the former generation."[45] Mayes, an architect of Mississippi's disfranchising 1890 constitution, was the son-in-law of L. Q. C. Lamar, author of Mississippi's 1860 ordinance of secession. For such men, assertions of white solidarity came easily and naturally, especially with their hands firmly on the reins of political and economic power.

To listen to most turn-of-the-century white southerners, one would assume that Jim Crow, the solid Democratic South, and a broader "Southern

Way of Life" were timeless features of the southern landscape, as C. Vann Woodward found when he began tracking the origins of the New South. "To doubt or to question the status quo and the received wisdom in any degree," wrote Woodward of the Arkansas of his youth, "was to affront if not insult one's fellow citizens and call in question one's very loyalty." Earlier, progressive reformer Walter Hines Page found in North Carolina that what appeared to be a collective white southern mind, at least in its public utterances, was in fact a realization that certain voices mattered more than others in the New South. Noting the absence of free speech in a southern college town, Page was told that public utterances must serve the public. "Who is the public?" asked Page. One person answered, "The Democratic platform, the Daughters of the Confederacy, old General So-and-so, and the Presbyterian creed."[46] Yet, when it came to racial matters, white southerners evidenced little of the cynicism of Page's North Carolinians about the forces that determined the limits of public discourse. While white southerners might profess to deplore unregulated violence in support of Jim Crow, or argue that race baiting on the campaign trail was beside the point, no significant white public voices argued anything other than the fundamental reality and importance of the differences between black and white southerners.

Without the work of many other scholars of southern history and culture, I could not have written this book. Two other studies that examine race and southern culture at the turn of the twentieth century have been especially influential. Joel Williamson's *The Crucible of Race: Black-White Relations in the American South Since Emancipation* (1984) is justifiably regarded as a classic reading of the power of the idea of race in the late-nineteenth-century South. Provocative and insightful, Williamson's book helped me see much more clearly the history of assertions of white culture and community in the South. However, my work is different from Williamson's in several significant respects. I approach southern culture through a narrative rather than a psychoanalytical analysis. Ultimately, I feel more comfortable examining what white southerners told themselves and others about who they were than I do exploring how those beliefs might be manifestations of certain fundamental psychological phenomena. Further, I doubt that it is useful to speak of a collective psychology of white southerners. I concentrate on speech and action, much as Williamson did, but I feel more assurance in writing about how a text works, rather than what it means. Second, and more important, I do not aim here to trace the history of race relations, which Williamson has done so skillfully, but rather to listen to the stories white southerners told about themselves and their region. Last, and perhaps most important, I differ from Williamson in not attempting to sort white thought on race into radical, conservative, and moderate camps. As I explain throughout this book, I wish instead to collapse those distinctions to show how an emphasis on rhetoric and tropes rather than on the identity of the speaker shows surprising commonalities in turn-of-the-century white southern discourse on race, community, and family.

The more recent book I have had in mind is Grace Hale's *Making Whiteness: The Culture of Segregation in the American South, 1890–1920* (1998). Hale's book has been deservedly well received for its sophisticated application of critical race theory to the early twentieth-century South. Theoretically informed and powerfully written, the work explains how "some southerners created a common whiteness to solve the problems of the post–Civil War era."[47] Hale and I share an interest in fiction and the role of the built environment in making whiteness. But on significant matters, we differ. This book begins with a chapter on politics, a subject to which Hale gives relatively little attention. And I do not share Hale's emphasis on the role of consumerism in the making of segregated southern culture.[48] A more fundamental difference, I think, is that I explicitly explore the shaping power of narratives, particularly narratives of family and community, both at the turn of the century and more recently. In attempting to understand how power worked, and how stories of white identity enabled and perpetuated power and inequality, I cannot find a more fundamental matter than stories of family and community and arguments about what must be done in their defense. Explicit attention to the tropes, metaphors, and narratives of white identity helps to show how white identity was made and operated. Further, this book differs from Hale's in the attention I give to the ways that literary criticism and historiography grew out of and shaped understandings of a common white experience in the American South. Finally, in my conclusion and in other parts of this book, I spend more time than Hale in attempting to show how narratives of a white South have continued to operate, especially in the years since the civil rights movement of the 1950s and 1960s.

One Homogeneous People is not a traditional monograph, and does not attempt to duplicate any of the other fine recent examinations of southern culture or race relations at the turn of the twentieth century. The book consists of three extended essays on related themes of narratives of race and power, framed by an introduction and a conclusion. These essays examine not only language and discourse but also literature and institutions that constructed discursive practices. Stephen Greenblatt writes: "In any culture there is a general symbolic economy made up of the myriad signs that excite human desire, fear, and aggression."[49] To analyze this symbolic economy, I use various texts: newspapers, magazine and journal articles, diaries, correspondence, and fiction among them. Placing political oratory alongside fiction, scholarship, and folkways demonstrates the remarkable similarity of discourses of pan-whiteness across formal and generic lines.

The state of Mississippi figures prominently in this book. As James Cobb has argued of the Mississippi Delta, the state has often seemed to observers "the most southern place on Earth."[50] All the South is not Mississippi, of course, and I try to take care not to generalize too broadly, and to provide evidence from white southerners who lived and worked in the geographical area stretching from Washington, D.C., to Texas. But Mississippi provides a useful touchstone for examining racialized notions of community, for in that state narratives of pan-white identity operated perhaps most openly, most tenaciously, and with the most destructive consequences of any of the southern states. White Mississippians argued vigorously and often about the "southern way of life," and demonstrated that they would willingly use violence to defend the things they professed to cherish. Many other white southerners felt the same way, and to that degree the example of Mississippi is representative, but neither universal nor unique. Finally, as a native Mississippian, I have been particularly concerned with difficulties that the state has had with the stories it tells about its past and present, and hope that this book will at least suggest some useful questions to ask about community and the way that it is conceptualized.

I begin this book with a chapter that explores a Mississippi political campaign and its participants' use of the language of white community and black danger. Political campaigns often occasion the concise articulation of matters otherwise left implicit. Political rallies and stump speeches were literally the stages upon which narratives of white identity were conjured and performed. At the turn of the twentieth century, white politicians argued that black voters—black men, that is—represented a unique danger to white interests and white homes. The 1907 campaign in Mississippi between U.S. Representative John Sharp Williams and Governor James K. Vardaman for the Democratic senatorial nomination shows both men, one a "moderate" and the other a "radical," to borrow Joel Williamson's categories, wielding essentially the same narratives of orderly white communities and politically inept but threatening blacks. It is tempting to view one racist harangue as being much like another. Instead, I argue that examining such speeches in relation to the larger culture that produced them yields tropes and stock figures and threads of other common narratives of white identity.

In the second and third chapters, I seek the literary and academic sources of some of the most compelling narratives of white southern identity. I examine works of fiction and then the texts that created canons of southern literature and history, arguing that through such texts post-Reconstruction narratives of a white South gained a tenacious cultural hold. I consider particularly two writers of fiction who will be familiar to students of southern literature and history: Thomas Nelson Page and Thomas Dixon. I try to find something new in the familiar, however, and I concentrate on the function of the domestic narrative within two representative works, "Marse Chan" and *The Leopard's Spots.* I also suggest how these texts worked: narratives of white distinctiveness and identity became naturalized and normalized in large part through popular forms of pleasurable consumption.

The southern histories and the anthologies of southern literature that I examine in chapter 3 will likely be less familiar ground to most readers. But their work seems just as vital as that of the better-known Page and Dixon. Writers of fiction such as Page and Dixon were popular in the broadest sense: their work circulated narratives of a white South to a wide national audience. Scholars and critics aided at the same time in a similar process by anthologizing and canonizing southern history and letters. Their work helped to normalize white southern narratives to a regional and national professional audience. Further, the historians' and anthologists' redefinition of the South as one region among a nation of regions served to deflect criticism from Jim Crow by suggesting that each region had its own organic culture and traditions—traditions that people outside the family, so to speak, had no standing to criticize.

In the conclusion I look at narratives of pan-white identity founded in the late nineteenth century and persisting to the present day, turning my attention again to Mississippi and an important but largely unexamined institution, the Neshoba County Fair. From its late-nineteenth-century origins as a camp meeting, the fair has grown into a weeklong summer festival drawing thousands of Mississippians; appearing at the fair is vital for would-be state office holders. In the fair's rhetoric of old-time family and community values, I see echoes and reformulations of turn-of-the-century narratives of white southern identity. Finally, I suggest that turn-of-the-century southern narratives of white order and black disorder still foster racial division in the South, even if the genealogy of those narratives typically goes unremarked. Some readers may be uncomfortable with my suggestion that current talk of "family values," a staple of many contemporary discourses, even when used ironically, has dark roots. I do not suggest something as simple as an easy, coded correspondence between celebrations of family and racialist practices. I do not mean that white southerners or other white Americans really mean something other than what they say. Most people do not live so consciously or deliberately within their culture's narrative structures. I do suggest, however, that narratives built within a certain cultural context carry the resonances of their origins whether we like it or not.

This story about the making of narratives of a white South also suggests something about the gradual weakening of those white southern narratives. Turn-of-the-century white southerners said loudly that they were white and proud of it. As I suggest in the conclusion of this book, those old narratives have morphed into new, seemingly color-blind stories of southern families and culture. The subtle changes in narratives of white southern identity help us to see their history and shaping power in contemporary southern culture. It is too soon to write obituaries for whiteness. But what has happened is that overt narratives of white southernness seem unpersuasive, dated, and to most white southerners, a relic of a past best not dwelled upon. The post–civil rights generation, however, has failed to produce a narrative of community that works. But that is another matter, one that speaks to the failure not only of southerners, but of all Americans in recent years to generate inclusive narratives of community and common purpose. In saying that these old narratives of white southernness failed, I do not mean that they disappeared. The rhetoric of James Vardaman and Thomas Dixon or, more recently, Mississippi's Governor Ross Barnett, whom I discuss briefly in chapter 1 and again in the conclusion, sounds dated not because we have rid ourselves of racism, but because their stories no longer satisfy contemporary cultural needs. Few office seekers speak like Barnett, for instance, because it does not seem right or natural or even prudent to do so. That sense of rightness or fit seems to me the key in judging whether or not a narrative works— whether it retains its explanatory power within its interpretative community, that is. But because certain elements of those narratives of a white South remain culturally resonant, there is all the more urgent a need today for new, more inclusive narratives of southern identity.

Narratives of southern culture with homogeneous, normative whiteness at their core—the South troped as *Volksgemeinschaft*—were long so tenacious in large part because the domestic ideology so central to this southernness was nationally accepted. Domesticity, in its mutable, evolving forms, was white, too, though domesticity's whiteness was less apparent, even (or especially) to those who lamented white supremacy as un-American. Contemporary white southerners often assert that the end of Jim Crow brought the end of history to the region, or at least the end of the need to reckon the cost of racism. Such assertions are premature. The New South—as an idea or a set of material conditions—was not simply a hierarchy of labor control or a set of Jim Crow laws and folkways. If that were so, the ameliorative liberalism (or more radical and untried solutions) of the twentieth century could perhaps have washed that sin away. But there is at least potential for change once we understand that for too long, stories about the South have depended upon certain historically specific, exclusive, polarizing conceptions of a pan-white community with a shared history and values. Fundamental elements of these narratives—the South, black and white, family and community—are built, rhetorically and physically, and can be interrogated, critiqued, and perhaps rewritten into broader, more inclusive stories about family, community, and belonging.

1

THE ROAD TO A CLOSED SOCIETY:

MISSISSIPPI POLITICS AND THE LANGUAGE OF WHITE SOUTHERN IDENTITY

A VOTE FOR VARDAMAN IS A VOTE FOR WHITE SUPREMACY, THE SAFETY OF THE HOME, AND THE PROTECTION OF OUR WOMEN AND CHILDREN.
—Slogan from James K. Vardaman Campaign Banner, 1903

Q: I'm wondering if you consider Negroes people in Mississippi.
Barnett: I would say that the Negroes, the Indians, the Eskimos, and all the whites—90 percent of them are against Kennedy in Mississippi.
—Ross Barnett at Western Michigan University, 1963

Racial bigotry transcends reason in Mississippi because . . . so many leaders are willing to exploit the nameless dreads and alarms that have taken possession of most white people.
—James Silver, *Mississippi: The Closed Society*, 1964

On the evening of Saturday, September 29, 1962, as the crisis over James Meredith's admission to the University of Mississippi came to a head, Governor Ross Barnett sat in Jackson, watching the Ole Miss Rebels play the Kentucky Wildcats at Veterans' Memorial Stadium. At halftime of the football game, the Rebels, ranked in the top five in preseason polls and headed toward their first unde-feated and untied season in the program's history, led the Wildcats 7-0, on their way to a 14-0 victory.[1] The stadium rang with the chant "We want Ross!" as Barnett began to address the enthusiastic crowd of more than 40,000 people as well as a statewide television audience. "My fellow Mississippians, I love Mississippi," he declared. "I love her people, our customs. I love and respect our heritage."[2] The Rebel faithful loved their governor, too; the crowd roared its approval. "On nights like this," a commentator wrote recently, "it's easy to forget the South lost the war. In some ways that's the point."[3] The previous Thursday, the *Jackson Clarion-Ledger* had printed the words to the "Never, No, Never Song," recalled University of Mississippi historian James W. Silver, "with the suggestion that it be clipped and taken to the Ole Miss–Kentucky football game":

> We'll never yield an inch on any field.
> Fix us another toddy,
> Ain't yielding to nobody,
> Never, never, never, never, no never.
> Ask us what we say,
> It's to hell with Bobby K.
> Ross's standing like Gibraltar,
> He shall never falter.
> Never shall our emblem go
> From Colonel Rebel to Ole Black Joe.[4]

Barnett "was a symbol of the South," explained his former campaign publicist; he "represented the traditions that emerged after Reconstruction, a way of life that white southerners had vowed to continue."[5] Awash in a sea of Confederate flags and rebel yells that night in Jackson, Governor Barnett, the son of a Confederate veteran, took his stand, assuring white Mississippians that the foundations of their society were solid. Yet twenty-four hours later, Ole Miss's campus in Oxford was engulfed in riot over the admission of Meredith, the first African American student to enroll at the University of Mississippi. Students, other Mississippians, and out-of-state supporters joined in an orgy of rock throwing, automobile burning, and federal marshal taunting. Two men were killed, dozens were injured, federal and National Guard troops occupied the campus, and the reputation of the University of Mississippi as a cauldron of racial hatred was fixed in the minds of a generation of Americans by nationally broadcast television footage. "The eyes of the nation and all the world are upon you," President John F. Kennedy counseled Mississippians that night. "The honor of your University and your state are in the balance."[6]

Four years before Barnett's gridiron apotheosis into Mississippi's most prominent massive resister, C. Vann Woodward undertook a "Search for Southern Identity," and recalled an earlier occasion when the South struck a defiant pose and vowed "Never!" Advising his fellow white southerners not to misread the changing national mood, signaled by the *Brown* decision, the first federal civil rights measures since Reconstruction, and the unmistakable emergence of a grass-roots civil rights movement in the South, Woodward wrote:

> Once more the South finds itself with a morally discredited Peculiar Institution on its hands. The last time this happened, about a century ago, the South's defensive reaction was to identify its whole cause with the one institution that was most vulnerable, and make loyalty to [it] the cardinal test of loyalty to the whole tradition.[7]

Woodward warned that to repeat the experiment—to insist, as did Governor Barnett, the stadium crowd in Jackson, and tens of thousands of other white Mississippians, that the Jim Crow racial settlement was the heart of southern identity—was to threaten the meaning and integrity of that identity after the federal government made it clear that the southern states would no longer be allowed to regulate their affairs after the old fashion. Days before the Oxford riots, the *Memphis Commercial Appeal* advised white Mississippians to accept the inevitable:

The answers may not be palatable. But not so bitter as hatred and violence. Finally, it is the young students—those now in the university and those who may attend in years to come—who must be considered. Mississippi needs their talents and services. It should not drive them away.[8]

How did Ross Barnett come to stand in Jackson that evening in 1962, cloaked with symbols of the Confederacy and invoking "the southern way of life," with its assertion of white community, tradition, and resistance to change? The drama, or farce, of the moment obscures the fact that Barnett's role in this unfortunate episode was in one sense a small one. He did not create the complex brew of politics, race, and southern identity that proved so galvanizing in the Deep South in those years; after this high-water mark of fame, Barnett's reputation quickly faded. When he ran for governor again in 1967, rumors of his behind-the-scenes attempts to salvage a compromise with the Kennedy administration over Meredith's admission haunted his campaign.[9] Unlike George Wallace, Barnett was politically irrelevant by the end of the 1960s.

Yet today in the Deep South, while Ross Barnett is no more, resonances of the Jim Crow years are still discernable.[10] Southern cities as large as Richmond and New Orleans, as well as numerous small towns, wrestle with divisive issues rooted in a lingering sense among many black and white southerners that they represent two groups, that they are people who constitute proximate but nonintegrated communities. These divisive issues range from the public commemoration of African Americans and the civil rights movement to the drawing of school district lines to the funding of community services. In Mississippi today, for instance, the majority-black city of Jackson meets stiff resistance when it attempts to expand into majority-white Rankin County. "It's a political issue, it's racial, it's historical," said one local politician.[11]

Questions of race, community, and identity in the South, then, remain matters of discord and urgency, but without clear answers. To trace the road to Ross Barnett and his stand in Memorial Stadium, and to understand the current South's difficulty in envisioning a post–Jim Crow community, it is vital to understand that these problems of racial discord and mistrust are fundamentally problems of imagination and narration. The legal mechanisms of Jim Crow have been challenged and dismantled. All but a few white southerners would denounce the use of direct force to ensure white domination of African Americans, if the issue were framed that baldly. Yet the language and ways of thinking about white identity and family and community in the region forged at the turn of the twentieth century have been less successfully confronted and challenged, thereby compromising attempts to built bi- or multiracial models of community and public policy in the recent South.

Today one can find southerners grappling to find workable ways to tell stories about community and connection. The *Jackson Clarion-Ledger* self-consciously looked to organic and mechanical metaphors to explain to white suburbanites why they should care about the city of Jackson and its problems: "Support for Jackson must cross city limit lines to ensure the future of the metro area. The trunk, the wheel, the core—the central city of Jackson—must be healthy for the entire area to grow and thrive."[12] The divisive problems of race and community with which contemporary Mississippians contend are rooted in turn-of-the-century narratives of pan-white southern identity. Without facing that fact, it will be difficult for Mississippi and other southern states to come to terms with those years, and to work out a vision of community that embraces blacks, whites, and other members of an increasingly ethnically diverse region. Hundred-year-old stories about white identity, family, traditions, and community, long a staple of southern political rhetoric, are not entirely vestigial, but still serve, however covertly, to explain and to delineate.

"The eyes of the world are upon Mississippi to-day," Governor James K. Vardaman advised the state legislature in 1904, "because Mississippi is the very heart of the race problem."[13] Warning white Mississippians of an impending crisis in race relations, Vardaman suggested measures to strengthen Mississippi's racial caste system: abolish state support for black education, he counseled, and repeal the United States Constitution's Fifteenth Amendment. During his three decades in public life, Vardaman, the "White Chief," became notorious for sensationalistic, racist rhetoric:

Forty years of freedom and public education have not fulfilled the utopian dream of the Negro-philist of the North and the North-flavored vagarist of the South. It has not improved the Negro's morals, awakened within him an intelligent love of country or cultivated an uplifting, passion-restraining self-respect. He is a barbarian still . . . and the education of forty years seems only to have increased his aspiration to arise in the world and stand on a dead level with the white man socially and otherwise manifests itself in beastly assaults upon white women.[14]

Antipathy for the North, pseudoscientific references to blacks' primitivism and ignorance, and especially the threats of sexual violence by beastly black men against white women, were all themes of the narratives of common white identity and black depravity that Vardaman wove into his newspaper editorials and campaign speeches from the 1890s through World War I. "A magnificent actor, he projected a magnetic personality on the platform, and his swelling oratory lifted his audiences out of themselves."[15] Though racist southern political oratory was not invented by James K. Vardaman, of course, his narratives of white community menaced by black men were particularly effective in turn-of-the-century Mississippi because of his bombastic, melodramatic style, and for his raw public use of visceral domestic, gendered issues, such as the specter of sexual assault.

Yet, Vardaman's melodramatic racism drew as much upon assertions of white commonality as it did upon assumptions of black difference. Assertions of white community—particularly of white men's common duty to defend family and home—were not separable from racist assumptions about African Americans. Indeed, white southern community—as an idea or a practice—was most easily conjured through culturally resonant stories about black southerners. In his 1904 gubernatorial inaugural address, Vardaman reminded his listeners that they could "scarcely pick up a newspaper whose pages are not *blackened* [emphasis added] with the account of an unmentionable crime committed by a negro brute." But in the same speech, Vardaman spent far more time asserting a common white community than he did in lambasting black Mississippians. The "White Chief" assured his audience that Mississippi was "home of the highest type of Anglo-Saxon manhood," and spoke without qualification of "the white people of Mississippi" and "the government of white men." Tellingly, Vardaman celebrated as well the sense of white community and reunion that suffused post-Reconstruction America: "the sections [have been] reunited by the spirit of Anglo-Saxon brotherhood."[16] Vardaman and his audience needed very little persuasion, then, to imagine that fundamental differences separated white and black

Americans and that racial difference was a sufficient basis for political as well as social identity.

In accounts of the Progressive Era South, Vardaman stands with Arkansas' Jeff Davis, South Carolina's Pitchfork Ben Tillman, and the lapsed Georgia Populist, Tom Watson, as the archetypal southern demagogue.[17] A state legislator from 1890 through 1894, Vardaman served as governor from 1904 through 1908, winning election in his third campaign, the first test of Mississippi's 1902 direct primary law. A U.S. senator from 1913 to 1919, Vardaman supported Wilson's New Freedom and Jim Crow in Washington, D.C., but strongly opposed American involvement in World War I, joining five other senators in voting against American entry. This stand cost him his seat after the 1918 election.[18] In the national press, Vardaman was widely reviled as provincial and vulgarly racist. At home, James K. Vardaman was one of Mississippi voters' favorite Progressive Era public figures.

How can we account for the fervor the flamboyant Vardaman inspired among white Mississippians?[19] Contemporary detractors, such as John Sharp Williams and LeRoy Percy, his opponents in three elections for the U.S. Senate from 1907 to 1911, judged him a vulgarian who rode redneck prejudice into public office.[20] In the biting words of William Alexander Percy, LeRoy Percy's son, Vardaman was a "kindly, vain demagogue unable to think."[21] A later Mississippi historian attempted partly to rehabilitate Vardaman by arguing that he was "at least as progressive as Robert LaFollette" and lamenting that Vardaman "sustained a peculiar mental compartmentalization that allowed him to ignore black poverty."[22] But Vardaman was no redneck savant or a "but-for-that-one-flaw" progressive, his defense of lynching an unpleasant contradiction in a reformer who also called, Bryan-like, for checking the excesses of predatory railroads and corporations.[23] Concentrating too narrowly on Vardaman's biography or character does not get us very far in understanding his electoral success or, more important, the prevalence and tenacity of racialist narratives in the politics and broader culture of turn-of-the-century Mississippi.

It is certainly tempting to treat some of the darker aspects of southern political history as the fruits of bad men. Without Huey Long, then, no Longism; without Vardaman, perhaps a more racially tolerant Mississippi. Thomas C. Holt has suggested that "the sheer incomprehensibility of racist phenomena" has led historians to treat racism "as if it were somehow outside normal historical and social processes."[24] Vardaman was popular and Vardaman was elected not because he was *sui generis,* as Huey Long said about himself, but because what Vardaman said about black sexuality and white domesticity struck most whites as both beyond debate and highly galvanizing. Vardaman proved skillful, then, not in persuading his audience of something novel, but in providing explanations of daily life in turn-of-the-century Mississippi that seemed rational, natural, and persuasive, if occasionally alarming.

Vardaman's success was more than a matter of his skillful manipulation of tropes and literary figures, however. As is the case with popular writers, Vardaman needed an audience receptive of his narratives. His rise to prominence came at a critical time of generational shift in Mississippi politics. The Confederate generation was dying off. And as in most southern states, Mississippi's post-Reconstruction Democratic establishment was challenged by third-party insurgency in the 1880s and 1890s, even after the state adopted its disfranchising 1890 constitution.[25] The Agrarian political challenge in Mississippi, as Bradley Bond persuasively argues, was built upon "a sense of homogeneity based on egalitarian notions derived from the Jacksonian era." However, that egalitarianism, so vital to the populist cause, never managed to overcome white Mississippians' convictions that racial difference existed and mattered; and upon that rock, the agrarian revolt shattered. By the mid-1890s the Democratic Party had assured its hold on state politics. For several generations, the only political campaigns that mattered in the state were the ones before the Democratic Party's primary elections.[26]

Mississippi Democrats (and by 1900 that meant the very great majority of white Mississippians) were not homogeneous: the black-majority but white planter–dominated Delta squabbled with the yeoman whites of the state's pine woods and hill regions for control of the legislature and for the distribution of political favors. White men differed vehemently at election time, but those differences were more apparent than real, certainly for black Mississippians. It is easy to exaggerate the significance of intrastate differences, and dangerous to force them too easily into stories of significant social class tension.[27] "Mississippi politics," argues one scholar, "was nothing more than a family affair."[28] A family very much in agreement, I would add, on the need for Jim Crow to protect a white people who were in the most important way one broad family. One turn-of-the-century observer wrote: "the rest of the country may be given over to Negro rule and Republican highway robbers, but old Mississippi, God bless her, will always remain true to the Democracy, Good Government, and White Supremacy."[29]

By the first decade of the twentieth century no Mississippi politician of any note would bolt the Democratic Party, as had the state's most prominent Populist, Frank Burkitt, who declared in 1892: "I was born a plebian and I prefer to suffer with my people than eat from the flesh pots of Egypt."[30] In fact, the egalitarian vision of the agrarian reformers served well among the foundations of narratives of white community in turn-of-the-century Mississippi. While Democratic primary elections continued to be strongly contested, the significance of racial difference and the need for maintaining white supremacy were shibboleths of the era and the region. Indeed, casting doubt on an opponent's zeal in defending white supremacy forced that opponent onto the defensive, much as charges of being soft on communism or family values would do later in the twentieth century.

The wide currency throughout the South of narratives such as Vardaman's confirms the centrality of race to public discourse in the Progressive Era South, a well-documented fact.[31] But close attention to Vardaman's speeches and writings reveals just how that centrality of race to twentieth-century southern culture was constructed, and why it was so tenacious. Vardaman's rhetoric was built upon broad, effective tropes of domesticity and order. Practically all white Mississippians were persuaded that racial difference existed and mattered. Dominant cultural discourses praised the sanctity of the family and a man's right to control his family and home. Vardaman's language reveals how inseparable were these narratives of white domesticity and racial difference. At the turn of the century in Mississippi, the overt celebration of white community (and its defining, shadowy other—potentially disruptive blackness) emerged not only as the language of politics, but as the language of identity as well.

Vardaman's rhetoric was in classic form during his 1907 campaign for the United States Senate. Though U.S. senators were not yet directly elected, candidates in Mississippi did actively campaign throughout the state, thus providing a prime moment to assess the broad circulation of political rhetoric that attempted to identify their interests, aspirations, and anxieties. In the campaign for the Democratic nomination, Vardaman and his opponent, U.S. Representative John Sharp Williams, deployed complementary narratives of white community and black difference that would dominate Mississippi politics for the next half-century and beyond. Vardaman moderated his earlier denunciations of wealth and privilege and concentrated instead on what his state campaign committee called the issue of "paramount, overshadowing importance": repeal of the Fifteenth Amendment to the U.S. Constitution. "The election of James K. Vardaman on this issue," they declared, "would be a fresh notice to the negro at home and elsewhere, that Mississippians never intend to furl the flag of white supremacy."[32] By spinning tales of black depravity and evoking the specter of an ever-present black threat, he attempted quite literally to make the election a referendum on the state's commitment to white supremacy.

Vardaman manipulated a language of race, domesticity, and violence that spoke to the deepest and most immediate concerns of the state's voters. As he championed the common man, he did so in a way that emphasized white commonalities, not differences. Candidate Vardaman spun narratives of whiteness and blackness, of manhood and womanhood; gender, as a discursive category, worked reciprocally with race at the heart of Vardaman's political language. He was a glowing orator and "a man of striking and attractive personality" in an age that still enjoyed listening to all-day preaching and speaking.[33] His language and plots were those of nineteenth- and early twentieth-century stage melodrama and popular fiction. "Melodrama," writes film theorist Linda Williams, is "the fundamental mode by which American mass culture has 'talked to itself' about the enduring moral dilemma of race."[34] For Vardaman and his audience, the chief moral dilemma was how best to protect white supremacy and white power. The sensationalistic plots and stereotyped characters of these melodramatic popular forms were immediately accessible, persuasive, and uniting to a broad audience of white Mississippians in a way that discussions of the tariff, political economy, and the constitutional process were not.[35]

The function of fiction within nineteenth- and early twentieth-century Anglo-American culture, argues literary historian Nancy Armstrong, was to turn "political information into the discourse of sexuality," to rewrite political conflict in personal terms that might be easily diagnosed and resolved.[36] Vardaman's novelistic and apocalyptic narratives conflated the public, white male–dominated sphere of politics and the "rest" of culture—the domestic, the female, the African American. These sorts of popular plots provided, writes Jane Tompkins, "a basis for remaking the social and political order in which events take place."[37] When Vardaman used novelistic, domestic discourse as the language of his campaigns, then, he not only brought the sexual into political discourse, he provided a popular plot through which a common sense of white Mississippi identity could be freshly imagined. His stories of rape and retribution brought his white audience together around a common fear, titillated them with the specter of black disorder creeping into white households, and provided reassuring narrative closure by implying or describing the legal or extralegal suppression of black Mississippians.

The flowering of virulent racism in southern political discourse in the early twentieth century puzzled some observers. Indeed, candidates such as Vardaman's 1907 opponent, John Sharp Williams, imagined that electoral "reforms" after the 1890 disfranchising of African Americans (and many white voters) would resolve the "race question."[38] Vardaman and others who followed him understood that eliminating the black vote did not eliminate race as a cultural and political force in Mississippi; Vardaman quickly learned the electoral reward of overt appeals to racial difference. Deploying narratives of racial danger, he offered contemporary Mississippians explanations and solutions for a host of deeply felt issues—economic status and gender roles as well as race relations.[39] In so doing, Vardaman modeled a political language and a campaign style that persisted until black votes counted in Mississippi once again.

In Vardaman's rhetoric, black education and black political rights led inexorably to black assaults upon white women. "The women of the southern states [are] today living in a state of siege," claimed the White Chief, "with more dread than in the days when the wild man and the wild beast roamed the frontier."[40] By rewriting the political in terms of the domestic, by insisting that wild men and wild beasts still threatened white ballots and white women, Vardaman's narratives redefined the persona of the politician in Mississippi and the language in which he carried his appeal to the voters. After Vardaman, anyone who sought public office in Mississippi had to be "right" on "the race question," and prepared to place it at the center of his political campaign.

The Candidates in 1907

Traditionally, the long hot summer months in Mississippi have been the season for political campaigning. The agricultural imperatives of sowing and reaping shaped hamlet and city as well as rural life. In a society attuned to agrarian rhythms, late-summer campaigning was a necessity if candidates wished to reach mass audiences. During the "lay-by" time of midsummer, the heavy spring work of breaking the land and planting and chopping the crops was done, and the furious labor of the harvest and the trial of the season-ending reckoning of accounts were still anticipated.[41]

People sought entertainment, but in Mississippi much of the population could not afford public amusements such as traveling circuses at any time of the year.[42] But simply coming to town held its own attractions. On weekends, roads were often packed with men and women on their way to town; the railroads brought in large crowds for more anticipated events. In the late summer, office seekers canvassing for votes competed with camp meetings, county fairs, and the occasional lynching for public attention.[43] The summer of 1907 in Mississippi was a busy one for political "speakings." Voters prepared to choose a senator and a governor, as well as a slate of other state and local offices. Though the Mississippi state legislature still selected the state's U.S. senators, candidates for the Senate ran during the state's regular elections; the legislature chose the candidate who won the most votes.[44] Thus, candidates and their supporters traveled from fairgrounds to courthouse public squares, creating hives of activity in the state's towns and crossroads hamlets.

In 1907, the most significant campaign being waged was for the Democratic nomination for U.S. senator, the office Governor James K. Vardaman had desired since incumbent Senator Hernando DeSoto Money announced in 1905 that he would not seek reelection.[45] During the spring before the election, Vardaman's longtime friend and confidant, the unreconstructed Confederate Dr. Benjamin F. Ward, released a pamphlet, "The Man, the Hour, and the Opportunity," that laid out Vardaman's chief campaign issue. "'The Man' was Vardaman; 'The Hour' was now; 'The Opportunity' was the repeal of the Fifteenth Amendment."[46] Before mass audiences, Vardaman preached the baseness and depravity of "the inferior races." He informed white Mississippians that theirs was a high and noble culture, their women the flower of the southland, and that he stood as their champion, their "White Chief," against predatory interests and violent threats ranging from Wall Street plutocrats to vicious and "uppity" blacks run amok. And always the governor reminded his audiences of the constant vigilance and common action needed by whites to ensure that blacks knew and stayed in their place. In his campaigns for governor and senator, Vardaman developed a national reputation for his apocalyptic rhetoric, lashing out at such targets as Theodore Roosevelt and Booker T. Washington.[47] "The Southern States," Vardaman declared, "must protect themselves. Mississippi must conserve her own civilization and by law maintain white supremacy." In Vardaman's estimation, ideas of racial harmony and black uplift had to confront hard and incontrovertible facts, wisdom that "the Southern people" had acquired during the years of slavery and Reconstruction: "they alone are capable of informing the world of the profound, God-stamped, time-fixed and unalterable incompetence of the negro for citizenship in a white man's country."[48]

Vardaman and the state's system of primary elections rose together. His mode of politics, the dynamic that he was able to establish with the state's voters, would not, in fact, have been possible without the state's primary law of 1902. Far from the longtime tilter against privilege that he sometimes claimed, Vardaman had sought to make his way within the existing system of Democratic alliances, not hammer it down. As a young man during the 1890s, Vardaman supported Mississippi's regular Democratic organization against the state's Populist challenge. Only after twice failing to win the party's gubernatorial nomination did he announce that the state's political old guard was thwarting the will of the people. In a 1902 letter to the editor of the *Meridian Weekly Star*, for example, Vardaman campaigned for governor by attacking the state's system of public education for blacks:

I make the assertion boldly that *education does not make the negro in Mississippi a more useful or desirable citizen.* . . . When you educate one of them you usually make an immoral woman, hypocritical preacher or bunglesome forgerer. . . . You dissatisfy him with his inevitable lot and then kill him for being dissatisfied. The Constitutional Convention of 1890 at a cost of $150,000 met and eliminated temporarily the negro from politics. Since that time under the absurd policy now in vogue we have spent $5,000,000 to bring him back. Now I submit . . . that is very faulty statesmanship.[49]

Later that year, President Theodore Roosevelt roused the ire of Vardaman and many other white southerners by inviting Booker T. Washington to dine at the White House. This clear breach of the color line in a domestic matter, more than any strictly political decision of the federal government, prompted angry headlines across the South. "When Mr. Roosevelt sits down to dinner with a negro, he declares that the negro is the social equal of the white man," declared the *New Orleans Times-Democrat*.[50] The *Memphis Scimitar* railed: "The most damnable outrage which has ever been perpetrated by any citizen of the United States was committed yesterday by the President when [he] invited a nigger to dine with him in the White House."[51] These attacks on Roosevelt were "mild, indeed" compared with the "vituperations" of Vardaman's own paper, the *Greenwood Commonwealth*.[52] "Let Teddy take coons to the White House," said the *Greenwood Commonwealth*, "I should not care if the walls of the ancient edifice should become so saturated with the effluvia from their rancid carcasses that a 'Chench bug' would have to crawl upon the dome . . . to avoid asphyxiation."[53] As always, Vardaman had his eye on a political target. In the following week's *Greenwood Commonwealth*, Governor Andrew Longino, Vardaman's political opponent, was linked to the "negro-philic" Roosevelt:

> WANTED, Sixteen big, fat mellow, rancid "coons" to sleep with Roosevelt when he comes down to go bear hunting with Mississippi's onliest governor Longy. . . . Teddy may bring Booker with him, and if he does Longy will have to entertain him. . . . [54]

Here, Vardaman tweaked his opponent by reminding his readers of Roosevelt's breach of the dinner table color line. He pushed the offense further by suggesting that Roosevelt, the man Vardaman called a "broncho-busting nigger lover," would transgress the bedroom color line as well, and implies too that the gender of the "coons" need not necessarily be female.[55]

Mississippi's gubernatorial race in 1903 had been the first test of the state's direct primary and gave Vardaman an opportunity to carry his racialist narratives directly to the people in a political contest. He proved a master of the mass campaign, drawing enthusiastic audiences throughout most of the state. The primary, replacing the old system of state conventions to select candidates for state office, finally gave Vardaman the gubernatorial prize. A contemporary historian argued that the rise of Vardaman coincided with a cruel turn in race relations: the campaign was "without precedent 'for low-down vulgarity and indecency. . . . There can be no doubt that the hostility of white to black is increasing.'"[56] A recent historian agrees: "Vardaman introduced the new politics and became its most flamboyant practitioner."[57] Vardaman's talent lay in realizing that the issue of racial difference, upon which essentially all white Mississippians were agreed, provided a sufficiently galvanizing narrative through which to build a political career.

In office, Vardaman continued to assert that blacks were unreliable, potentially dangerous, and unfit for the privileges of Mississippi citizenship. "There must be a moral substratum upon which to build," he reasoned, "or you cannot make a desirable citizen. The negro as a race, is devoid of that element."[58] While Vardaman argued that African Americans were unfit for political participation, his larger message was clear. Vardaman stressed to his audiences of white voters the underlying lack of "moral substratum" in blacks and from that extrapolated a host of possible dangers, ranging far beyond the world of politics. In Vardaman's rhetoric, the specter of black men assaulting white women was never far below the surface.

Some of Vardaman's contemporaries insisted that he was substance-less, a mere race-baiting demagogue. William Alexander Percy, his father defeated by Vardaman for a senate seat in 1911, did much to fix this image with his autobiography *Lanterns on the Levee: Recollections of a Planter's Son* (1941). Casting a wearied eye on the state's affairs, the aristocratic Percy concluded that Vardaman was, in truth, a man of the people.[59] The Columbia-trained Mississippi historian of Reconstruction, James W. Garner, wrote of Vardaman during his 1903 gubernatorial campaign: "He is a most violent negro-hater, and has taken advantage of the passions and prejudices of the ignorant white population to arouse their hostility to the blacks, and by this means to ride into office."[60] But it was not solely the "ignorant white population" that provided Vardaman with so many votes in his campaigns. In several elections Vardaman drew a large vote across the state, with strong showings in urban and "progressive" areas. He showed special strength in rapidly growing, relatively white, and underrepresented south Mississippi.

Why did some of his white contemporaries scold Vardaman for his flamboyant racism? They objected to Vardaman's race baiting mainly because they viewed it as counterproductive, or at best unnecessary. It is vital not to misread objection to Vardaman's candidacies for office as rejection of Vardaman's racist assumptions. In 1903, the state's major newspaper objected to Vardaman's "extreme and unceasing appeals to racial prejudice" and went on to assure its readers that not "in the remotest degree" did blacks threaten white "social, industrial, or political supremacy" in the state.[61] But clearly, contemporary white Mississippians found something appealing in Vardaman's message. Revisiting the question of white supremacy over blacks was necessary, or at least satisfying, as if the matter were not permanently settled, or simply needed periodic renewal. To their regret, Vardaman's opponents discounted white agreement upon white supremacy as a powerfully sufficient basis for a language of politics and a political campaign. Vardaman understood that narratives of white community threatened by blacks were viscerally effective because so many people believed them so strongly.

John Sharp Williams, Vardaman's 1907 opponent for the Senate, was one of those people who underestimated the power of Vardaman's rhetoric. Williams seemed the very image of the Bourbon southern politician, in sharp contrast to the White Chief, the demagogue scornful of constitutional niceties. John Sharp Williams believed with Vardaman that blacks should not vote, but thought that disfranchisement was a sufficient safeguard. Intelligent and decorous, Williams was well respected across party and regional lines. Northern newspapers applauded his "good understanding" and "sheer force and merit," as well as his ability to work with the Republican House leadership. The *New York Times,* for instance, believed that Williams had "upon the whole exercised his control wisely and in the interest of sanity and safety," and went on to worry that the next Democratic leader in the House might not be so amenable.[62]

A member of the U.S. House since 1892, Williams was esteemed by his own party. At the time of the 1907 election he had been House minority leader since 1903, and seemed destined for one of the long careers so common to Democratic congressmen in the era of the Solid South. Everything in Williams's manner bespoke regularity, order, and tradition. The scion of an old southern family, Williams enjoyed, as the son of an officer killed at Shiloh, great public respect in an age when evocation of the Lost Cause still stirred the hearts of white southerners. His education at the Universities of Virginia and Heidelberg and career as a planter and lawyer completed the stereotypi-cal image of a "planter-statesman of the Deep South." Republican James E. Watson wrote that "[n]ext to Henry Cabot Lodge, John Sharp Williams was the most scholarly man in either branch of Congress."[63]

Unlike Vardaman, however, Williams seems today a little-known figure. "Who remembers [Williams] now," wrote the Mississippian Willie Morris in 1967, "who knows much about [Williams] or cares?"[64] Even to southern historians, Williams is a vague figure. Standard works of southern history barely mention him; Williams appears not at all in Ayers's *Promise of the New South* and is quoted once in Woodward's *Origins of the New South.*[65] Occasionally, even in Mississippi, he is confused with later Mississippi congressman and governor John Bell Williams. Other than a bridge named for him in his native Yazoo County and a portrait hanging in Mississippi Senator Thad Cochran's office, Williams seems largely forgotten. In *The Crucible of Race,* Joel Williamson notes Williams's support of segregation in Wilsonian Washington, D.C. But Williamson says that the southern conservatism (as opposed to Vardaman's radicalism) represented by Williams had by World War I "neither anchor nor direction, and [was] in effect rudderless."[66] But it would be a mistake to read Williams merely as a type of politician overtaken by the rising tide of Vardamanism.

Like Vardaman, Williams told stories about white community. Unlike Vardaman's stories, though, Williams's narratives emphasized the permanence and inevitability of white control over blacks. Consider the following passage:

> There is no grander, no more superb spectacle than that of the white men of the South standing from '65 to '74 and quietly, determinedly, solidly, shoulder to shoulder in phalanx, as if the entire race were one man, unintimidated by defeat in war, unawed by adverse power, unbribed by patronage, unbought by the prospect of present material prosperity, waiting and hoping and praying for the opportunity which, in the providence of God, must come to overthrow the supremacy of "veneered savages," superficially "Americanized Africans" waiting to reassert politically and socially the supremacy of the civilization of the English-speaking white race.[67]

Williams's story of Reconstruction and Redemption is rooted in the same assumptions about black disorder and a pan-white common southern identity that one could find in Vardaman's rhetoric. One difference between the two is the overt maleness of Williams's account. Any Vardaman account of Reconstruction would, as I indicate below, raise the specter of unmastered black men threatening white women as well as white ballots. But not Williams, for whom white male mastery seemed self-evident and secure. Their stories, however, complement each other at base, and thus worked together to build a sense of white community.

Williams and Vardaman agreed that whites should control politics and society, and that blacks were inferior. Vardaman persuaded audiences by conjuring a vision of black assault before reassuring whites that they were in fact in control, in control by virtue of solidarity based upon color. Williams invoked the instinctual race consciousness of the white community as a self-evident guarantee of white rule.

Not only was Williams careful in his rhetoric and manner to convey a personal image of order and tradition, but he played as well upon contemporary impressions of the Mississippi Delta as a land of southern ladies and gentlemen. His family plantation, Cedar Grove, was located near Yazoo City, in Yazoo County. The Yazoo-Mississippi Delta covered roughly seven thousand square miles of the state, and was the center of Mississippi's cotton production.[68] Some Delta counties had a black population of well more than 80 percent. The majority of these black Mississippians worked as sharecroppers and tenants on what was described by a geologist in 1906 as land "probably unexcelled by any soil in the world thus far examined."[69] As one who knew black Mississippians as agricultural laborers and servants, Williams took great pains to assure voters that he discerned no crisis in American race relations. In Williams's rhetoric, contemporary African Americans were very much as they had always been—with the instructive exception of Reconstruction—content and best "handled" with a mixture of noblesse oblige and occasional firm correction.[70]

Williams argued that Mississippi had attained equilibrium in race relations, in state politics, and with the national government. This settlement was predicated upon the removal of black Mississippians from state politics, with the tacit agreement of the national government that Mississippi would be allowed to run its "family" affairs as it saw fit. Given Williams's conception of the polity as patriarchal household, such an understanding was both essential and sufficient. Williams's views on race and community are best extrapolated from a situation he imagined several years before the 1907 election. The central problem of society, he asserted, is the necessary foundation of good government:

> You could ship-wreck 10,000 illiterate white Americans on a desert island, and in three weeks they would have a fairly good government, conceived and administered upon fairly democratic lines. You could ship-wreck 10,000 negroes, every one . . . a graduate of Harvard University, and in less than three years they would have retrograded governmentally; half of the men would have been killed, and the other half would have two wives apiece.[71]

Williams and Vardaman agreed that blacks were irrational and incapable of restraining their passions. Williams argued, much as Vardaman did, that black political participation would bring chaos and governmental retrogression. At first glance, Williams appears to argue that the race problem is a matter for political science, not eugenics. But while Williams did not raise the specter of miscegenation, he, like Vardaman, elided disordered government and disordered families. Most white southern accounts of Reconstruction sympathized, recalling the years before "Redemption" as ones of wholesale black malfeasance. But as Williams constantly pointed out, the framers of the 1890 Mississippi constitution had ensured that the blacks would never again have such an opportunity. The Supreme Court in effect agreed when they upheld that constitution in 1898.[72]

There is no doubt that in the first decade of the twentieth century black Mississippians posed no real threat to white economic and political power. At the 1900 census, Mississippi was home to almost 10 percent of the nation's African Americans, with a black population of nearly 60 percent, numbers approached only by South Carolina.[73] "The South cannot raise cotton without the negro," went a typical and frank refrain. "Southern farmers are accustomed to domineer over the negro, having once owned him as a slave; and the negro being used to such a policy, could not work without it, because he has never been trained to work by direction of his own mind."[74] With the law affording black labor practically no redress for fraud or other grievances, the landowners' preference for black rather than white workers is hardly shocking. John Sharp Williams was somewhat less admiring of black farmers' skills: "one of the best plantation hands in the world and about the poorest farmer that God ever made."[75] Whatever their opinion of his services as a laborer, however, white Mississippians were adamant that the black man's realm of endeavor did not include politics.

While they took great and often violent steps to keep the color line drawn at the ballot box, white Mississippians loudly asserted that black Mississippians were thoroughly uninterested in politics. An editor from Williams's hometown, for instance, argued,

> If it were not for the agitators one half the people would not know that there were such a thing as the race issue. . . . There never was in this state a race issue, except when the negroes were incited by bad white men, and this was in the days of reconstruction. . . . The whites will always control the state's public affairs, and this fact the negroes now realize.[76]

As one who agreed with this reading of black Mississippians, Williams was particularly disgusted with Vardaman's incessant stress on the "negro question." The state's government, Williams assured voters, was safely in the white man's hands. "I think that the South ought to take its part in the solving of the great questions," he wrote, "and not occupy itself 'baying at the moon.'"[77] But at the same time, Williams left no doubt about his conception of the meaning of citizenship for black Americans: "the Democratic party is the white man's party." He proclaimed: "Every young man wants to know that he is living in a country whose destinies will be controlled by the white race."[78] For Williams, fidelity to the Democratic Party was the mark of a southern man. Because political participation was in effect closed to Mississippi's African American men, they could not be the threat that Vardaman claimed, since to Williams they were something less than men.

To Williams, then, Vardaman's race baiting and, moreover, his insistence that the state and nation were hurtling toward racial Armageddon, appeared self-serving and dangerous. "If the agitators would cease their passionate appeals," agreed the *Yazoo Herald,*

A feeling of harmony could be established between the races. . . . But these incessant appeals to the prejudice . . . will ultimately lead to results that will make
the peaceful settlement of the question an almost utter impossibility. Those
who are sowing the wind will eventually be called to reap the whirlwind.[79]

Defenders of the status quo insisted that black Mississippians were effectively disfranchised—and hence removed from the realm of politics—by the
1890 Mississippi Constitution, with its provisions for a literacy test, poll tax,
and complex registration and residency requirements.[80] If Vardaman were
elected to the Senate, Williams asserted, his wild schemes for constitutional
tinkering would only invite ridicule: "I have noticed in a somewhat extended
public life that men with hobbies have no influence."[81] For Williams, a public
man was decorous and orderly, unlike the firebrand Vardaman.

Through the 1907 campaign, Williams traded on his image of genteel effectiveness while encouraging the caricature of Vardaman as a bumbling ig-
noramus. Vardaman's supporters spread rumors that Williams was a drunk;
the "White Chief" scored points as a self-made man. The candidates had
spent months attacking and lampooning one another in the state press and
by personal correspondence. The Meridian debate would prove a powerful
demonstration of the effectiveness and essentially complementary nature of
Vardaman's and Williams's narratives of white identity.

The Debate

By the afternoon of July 4, 1907, more than twenty thousand people had ar-
rived in Meridian, Mississippi, for the climax of the Democratic senatorial
campaign, victory in which was tantamount to election as the state's next
United States senator. They came from Marion and Daleville, Kewanee and
Toomsuba, the hamlets of Lauderdale County; they came from all parts of the
state, from cities throughout the South, and included among their number
correspondents from national newspapers and magazines.[82] Arriving by railroad, in ox-drawn carts, and in automobiles, they quickly packed the streets
and strained the public accommodations of the small city. On that hot July
day Meridian turned out in force to hear Governor James K. Vardaman debate U.S. Representative John Sharp Williams in their only joint appearance
before the August election.

In this charged atmosphere, enthusiastic crowds lined the streets of Meridian, a city that epitomized the uneven growth and change that Mississippi had known since the end of Reconstruction. In the antebellum period, the city had scarcely existed at all. By 1880 it boasted a foundry and a machine shop and a population of four thousand. By 1907 the population had increased to more than twenty-five thousand. Near the eastern edge of the state, some fifteen miles from the Alabama border, Meridian was a manufacturing center and shipping point surrounded by booming lumber towns, and at the turn of the century was experiencing spectacular growth.[83] The city's streets were paved and sidewalks had been laid. Its paved streets, sidewalks, modern sewerage system, and electric streetcar lines caused a contemporary to label it "a modern city in every sense of the word."[84]

Located in John Sharp Williams's old congressional district, the debate allowed Williams a chance to campaign among people who knew him well. Despite Meridian's fondness for Williams, however, a recent flash of interracial violence prepared the people there to hear with piqued attention the tales of racial danger and tumult that Vardaman regularly delivered. The previous Christmas Eve, Governor Vardaman had ordered state troops through Meridian on their way to the Kemper County settlement of Wahalak, some forty miles away. Three days earlier, Alabama's Governor William Dorsey Jelks wrote Vardaman: "I have received yesterday this telegram. . . . 'Have you been notified by Governor of Mississippi to be prepared for uprising of negroes Christmas Eve night.'"[85] Jelks suspected that the report was a false alarm. Despite Jelks's suspicion that the report merely was one of the periodic rumors of black uprisings that haunted the imagination of white southerners, the Christmas Eve violence did erupt.[86]

The circumstances of the Kemper County violence are unclear, but it appears that in the aftermath of a lynching, whites decided to inflict general punishment upon Kemper County blacks, "who had been getting defiant of late."[87] White Mississippians did not like to dwell on black resistance to Jim Crow, but contemporaries knew that a number of the Wahalak community's African Americans were armed and vigilant.[88] These black Mississippians had recently taken up arms again to defend themselves, and at least seventeen men (one white and sixteen black) were killed before the status quo was restored. The state press gave the incident prominent coverage, as it did whenever incidents of black "defiance" were quickly and harshly punished.

Nor was this occurrence an anomaly: the state regularly led the nation in documented lynchings, with seventy-four during Vardaman's years as governor—one every twenty-five days, on average. "To my mind," declared Piney Woods School Principal William Henry Holtzclaw in 1915, Mississippi "was the darkest section of the South for a colored man."[89]

Ironically, a dominant message of Vardaman's campaign was his claim that as governor he had not only reduced the number of "serious crimes by negroes" to an all-time low, but that he had reduced the number of lynchings in the state as well.[90] Supporters asserted that by making discriminatory acts against blacks legal, Vardaman had made white vigilante justice less necessary; Vardaman himself took pride in his use of state troops to stop mob violence against black prisoners (some of whom were later hanged under the aegis of the law). "Several instances of troops mysteriously appearing in time to frustrate lynching plans have had a wholesome effect," reported Mississippi journalist Garrard Harris in 1905. Now, claimed Harris, "there is little disposition to interfere with the routine of the law" under Governor Vardaman unless, he noted, "the crime is of violence against some woman."[91] This exception is, of course, a significant one and goes far toward explaining the particular contours of Vardaman's racist narratives. As a sitting governor in 1907, he did not want to imply that his was a lawless state; therefore, again and again he conjured up the one crime that white southerners said they could not help but avenge with violence, law or no law.

In his "Biennial Message" as governor in 1906, Vardaman all but encouraged mob lynching for rape. After citing several recent cases of rape, Vardaman declared that in each case "the disgusting brute would have been hung if the law had permitted," and that "they should have been hung, all decent white people will admit." If, he warned, the legislature does not

Correct this fatal defect in the laws . . . the people—the source of all political power . . . will take the law in their own hands. . . . The white people of Mississippi . . . will not suffer a brute to enter the sacred precincts of their homes and despoil them, or waylay their wives, mothers, daughters and sisters and with brute-like ferocity assault them upon the highway and then go unwhipped of justice.[92]

For Vardaman, rape was by definition a crime committed by a black man upon a white woman; this assumption need not even be voiced because no other possibility existed within his representation of the act. Moreover, this assumption that all rapists were black men (and, by implication, vice versa) made it easy for Vardaman to translate this message of black sexual corruption into broader social and political terms. Vardaman declared himself

> Unable to account for the frequency of rape upon any other theory than the growing disposition and consuming aspiration among the negroes to break down social barriers which debar them from equality with the white race.... This crime is the cruel and horrible manifestation of the negroes [*sic*] hope for the unattainable.[93]

The social and political aspirations of black men, argued Vardaman, were indistinguishable from their sexual aspiration to conquer white women. White southern men thus faced a common enemy, and thus had a common identity and purpose.

Despite Vardaman's claims of an orderly and lawful state, even the most cursory look at a Mississippi newspaper from this period suggests that white violence against blacks was both common and extreme, and that blacks did not always accept this violence passively. On the front page of the *Jackson Clarion-Ledger* for October 7, 1906, for instance, six of the eleven lead stories involved blacks being chased and beaten or lynched by angry white mobs: "Negro Shoots Two White Men and Mob of Two Hundred is Storming Jail," reads one; "Two Negroes Kick Souls into Eternity at Rope's End," reads another.[94] Vardaman's narratives, then, fell upon an audience accustomed to a very high degree of everyday racial violence.

Meridian's dawn on the Fourth of July was broken by a cannonade, eerily reminiscent, to Confederate veterans at least, of spring and summer mornings more than a generation earlier. Later that morning, the air began "resounding at intervals with the music of brass bands," as the supporters of each candidate made their way to the Southern Hotel, the headquarters of John Sharp Williams, and the Grand Avenue, the headquarters of Governor Vardaman. Vardaman's supporters wore badges of white silk, labeling themselves as the "White Chief's" men. In honor of Independence Day, and apparently intending a commentary on that summer's campaign, the *Meridian Weekly Star* ran on its front page a tribute to the heroes of 1776: "There is no call to arms today; / This is a silent fight, / With demagogue arrayed 'gainst, they / Who would their country's might, / Guard well from day to day."[95]

Vardaman was at his best in this carnival-like atmosphere of parades and campaign rallies. In the year before the election, he rejected Williams's frequent calls for a series of formal, structured debates, insisting instead that he preferred to talk to the people, "the source of all political power," rather than to Williams.[96] Letters between the two men show that Williams was trying in vain to organize "joint discussions" between them as early as November 1906. By February 1907, both Williams and Vardaman had become quite plain about the question of public debates. On February 16, Williams wrote to Vardaman that he wanted to have scheduled "in all about a hundred joint discussions up to the time of the Senatorial primary." He continued:

> I think the people of Mississippi would like to hear us discuss our points of difference in their presence . . . so that the great question before the country could be evolved in the course of debate and presented by each of us in accordance with our ideas of what was good for the public welfare.[97]

Perhaps because of Williams's national reputation as an excellent debater, Vardaman firmly and repeatedly rejected the speech, rejoinder, and surrejoinder format that Williams suggested:

> As the campaign . . . progresses we shall be permitted, I trust, to speak from the same platform but under no circumstances will I consent to an arrangement for the order of speaking as you suggest. . . . [M]y time will be limited and instead of listening to your always interesting speeches I prefer to devote my time to speaking at other places.[98]

Vardaman may have feared Williams's rhetorical skills. Historian George Osborn also speculates that Vardaman knew that as a highly popular governor he would draw large audiences that would otherwise not be available to Williams.[99] A third possible motive for avoiding a series of traditional debates was that Vardaman's political style simply demanded a different sort of spectacle. The show that Vardaman put on in Meridian on July 4 and the enthusiasm of the crowd's response imply that this third motive may have been strongest.

Making his way to the speakers' stand in a lumber wagon drawn by "fifteen or twenty yoke of oxen," the "White Chief" was dressed in his traditional outfit of a white suit, white shoes, shirt and tie, a white carnation, and a broad-brimmed black hat. At forty-six years old he wore his black hair long—well below the collar, a match for his "long, flowing coattails." "He probably looked to his opponents," writes one biographer, "like an overdressed medicine show man." "When Vardaman alighted from the wagon, 'his ardent supporters took his broad brimmed black hat . . . and cut it into small bits which were sold [as fund-raising souvenirs] for one dollar each.'"[100] This desire to possess what seemed almost a holy relic of the White Chief suggests both the enthusiasm and atmosphere he and his supporters generated.

Shortly after ten o'clock that morning the candidates moved to the speakers' platform, surrounded by some ten thousand spectators. After an introduction by the president of the local board of trade and cotton exchange, Williams prepared to speak. Throughout the campaign, Williams condemned Vardaman's unorthodox style, his refusal to debate formally, and his emotional appeals for the repeal of the Fifteenth Amendment. The real issue for the voters to decide, Williams argued, was which of the two men was better suited, by experience and temperament, to represent the state in debates over the "issues of the gravest and most vital sort knocking at our legislative doors for solution." Moreover, he added, the "negro question" needed no attention in Washington. It was a distinctly southern problem, best handled by the southern states themselves, long familiar with "the general incapacity of the negro race for self-government."[101] In short, Williams tried to persuade Mississippi voters that Vardaman's calls for constitutional amendment were neither necessary nor wise. Though he never disagreed with the governor about the wisdom of black disfranchisement, Williams balked at Vardaman's attempts to cloud what he saw as the substantive issues of the campaign, such as government ownership of the railroads, tariff reform, and trust regulation. Above all, Vardaman's stories of rape and violence seemed indecorous and unnecessary.

Williams began his address by challenging Vardaman to confine his remarks to relevant matters. Williams at once congratulated and reminded the audience that they were gathered to educate themselves on matters that were "the subject of all the contemplation, study and determination of a self-governing people." He added: "you must keep before your mind that the senate of the United States is a legislative body and to which men are sent with the expectation of doing things and not for doing things they profess impossible to do." One such impossibility, he assured them, was the repeal of the Fifteenth Amendment and the modification of the Fourteenth Amendment that Vardaman had made the centerpiece of his appeal to the voters. Obviously surprising Vardaman, Williams handed the governor a copy of the U.S. Constitution, and invited him to "take a lead pencil, strike out that part of it which he does not want, and insert the part that he wants put in there." Williams then admonished Vardaman for implying that he was less vigilant than the governor on the question of white supremacy. There was no "real issue between them," he maintained, "upon the desirability of white political supremacy and the undesirability of black political domination."[102] Indeed, in a newspaper interview for the *Jackson Clarion-Ledger* in February, Williams had scoffed that Vardaman "seems to think that he has a monopoly on 'nigger issues.'"[103]

Again, it is vital not to mistake Williams's more "genteel" style for a position that was fundamentally less racist than Vardaman's. Though they were delivered with decorum, Williams's speeches were unapologetic defenses of Mississippi's white homes, communities, and racial caste system. In an important speech that he made in Walthall, Mississippi, in November 1906, Williams had attacked Vardaman's proposal to repeal the Fifteenth Amendment by arguing that Mississippi's 1890 Constitution effectively and legally solved the problem posed by the Civil War and Reconstruction—how "to save the white man's civilization, based upon his peculiar code of ethics, which code, in its turn, has for its keystone, the sanctity of his family life."[104]

As they were for Vardaman, white civilization and white domestic life were of primary importance to Williams; but whereas Vardaman exercised fears about the violation of these things, Williams emphasized their sanctity and security. Replying in a 1902 congressional speech to a northern congressman who asked him to defend the 1890 Constitution and especially the grandfather clauses that some southern states had adopted to disfranchise black voters, Williams replied in calm legal and then in stirring emotional terms:

> If the Supreme Court decides that the "grandfather clause" . . . is unconstitutional, that clause will go by the way; and when it goes by the way, if it shall, it will still leave us what our race has always possessed, and especially that superb part of the race to which I belong—the Southern white people, almost purely of English-speaking blood in their derivation—it will leave us with the intelligence, with the ingenuity, with the courage and the resolution to take care of the white man's code of ethics—his sacred family life, the capstone of it, and Caucasian civilization, the fruit of it all [loud applause]— without violating one word of the Constitution of the United States.[105]

And though Williams avoided Vardaman's campaign narratives of rape and miscegenation, in 1904 he attributed to the Civil War, with its discipline and "racial organization," the prevention of "the Africanization of the South," the "hybridization of races, a lowering of the ethical standard and a degradation, if not loss, of civilization." Only the lessons of the Civil War led the white South through the "ten long years [of Reconstruction] during every day and every night of which Southern womanhood was menaced and Southern manhood humiliated."[106]

Similarly, Williams repeatedly dismissed Vardaman's calls for the repeal of the Fifteenth Amendment not because he supported the right of African Americans to vote, of course, but because he saw it as dangerous and vulgar showmanship. "Nobody but a man with his head in the clouds, or in a dark closet," he said wryly, "has the slightest notion that two-thirds of the Representatives in the National Congress and three-fourths of the States of the Union can be prevailed upon . . . to endorse this movement."[107] A more likely scenario, he argued, was that Vardaman's pronouncements would reawaken the North's interest in civil rights, in which case only a majority vote of both houses would be required to test the resolve of Mississippians to defy the federal government.

The structure and substance of the Meridian "debate," then, assumed a familiar pattern. As he had in countless congressional speeches and newspaper interviews, Williams began by speaking on what he felt were the substantive issues facing Mississippi and the nation: economic growth, the tariff, and nationalization of the railroads. Throughout this 1907 campaign, he had sought to impress upon voters that Vardaman was soft on such substantive issues. Most significant, Williams accused Vardaman of waffling on the question of the federal purchase of the railroads. "What is the Governor's position?" he asked in a February interview. "As I understand it, he opposes the proposition of railroad ownership by the Federal government 'for the present' or 'at this time,' but says that 'ultimately' he may or may not."[108]

But in Meridian as in previous forums, Vardaman almost immediately pulled the debate toward the question of race and, especially, toward the social and cultural need to repeal the Fifteenth Amendment. After Williams finished speaking, Vardaman rose and acknowledged the enthusiastic audience. The following day's *Meridian Weekly Star* provided an admiring, even fawning, physical description of the governor, a description that unambiguously suggests the model of white masculine authority that Vardaman embodied to his supporters:

He stepped forward, brushed back those long, silky lionel locks, wiped the sweat from his massive head and faced the vast audience: The picture of one of the world's noblemen, open of countenance and fearless of eye, handsome of men and beautifully symmetric in physique—a master of men and the champion of all women.

Vardaman "then read an extract from the declaration of independence and proceeded to take up the white man's rights of supremacy."[109]

Next, Vardaman briefly answered his opponent's charges that he was a novice in national and international affairs. Had he not long been, Vardaman asked, a foe of imperialism? Not only did Roosevelt's imperialist ventures aid business interests, but they threatened to give America just what it did not need—more members of inferior races to oversee.[110] As for his services as governor, he had fought for a series of progressive measures, including limits to corporate landholding, support for public education (for whites only), and modification of the state's horrific penitentiary system. Vardaman also introduced a law requiring "equal but separate accommodations for white and colored races" on streetcars, leading to a black boycott of the segregated lines. "Since the coming of Governor Vardaman," one black commentator understated, "the thinking Negro has come to realize that conditions are changing somewhat."[111]

While Williams may have been sounder and better informed on the issues he wished to debate, Vardaman swayed the crowd. Vardaman's immersion within popular culture is most evident in the way that he borrowed the language of the stage and popular fiction to narrate his political message to voters. This language carried such appeal because "the clash between good and evil found in all melodrama provided the means for exploring social and political issues in personal terms. The exploration of contemporary concerns about class and gender [and race] gave melodrama its immediacy, while the placing of these issues in a personal context gave it emotional force." The heart of Vardaman's message was domestic melodrama, which presented "primal fears clothed in everyday dress."[112] His favorite was a story that in various forms ran throughout his speeches and writings, from his earliest days in Greenwood as a newspaper editor through his political campaigns to his later days on the Chautauqua circuit. "My friends," he told the audience at Meridian:

> The mounted constable gets on his horse and starts out for his ride. He meets a young buck negro. He accosts him. Where are you going, Buck? Going to town. Where have you been? Been out here working at a saw mill. Buck passes down the street. He spies a little cottage; he enters that cottage; he finds a mother and daughter there, the husband and brother out in the field at work. The beast goes in and commits that crime which forever blasts the peace, the purity, and the happiness of that home. The constable comes along. He may possibly arrest him and visit upon him punishment. But he has not brought back the love and light and purity of that home.[113]

The governor prefaced this cautionary tale with a disclaimer that he did not bear hatred for blacks, citing the affection that he felt still for the antebellum mammy.[114] Contrasting this maternal, nurturing, yet dependent mammy with the "negro fiend," "Buck," we may better understand the threat Vardaman was delineating.

Buck is the stereotypical hypersexualized black man. No tenant or farm laborer, he looms more threateningly here because of his employment in a sawmill, with the greater financial and social independence that wage labor brought. Sawmills and lumber camps of the Deep South were infamous for their violence and, more important, for the transience and anonymity of the men who worked and played there. Like Thomas Sutpen's domain in *Absalom, Absalom!,* the lumber towns of southern Mississippi saw the arrival of what whites viewed as strange, anonymous black men to an area undergoing a particularly visible and dislocating transformation. As the great longleaf pine forests of southern Mississippi were extracted, thriving towns grew from the rough logging camps and railroad junctions.[115] Governor Vardaman's desk was crowded with petitions for incorporation from communities throughout southern Mississippi, and he was quick to calculate their growing electoral weight. White landowners throughout the state hated the labor recruiters who came to take away "their" blacks, holding out the lure of higher wages and greater independence. The white farmer, squeezed by the railroad, the bank, and the merchant, found in Vardaman's tales confirmation of what he saw each day, and sometimes took his appeal to the "White Chief" himself. B. W. Whittington, a Mississippi farmer, wrote this appeal to the governor:

> It does look to me like if it was looked in to the state would take back some of her land men has come in here & bring negros to take up home steads. . . . A poor man cant get it but a rich man & turpentine men came in with negros From Ala & takenup land & they boxd the timber & then left it. I wish you could see This Robery you would be Surprised. . . . I expect to vote for you a gain.[116]

The other current running through Vardaman's "Buck" story is the highly resonant Victorian narrative of the home as a sacred refuge. In Vardaman's tale, the violation of home and wife and daughter might well be read as the violation of a white man's sacred trust, making this part of his story equally effective to the rural whites and the townspeople of the middle class. This domestic ideology, central to middle-class capitalist individualism, broadened the rhetorical impact of Vardaman's message. Williams, too, had long argued that the overthrow of "black rule" in Mississippi was necessary "to save the white man's civilization" and "the sanctity of his family life."[117] For Williams, though, the familial, the domestic, remained secured by white men's control of politics. Not so for Vardaman, whose message collapsed this distinction, making the "black threat" seem all the more immediate to white Mississippians.

Vardaman's narratives of the embattled white family played upon and underscored the tales of racial violence that dominated Mississippi newspapers. The day of the Meridian debate, the *Meridian Weekly Star* reported a story that could have been one of Vardaman's own: "Negro Assailed White Girl, Meets Usual Fate; Brute Lurking in Bushes Rushes Upon His Victim at Work in the Fields as Soon as Her Brother Leaves Her Alone—Identified by Girl and is Mobbed."[118] There is an obvious and telling difference, however, between Vardaman's narratives and this one. Unlike Vardaman's "Buck" story, the victim here is assaulted not in the home, but at work in the fields. Field labor, in fact, was an experience that many women of both races shared, though white Mississippians went out of their way to downplay such commonalities. Attempting to craft a shared white identity, Vardaman's anecdote evoked the white home. Such narratives of domesticity erased class difference by drawing on a model of shared white domesticity and identity, in which all white readers or listeners could comfortably participate. For Vardaman to have pointed out the assault of a woman working in the field would have immediately foregrounded economic differences among members of his white audience. The white audience would have been divided between those whose sisters, wives, and daughters worked in the fields, and those whose did not. Instead, Vardaman's narrative carefully divided southern culture along racial rather than class lines. The repeal of the Fifteenth Amendment rather than, for instance, an equitable economic system for all citizens, was the solution to the working family's ills.

In his rejoinder to Vardaman, Williams suggested that only "fools" would "suppose that the Fifteenth Amendment had something to do with [black] crime," and that by asserting as much Vardaman was side-stepping the real issues of the campaign.[119] Although most national and even Mississippi newspapers agreed with Williams on this point and believed that the senator had won the debate, Vardaman's message nevertheless appealed to the Meridian audience. A Georgian in the audience assessed the debate this way: "When I came here, knowing that Mr. Williams was a man of national reputation, I expected to find the sentiment [of the crowd] largely for him, but much to my surprise I find that Vardaman certainly has the crowd."[120]

Responses to the White Chief

Vardaman played the role of White Patriarch to full effect some three weeks later in the southern Mississippi town of Brookhaven. The prosperous village of 3,500 lay on the Illinois Central Railroad, and had ripened into middle-class respectability as a shipping point for timber and cotton.[121] Brookhaven turned out to hear Vardaman speak at one of the town's proudest accomplishments, Whitworth Female College. Vardaman's campaign now approached high theater, directed by the audience as much as by the "White Chief" himself. Brookhaven offered the governor a hero's welcome:

Mary Thomas Flood, a bright and sweet little Brookhaven miss of 9 . . . presented the Governor . . . with a large bouquet of beautiful white flowers, tied with white ribbons and accompanied with this greeting in verse:

TO THE "WHITE CHIEFTAN [*sic*]."
White flowers to our chieftan white,
Brookhaven's daughters send;
To welcome him with glad delight
The Southland's truest friend.
Be not afraid! Thou white man's chief,
The Anglo-Saxon race
Has yet to bend its neck beneath
A victor's cruel mace.
The blood is yours on land and sea
Uphold thro' its supremacy.

All the elements of Vardaman's narratives of white identity are present in this scene. The "sweet little miss" herself stands at once as the flower of whiteness, and also of course a potential object of black lust. Anglo-Saxon supremacy rings out, with the poem's declarations of defiance and racial victory. No one in Brookhaven that day wrangled with questions of the tariff or income tax, banking or the ownership of railroads. Instead, in this campaign Vardaman's idiom was the language of politics.[122]

Logically enough, an African American newspaper published in Brookhaven, *The People's Relief*, reacted more skeptically to the governor's candidacy. "'In what respect,' asked the editor, "is Mr. Vardaman like a negro woman with a wig on her head? He's always got something on to fool his people.'" The white-owned *Brookhaven Semi-Weekly Leader* thundered back: "Another Negro Editor Siding With Mr. Williams," claiming that Williams was regarded "as the negro's defender and champion in this senatorial race."[123] But *The People's Relief* was doing more than taking sides in an election. In lampooning Vardaman as a dissimulating black woman, the newspaper was subverting the very essence of Vardaman and his message. Not the virile champion of whiteness of his own sensationalist melodrama, Vardaman became in this mocking caricature a fraud and a sham, the antithesis of what he purported to be.

Less than three years later the white citizens of Brookhaven had tired of this brand of journalism from *The People's Relief* and its editor, Eugene N. Bryant. Bryant, the *Brookhaven Semi-Weekly Leader* reported, had "made himself obnoxious by certain publications made in his sheet; the negro is a menace to any community in which he resides." On May 17, 1910, a "few determined citizens" delivered an ultimatum to Bryant: leave town on the Number Four train that evening or face their wrath. According to the *Brookhaven Semi-Weekly Leader,* Bryant did not wait for the deadline, but fled town that afternoon, "Accompanied by his big fat wife." Bryant was accused of stirring up "race hatred" by reprinting material from other black newspapers. Any black editor in Mississippi risked such a reaction when venturing to comment on substantive public issues.[124] Forced to flee town for "'dabbling in politics,'" his home and press were destroyed, and no file of Bryant's newspaper survives. The irony here is blatant and telling: in the name of white civilization and the white family, a black man's home and livelihood were destroyed, his wife insulted, and his family chased from town. The white male defenders of the white home rejected with violence the sanctity of the black home.

Effectively disfranchised by Jim Crow legislation and largely silenced by actions such as those in Brookhaven, African Americans nevertheless played a significant role in the politics of Vardaman's Mississippi. Racial difference was at the center of Mississippi's social and cultural life and at the center of political campaigns. Blacks may not have voted in the 1907 Democratic primary, but their mere presence at some of Williams's speeches was powerful propaganda for Vardaman supporters. When the Vardaman-backing *Brookhaven Semi-Weekly Leader* published articles claiming that blacks had been present at Williams's speeches in Hattiesburg and Poplarville, the congressman was forced to respond, denying that black attendance was large.[125] And when Vardaman supporters accused Williams of arranging for the registration of black voters, who would presumably vote for him, Williams replied angrily: "Anybody who says that any Negro has been registered at my instance or knowledge or would be, is a liar."[126] The fear that blacks *might* vote endangered Williams's candidacy and their public presence alone made an impact upon the campaign, especially its rhetoric. Because of Vardaman's success in manipulating what Williams called "nigger issues," Williams found it expedient to sing to Vardaman's tune.

Conclusions

The narrative "participation" of black American men and white women in this 1907 campaign demonstrates that we cannot assess the strength and appeal of "Vardamanism" solely in terms of votes cast. To do so overlooks a more fundamental reason why narratives of white identity retained a tenacious hold in Mississippi long after the White Chief's political demise. Ironically, the people of the state who reviled Vardaman and his successors, Theodore Bilbo, John Rankin, and Ross Barnett as unsophisticated bigots, shared with them perhaps more than they knew. White supremacy, whether enforced by the coarse hatred of a lynch mob or by the paternalism of a planter who benevolently asked the opinions of his tenants and croppers, was a doctrine that precious few Mississippians, white or black, publicly challenged.

Vardaman did not invent race baiting in Mississippi or the broader South. The period from the 1890s through the First World War remains the most virulently racist period in our nation's public life—the nadir for African Americans, in historian Rayford Logan's judgment.[127] But few public figures, and no other Mississippi politician, had made the issue as central to his message or to his persona as Vardaman did. The electoral rewards were potentially enormous. Perhaps no other state was as race conscious as Mississippi, although it bears repeating that consciousness to race was not a sin unique to the South or to Mississippi. Nevertheless, racial mores governed the actions and thoughts of all Mississippians. That they were uncodified, often unspoken, and frustratingly variable from place to place made them all the more hazardous to black Mississippians, and contributed to a self-policing by both races probably more effective than any codification could have ensured. Whites, too, were early on schooled in the racialized rudiments of conduct. No one growing up in the state, then or later, could fail to be aware of what felt like essential differences between the races. Language, work, recreation, food, sexual conduct, and the most basic gender roles all were fundamentally shaped by the subtle, pervasive, and all but overwhelming doctrine of racial difference.[128]

Most important, the scholarship, popular literature, public celebrations, and public spaces of the state enforced an ideology that taught that Mississippi history was white history, that stability and orthodoxy were the hallmarks of southern culture, and that men and women had natural and separate spheres of action, spheres that white men were to dominate and protect. The 1890 Mississippi Constitution, so its framers and defenders claimed, killed the race question as a substantive issue in Mississippi politics. Yet thirteen years later, Vardaman campaigned and won on a platform in which narratives of racial danger were the basis of his appeal to the voters, no matter what defenders of his progressive record may claim. Politics, far from being removed from the realm of racial partisanship, was in fact linked with a construction of whiteness and southernness, with the Jim Crow settlement as its foundation. Though Vardaman and his more polished opponents, LeRoy Percy and John Sharp Williams, disagreed on such questions as the nationalization of the railroads or American involvement in the Great War, they shared fundamental beliefs about the shape and nature of southern culture. Seemingly in disagreement, their actions and rhetoric in fact reinforced the prevailing Jim Crow orthodoxy as the essence of southernness. Vardaman built upon and at the same time restructured ideas already present in turn-of-the-century Mississippi. "Vardamanism," then, was not the house that James K. Vardaman built, but a world that white Mississippians made together.

Williams's allies predicted that Vardaman stood no chance against a man of Williams's stature; some estimated that Williams would win by twenty thousand votes. A newspaper supporting Williams argued that Vardaman had erred in agreeing to the Meridian debate: "Goliath had his David, Roland his Oliver, Napoleon his Waterloo . . . and Vardaman his Meridian."[129] For weeks, the result of the primary was in doubt. In the end, Williams did prevail by 648 votes, the closest senatorial election in state history. But as the campaign progressed, many noticed that Williams took great pains to assure audiences that he was fundamentally in sympathy with Vardaman on the Fifteenth Amendment question. As for the danger Vardaman saw stalking Mississippi's white women, Williams admitted that "race is greater than law now and then, and protection of women transcends all law, human and divine."[130]

After his defeat by Williams, Vardaman had vowed to run for the next vacant senate seat. The seat opened in 1909 with the death of Senator Anselm McLaurin. Early the next year the state legislature, meeting as a party caucus, chose a candidate to fill the remaining two years of McLaurin's term. Anti-Vardaman forces combined behind Greenville planter and lawyer LeRoy Percy. Vardaman's supporters quickly levied charges of a "corrupt caucus," complete with bribery, proffered offices, and freely flowing whiskey. Percy spent the next two years enduring the sniping and complaints of Vardaman's supporters, led by the state's rising political star, Theodore Bilbo. Bertram Wyatt-Brown argues that "few senatorial incumbents ever faced more daunting prospects for reelection than LeRoy Percy."[131] Sensing victory, Vardaman's campaign was more restrained than his 1907 race; he and his supporters painted Percy as a high-living Delta planter whose 1910 victory had thwarted the true will of the people. In a fit of pique, the Sewanee- and University of Virginia–educated Percy allegedly referred to Vardaman's supporters as "rednecks" and "cattle," a statement that pro-Vardaman forces latched onto with glee.[132]

On the evening of July 4, 1911, Vardaman brought his triumphant campaign processional back to Meridian. Bands, men with torches, and men on horseback led Vardaman's wagon, drawn by eighty oxen, into the city. They carried signs and banners declaring themselves "Hillbillies," "Rednecks," and "Cattle," and bore before Vardaman a sign proclaiming him "The White Chief." The son of his opponent, LeRoy Percy, observed the campaign with disgust:

> I looked over the ill-dressed, surly audience, unintelligent and slinking, and heard [Percy] appeal to them for fair treatment of the Negro and explain to them the tariff and the Panama tolls situation. I studied them as they milled about. They were the sort of people that lynch Negroes, that mistake hoodlumism for wit, and cunning for intelligence, that attend revivals and fight and fornicate in the bushes afterward. They were undiluted Anglo-Saxons. They were the sovereign voter. It was so horrible it seemed unreal.[133]

In 1911, Vardaman carried sixty-one of sixty-six counties and took well over 60 percent of the vote in a three-man race; Percy finished a distant third.[134] Vardaman had not toned down his unmistakable message: "In my state next to the virtue of our women the most sacred thing is the ballot."[135] Both, he no longer needed to add, were for white men only.

For the rest of his public life, "the negro question" remained for Vardaman the central and nearly all-consuming issue. As late as 1919, Vardaman attacked state and national politicians by questioning their position on the issue. In his newspaper, *Vardaman's Weekly,* he repeatedly criticized Mississippi Governor Longino's "Negro Record." When Longino proposed in his inaugural address that county governments should reimburse families of lynching victims, Vardaman asked if Longino could have "ever felt in his heart that the good people of any county should pay . . . damages to the family of the brute who put his filthy lustful black hand to the lovely white throat of one of their sweet, fair, lovely daughters. . . ."[136] Borrowing the same Bible verse that Thomas Dixon used as the title for his novel *The Leopard's Spots,* Vardaman added, "Can a negro change his color or a leopard change his spots?" Not only was such rhetoric employed to justify lynching black rapists, it assumed that all lynchings were in response to rape. In this way, Vardaman's rhetoric made lynching a completely justified act.

Vardaman made an even wilder leap of logic in a short comment of June 19, 1919, "Hanging Negroes for Rape." "There was a cessation of rape crimes for a few days and consequently an adjournment of the mob court for the same length of time," Vardaman began; but, "Last Saturday the mob court resumed its operations in Arkansas and the unfortunate work goes on." Without transition, Vardaman tied this vague, unsupported statement to an attack on Woodrow Wilson:

If Wilson gets his League of Nations adopted this domestic problem will in
all probability be brought to the attention of the League by the Sovereign
Governments of Liberia and Haiti, who will, by the way, have the same vote
each in the League that the United States has. The "melting pot," otherwise
called the "brotherhood of man," will then begin to boil in earnest.[137]

With its intermingled threats of miscegenation and black political power,
this is classic Vardamanism, but on a worldwide scale. Through such narratives of racial danger, Vardaman explained for Mississippians many troubling developments not only in a volatile New South but also in a changing
nation and world. By fashioning his persona as the "White Chief," by wrap-
ping himself in whiteness, as it were, James K. Vardaman helped make public
racial antipathy a litmus test for would-be Mississippi officeholders for the
next half-century.

But again, Vardaman's narratives of white identity and racial danger
were so resonant and popular because they drew upon elements common to
Vardaman and to his political enemies. John Sharp Williams, a more careful
and systematic thinker than Vardaman, surveyed the field of southern history and found a central theme:

The philosophy of our sectional history—the purpose, conscious or uncon-
scious, of our sectional strivings—will be shown to have always been consis-
tent. And that purpose, whatever the shibboleth of the hour, State's Rights,
secession, sanctity of slavery, equal citizenship in the Territories, anti-
reconstruction, or what not, may more or less have obscured it to the eyes of
others and for a time to our own—that unvarying purpose is this—the preservation of our racial purity and racial integrity; the supremacy of the white
man's ethics and civilization. There has been no "lost cause," but a preserved
cause, though many things thought at many times to be a necessary part of
the cause have been lost.[138]

In 1907 and later, the white male voters of the state were not choosing
between men with radically divergent platforms. They chose in the 1907
Democratic campaign not between a progressive and a traditionalist, or

even between a radical and a moderate, but between variations on what was essentially the same cultural theme. Given the state's firm devotion to the Democratic Party, and its decentralized system of government, the actual performance of a senator, or governor, for that matter, made little difference to the life of the average Mississippian. They were in fact endorsing a language of politics, a way of talking about who they were as white men and a white community. There were always men and women, especially black southerners, who denied the authority of these white supremacist definitions of the South. But at the turn of the century their challenges were muted, and would not bear fruit for more than a generation. In the meantime, the region and the nation increasingly imagined Mississippi and the South as a tale Vardaman told.

Vardaman and Williams, for all the differences in style, manner, and stands on particular political issues that their contemporaries found significant, in fact shared fundamental beliefs about the sanctity of family and home and a (white) man's right to defend it. Vardaman and Williams offered similar narratives and examples to explain what factors had made the white South into a community with a common history and interests. While Vardaman emphasized the potential for danger, disorder, and the potential menace of black men, Williams confidently assured white Mississippians of the rightness and permanence of their control. But like many of their white southern contemporaries, they consistently believed and asserted one thing: white southern homes, families, and communities constituted one common people.

2

MANHOOD, FAMILY, AND WHITE IDENTITY IN THOMAS NELSON PAGE'S "MARSE CHAN" AND THOMAS W. DIXON'S *THE LEOPARD'S SPOTS*

"Listen, dear," he went on, eagerly. "Last night I dreamed the South had risen from her ruins. I saw you there. I saw our home standing amid a bower of roses your hands had planted. The full moon wrapped it in soft light, while you and I walked hand in hand in silence beneath our trees."
—**Thomas W. Dixon Jr., *The Clansman***

Amiable and orderly as the colored race were when the whites were in control, as soon as an election approached they showed every sign of excitement. When they were in power, life became intolerable, and a clash was imminent at every meeting; many families, unable to endure the strain, abandoned their homes, and moved to other communities or other States.
—**Thomas Nelson Page, *The Old Dominion***

At the turn of the twentieth century, southern writers such as Thomas Dixon and Thomas Nelson Page crafted highly influential representations of the South that helped to establish the broad category of white identity in the post–Civil War South. Both writers suggested that expansive history and recent experience had provided the white South, particularly white southern men, with lessons about race and order that they could teach the nation. During a period of intense American concern with issues of race, region, gender, and national purpose, Dixon and Page helped redefine the South's place in the American nation and popular conceptions of the American nation itself. Their representations of southern history and identity and of African Americans shaped popular discourse, directly or indirectly, for much of the twentieth century.[1] Their work helped as well to cast a nationally pervasive image of Progressive Era white American manhood.[2] Popular American literature of the period, as Alexander Saxton noted of westerns such as Owen Wister's *The Virginian* (1902), mixed "white egalitarianism with imperial authority and Christian mission" and thus "swept the heights of American national consciousness."[3] Similarly, Page's and Dixon's explorations of race and community created literary models of common white identity and benevolent white masculine authority for a post-Reconstruction America. Their narratives of family, order, and identity worked to assuage any lingering qualms a white national audience might have felt over slavery or the disposition of the Negro Question, and aided in the naturalization of the same Jim Crow South that contemporary southern politicians were building so assiduously. "White southerners," writes historian Glenda Gilmore, "had gone from pariahs to patriots in the national imagination, and white northerners had taken up the 'white man's burden.'"[4] By conceding that Confederate defeat was for the best, Page and Dixon contributed to the sense of reconciled white national community so strong during the period. By insisting that white men must continue the mastery and control of black men, their fiction persuaded readers of the legitimacy of the emerging Jim Crow order.[5]

Economic flux, political struggle, and harsh racial conflict were common characteristics of the New South. But much popular southern fiction of the period advanced a benign, placid, and reassuring vision of the South and its people. In the plantation tales of such best-selling authors as Thomas Nelson Page and Joel Chandler Harris, the South is a stable, coherent, and integral region of the United States. This South, with its benevolent order, both domestic and public, is a far cry from the stereotypical Slave Power–dominated land of mid-nineteenth-century northern rhetoric. During Gilded Age years of violent class conflict, especially in the industrial North, southern writers provided bucolic images of fundamental accord among white southern people. In "the aftermath of Civil War and Radical Reconstruction," writes Caroline Gebhard, "southern-identified male writers sought to renegotiate their generation's ideals of masculinity and patriotism."[6] On race, white writers such as Page emphasized not the record-setting lynchings of the post-Reconstruction period, but contended that racial harmony was the South's hallmark; in Page's fiction, black southerners are a contented and colorful labor force, and a reassuring symbol of benevolent white male authority.

According to writers such as Thomas Dixon, southern homes and communities found common cause in the threat posed by potentially violent black men. Against such threats white men must unite and remain vigilant, argued Dixon. Only a determined effort by white "Christian manhood" to control black southerners could solve that nagging problem of Progressive Era southern life, the "Negro Question." Dixon even broadly hinted, writes Eric Sundquist, that the struggle for mastery might take the form of "a new war against African Americans."[7] Further, argued Dixon, the problem of the color line was not merely a southern problem, but a national, even a world crisis, one in which white southern men were prepared to take a leading role. On tensions between England and Russia, Dixon asserted: "the Slav and the Anglo-Saxon have nothing in common."[8]

Both Thomas Nelson Page and Thomas Dixon saw black southerners and black Americans generally as subjects to be ordered and as potential violators of both domestic and public harmony. Both viewed the white South as essentially one people—with their own history and identity, but also unimpeachably American. More important, the fiction of both men is driven by a vision of white male mastery: in politics, of white women, and of black men and women. As Mason Stokes writes of Dixon's fiction: "white supremacy is more properly understood as white-male supremacy."[9] As did John Sharp Williams and James K. Vardaman, Thomas Nelson Page and Thomas Dixon provided complementary, overlapping narratives of white southern identity and egalitarian white southern manhood for America and the New South in the post-Reconstruction era. Page's and Dixon's sympathetic white male characters presented a model of masculinity fit for an emerging managerial age: the white southern man was masterful, competent, and regulatory, both of self and others, yet retained a satisfyingly exotic hint of racial mastery and honor, though not the kind of honor whose satisfaction would demand dueling or seceding from the Union.

This chapter assesses the operation in their work of a particular genre of Progressive Era southern fiction, the domestic narrative. This was an immensely popular form at the turn of the century, and the one that best reveals their arguments about white identity and community, as well as white masculinity and its stabilizing work in southern and American culture. Thomas Nelson Page wrote largely of the antebellum South, while Thomas Dixon examined the rise and fall of Reconstruction; both provided critiques of contemporary African Americans. It is not new to suggest that Page and Dixon provided racist representations of black southerners and a romantically heroic view of slavery and white attempts to assert their power over blacks. What this chapter attempts to show is how their particular representations of white manhood, family, and domestic order made their southern stories persuasive to so many white Americans and helped to further regional and national understandings of the South as one common people.

Dixon and Page helped conjure into being an imagined white South and a new model of white southern masculinity through their conflation of the domestic and public realms. Their closely knit racial and domestic tropes lead directly to larger questions of politics and citizenship. Economic, political, and racial instability coalesce around the figure of the embattled white family and the masterful white man. Page asserted that in the antebellum period, domestic and political order were one. For Dixon, as for his political and rhetorical double, Vardaman, the desire of black men for interracial relationships could not be separated from their desire for political participation. Both writers' use of the southern home as the heart of their fiction helps explain the persuasiveness and tenacity of their visions of white men, white families, and the dangers posed by black men.

Thomas Nelson Page: Benevolent White Mastery of the Old South

Thomas Nelson Page's romantic tales of Old South plantation life such as "Marse Chan" (1884) and "Meh Lady" (1886) and his Reconstruction novel *Red Rock* (1898) enjoyed a wide national audience and fostered representations of slavery and benevolent white southern manhood that were influential well into the second half of the twentieth century.[10] One critic argues that Page was "the literary spokesman of the South during the 1880s and 1890s," crafting "forceful, compelling legends which persuaded a generation of their author's accuracy and which still linger in the popular mind even though Page's fiction is rarely read today."[11] Page's contemporary Grace King, herself an excellent writer on New Orleans' Creole culture, asserted that he "was the first Southern writer to appear in print as a Southerner . . . [he] showed us with ineffable grace that although we were sore bereft, politically, we had now a chance in literature at least."[12] Page claimed that his stories were written in the spirit of that great late-nineteenth-century project, the reconciliation of North and South. He disavowed any intention that his romances of the Old South should nurse old wounds, claiming that he had "never willingly written a line which he did not hope might tend to bring about a better understanding between the North and the South, and finally lead to a more perfect Union."[13]

Perhaps because of his easy, conciliatory tone, Page was long dismissed by scholars as a lightweight "moonlight and magnolias" writer. Critics point to his use of the plantation romance as evidence of limited imagination. "He had, really, one talent in writing: he could weave a romantic setting around a situation."[14] However unprovocative Page's work may have seemed to critics steeped in a modernist aesthetic, reading his use of plantation settings as lack of imagination misses a strain of fundamental and calculated realism in Page's work. Page's decisions about fictional topics and narrative strategies prove him an adept interpreter of the literary marketplace. Late-nineteenth-century writers looked calculatingly at their fiction and its audiences. In *The Romance of Reunion,* Nina Silber shows how post–Civil War readers devoured stories of romance between southern belles and northern men.[15] Page knew as much, and he counseled Grace King, who came to him for advice on a rejected novel:

> Now I will tell you what to do; for I did it! . . . It is the easiest thing in the world. Get a pretty girl and name her Jeanne, that name always takes! Make her fall in love with a federal officer and your story will be printed at once! The publishers are right; the public wants love stories. Nothing easier than to write them.[16]

In an unpublished interview, Page was equally blunt about the marketability of his fiction: "My motive [for writing], as far as I can recall it, was the fact that I felt the romance of it [the Old South], and wanted to make a reputation and money. . . . The only way the North entered into the matter at all, was that the magazines were published at the North, and I assumed were largely read there."[17]

But does this clear statement of financial interest contradict Page's stated aim to promote reconciliation between the North and South through his writing? Michael Flusche takes Page at his word when he argues that "[Page] was not out to make converts to the Southern cause . . . he was simply trying to discover the proper literary formula that would earn him a little money."[18] These need not be mutually exclusive aims; Page, who "felt the romance" of the Old South, almost certainly did have motives other than money for his writing. The reconciliation Page and many other white southerners had in mind was less the South's joining modern America than modern America's reconciling itself with their particular vision of the New South. But leaving aside the unknowable question of Page's motivations, one thing is sure: it is precisely his gossamer representations of the Old South and his refusal to adopt a didactic tone that won such favor with a national audience.

Page offered not only imaginative reconstructions of the South's past, but also strategies for reimagining the structure and terms of the twentieth-century American nation. A central component of this rhetorical strategy is Page's assertion that the South is usefully seen as one people. Page's work, both fiction and nonfiction, is largely set in Virginia. But his Old Virginia stands for the Old South as a whole, in a blurring of state lines and assertion of a regionwide southernness that in fact worked to obliterate great economic, religious, and ethnic diversity in the region. Edmund Wilson notes:

> Not only is Virginia before the war made to fuse with the colonial Virginia of [John Esten] Cooke and other writers, so that both hang in the past as a glamorous legend. The attitudes of the North and South themselves have now become somewhat blurred. Animosities must be forgotten; the old issues must be put to sleep with the chloroform of magazine prose.[19]

Page's contemporaries, whether scholars or a popular audience, did not share Wilson's aesthetic judgments of his writing; he was in great demand in the North as a reader and lecturer. In Boston and at Yale, Page read to enthusiastic audiences.[20] Writing in 1903, Edwin Mims, professor of English at North Carolina's Trinity College, described Page's performance: "Tone, manner, distinctness of utterance, attitude toward the subject, were all that could be desired. The reader seemed full of the story he was reading and to have no thought of himself, and he captured everybody."[21]

Page ultimately "captures" his audience, as Mims implied, by luring them into an exotic regional theme park and letting them feel at home by stressing domestic details of courtship, romance, and family. His beautiful and gracious Old South was well ordered, politically and domestically. No strident Confederate apologist preaching sectional dissent, Page conceded the political right to the North: secession and slavery are behind us; we can be glad that the nation is one, since, of course, we are all one (white) people anyway. Fred Hobson is correct to suggest that Page "was not the uncritical admirer of the Old South he is sometimes depicted as having been." But consider his characterization of the Old South in the preface to his novel *Red Rock:* "The [white] people of that section were the product of a system of which it is the fashion nowadays to have only words of condemnation. Every ass that passes by kicks at the dead lion."[22]

While Page did occasionally criticize certain features of antebellum southern life, one thing is clear: while set in the Old South, his fiction and nonfiction spoke very directly to racial concerns of the New South. Page's fiction argues that the ordering and control of African Americans is one of the most pressing issues of contemporary American life, and that the white South, with its long experience in mastery of a lower race, has the answers the rest of the nation needs. Further, his writings suggest, white men as gracious and kind to their slaves as Page's southerners could not be wrong about race relations, either then or now.

Born into a distinguished Virginia family (Nelson and Page ancestors were both Virginia governors) on the eve of what he saw as the great caesura in southern life, Page lived a happy and, by contemporary material standards, enviable life. He was a member of a close and multigenerational household, in which the deeds of famous ancestors were kept green through retelling. Both his father and uncle served in the Confederate army, and returned to tell the tale. After the Civil War, Page was educated at home, and later enrolled at Washington College when Robert E. Lee was president, though Page never took a degree. He went on to study law at the University of Virginia, and retained lifelong ties to Charlottesville and the university. Page practiced law in Richmond for nearly twenty years, during which time he was widowed and began to write. Published in 1884, his story "Marse Chan" brought him a national audience. A fortunate marriage to Florence Lathrop Field, the widowed sister-in-law of Chicago department store magnate Marshall Field, brought him financial security and a widened social circle. They moved from Richmond to Washington, and Page became "a fashionable man of the city."[23] His wealth and fame made him a power in Virginia politics, and at the 1912 Democratic presidential convention in Baltimore, he helped unite the Virginia delegation behind Woodrow Wilson after initially opposing Wilson's candidacy, and was eventually named ambassador to Italy.

Page's first published work, "Uncle Gabe's White Folks," a dialect poem that appeared in the April 1877 *Scribner's Monthly*, established the representation of slavery and race Page would pursue throughout his literary career.[24] It is a treatment of black southerners seemingly characterized by a lack of rancor, patient understanding, and intimate knowledge. This claim to special knowledge of blacks and slavery anchors practically all his writing. By inviting white readers—both North and South—to suspend disbelief before the judgment of this "native" guide, he makes it possible for a broad national audience to romanticize a benevolent white South. It is an understatement to say that Page and his contemporaries were successful. One who was not persuaded, the Reconstruction judge and novelist Albion Tourgée, wrote in frustration in 1888 in an oft-quoted passage: "A foreigner studying our current literature, without knowledge of our history, and judging our civilization by our fiction would undoubtedly conclude that the South was the seat of intellectual empire in America, and the African the chief romantic element of our population."[25] Page helped turn slavery from national tragedy to national romance.

As if to mock Tourgée, not to mention the millions of freedpeople who had somewhat different memories of the recent past, Page's black speaker waxes nostalgic on the glories of old plantation days and the social standing of his owners:

> "Live mons'ous high?" Yes, Marster, yes;
> D' cut 'n' onroyal 'n' gordly dash;
> Eat and drink till you could n' res,'

My folks war n' none o' yo po'-white-trash;

Nor, suh, dey was of high degree—

Dis heah nigger am quality![26]

Page dons this black narrative mask not to give voice to the freedpeople, of course, but to spike any objections that the Old South was based on brutality. Consider how quickly such apologetics for slavery became nationally popular. "Uncle Gabe" was written in 1876, when federal troops were still stationed in Florida and Louisiana and when denunciation of Democrats and southern rebels was a Republican campaign staple.

"Uncle Gabe's White Folks" integrated antebellum plantation romance with literary realism, placing Page alongside other local color writers as a quasi-scientific chronicler of place. Page's stories were generically advanced for their day. Though twenty-first-century readers are rightly suspicious of dialect-based ethnic humor, late-nineteenth-century readers had no such reservations. Dialect was integral to the "authenticity" of local color stories. But while generations of readers have noted with pleasure or disdain Page's representations of black southerners, in fact just as successful and influential were Page's characterizations of white southern men as masterful and wholly admirable.

Perhaps Page's best-known story, "Marse Chan, A Tale of Old Virginia" (1884), was originally published in *Century* magazine, part of the Scribner's house that published his novels and collected works. The story introduces a pattern to which Page would return throughout his later work: he narrated southern public and racial order in terms of domestic order preserved by benevolent, masterful white men. Aware of its success, Page chose it to open his 1887 collection, *In Ole Virginia*. The dedication of this collection makes explicit Page's desire to reconcile not only whites of the North and the South but also his historical subject with contemporary literary techniques. First, Page dedicated the collection (a "Fragmentary Record Of Their Life") to "My People. . . ." But who are Page's people? Are they Virginians past or present? Southerners? Whites generally? When? Who, in other words, is being called to membership in Page's community? "My People" likely refers to white southerners or even just Virginians. But even that identification is uncertain. Literally, Page's "people" (that is, his family) would have included slaveholders and, in the common southern euphemism of the day, their slaves. Here is another of Page's effective slippages, in this case from an exclusive identity, cut off from the contemporary reader through time and legal sanction, to a broad white national audience. Any white reader of the story is a member of the family, or at least a welcome visitor to Page's Old South.

After establishing its audience, the second effect of the introduction is to fix one of the landscape's native but exotic features, the African American. In Page's fiction, black southerners are a primary object of white curiosity. Page accomplishes this exoticization with a quasi-anthropological note on "Negro" dialect:

> The dialect of the negroes of Eastern Virginia differs totally from that of the Southern negroes, and in some material points from that of those located farther west. The elision is so constant that it is impossible to produce the exact sound, and in some cases it has been found necessary to subordinate the phonetic arrangement to intelligibility (vii).

Page positions himself as our guide—one more experienced than we are with the natives, both black and white. The white nonsouthern reader needs an expert both to understand their spoken English and, just as important, to interpret them psychologically and culturally. Presumably steeped in the culture of black southerners and race relations, Page appears to approach his subject with a scientific precision that establishes him as an expert. But when he tries to reproduce the dialect in which black southerners speak, occasionally even he, an "expert," is thwarted by their sheer exoticism. They are so near savagery that Western orthographics can barely contain them.[27] As Toni Morrison argues, "equating speech with grunts or other animal sounds closes off the possibility of communication."[28] Or at least, one might add, the possibility of a competing narrative of the Old South. Finally, Page's anthropological note makes no distinction between black language before the Civil War and in the present. Though categories like "servant" and "freedman" may come and go, there is an essential "Negro-ness" that neither law nor time can change.

Through the eyes of an unidentified white male rider making his way down an eastern Virginia road, Page guides his reader through this landscape, which we meet before any of the characters.[29] Page's imagined Old

South for white Americans, then, is not only rhetorically anchored in the nineteenth-century science of race, but also physically anchored in the maternal southern land itself. Page's South is elusively and tantalizingly poised between Old and New; the story moves from 1872 to 1850 and back. Elusive too are Page's claims that techniques of formal realism can capture the region. With black southerners, for instance, Page likes to have it both ways: blacks are at once demonstrably inferior and outside some Western conceits entirely, as in his purported inability entirely to capture their dialect. So too Page's South is at once accessible and friendly to the (white) northerner, but there are features of the land beyond measure or the nonnative's ken. The white male southerner, then, whether Page, the narrator, or a character in his story, occupies the position of mediator between the southern region and the larger American nation.

The landscape in "Marse Chan" is curiously empty and enervated. The old southerners are gone, but still a palpable presence, an ancient yet faded "race," though in fact they could not have been gone more than a decade. The narrator emphasizes their isolation from and indifference to the outside world: "distance was nothing to these people; time was of no consequence to them" (1). He implies their moral virtue through Puritan imagery: "They desired but a level path in life, and that they had, though the way was longer, and the outer world strode by them as they dreamed" (1).

Why this curious emphasis on the passiveness of the antebellum Virginians, a people not disengaged from the cultural and economic life of the larger South and nation, and hardly uninterested in news from, for instance, Washington, D.C.? The effect is like that of a later portrayal of a vanished race, Margaret Mitchell's *Gone With the Wind* (1936). Both texts undercut potentially difficult questions of public policy and electoral politics by emphasizing the domestic arrangements of the vanquished South. The emphasis on southern domestic life orders the reader's thinking about both the Old South and the New, but particularly about slavery and its New South equivalent, the Negro Question.

A black character (later identified as Sam) speaks first, though they are hardly words at all, but a call to a dog ("Heah!—heah—whoo-oop, heah!") that arouses the narrator from his reverie. Not noticing the narrator, the black man scolds the dog, which waits for him to take down a fence rail so he can pass through: "Jes' like white folks—think 'cuz you's white and I's black, I got to wait on yo' all de time" (3). Although the black man's scolding of the dog might seem evidence of his discontent with the racial order, more significant is the black man's characterization of the dog as white, and thus able to command subservience from him. The black man addresses the narrator, "Sarvent, marster," and apologizes for having spoken roughly to "Marse Chan's dawg." Only later does the narrator realize that Channing (Marse Chan) is long dead. One of the stories white southerners loved to tell was that of the faithful slave. Here is a faithfulness that endures beyond the grave and beyond the species line.

The "darky" seems a person out of time, immune to the changes the end of the war brought: "Dey don' nobody live dyar now, 'cep' niggers," he explains. "Arfter de war some one or nurr bought our place, but his name kind o' slipped me. . . . I jes' steps down of a evenin' and looks arfter de graves" (3–4). Sam's use of the words "our place" and his care of the white graves signal his identification with his antebellum master and Old South civilization; now holding only "niggers," the land is as empty of civilization as the Africa of any imperialist tale.

In a recent introduction to Page's *In Ole Virginia, Or, Marse Chan and Other Stories,* the historian Clyde Wilson argues that this black speaker has a "bardic voice," and is "the survivor of a vanished regime who remains to tell its story . . . a post of honor in Western literature from time immemorial." But the honor of this position is certainly problematic; Page's black characters rival any white apologist in their hymns to the peculiar institution's benevolence. More accurate is Wilson's claim that the "virtues of Page's white Virginians are not imaginable or possible without the context of black Virginians."[30] Although the basic plot of "Marse Chan" is that of *Romeo and Juliet*'s star-crossed lovers, the black slave/narrator renders what could otherwise be an ahistorical tale of love and family feuding specifically within the context of southern culture and race relations. Indeed, Caroline Gebhard sees the bond between Sam and Channing as central to the story: "the women's presence merely underlines the men's bond."[31]

The reader is transported to Page's mythical Old South as the ex-slave, Sam, tells the traveler a story set before the war about "his" family, the Channings, and their neighbors, the Chamberlins. When the Old Master's son, Marse Chan, is born, the baby is given into the care of Sam, then five years old. Sam is charged to "tek keer on 'im ez long ez he lives" and follows young Channing to school, out courting, and later to war, becoming a double or shadow to the young white man, uniquely capable of telling his tale. In an oft-quoted passage, Sam explains that life on the old plantation was sweet:

> Dem was good old times, marster—de bes' Sam ever see! Dey wuz, in fac'! Niggers did' hed nothin' 't all to do—jes' hed to 'ten' to de feedin' an' cleanin' de hosses, an' doin' what de marster tell 'em to do; an' when dey wuz sick, dey had things sont 'em out de house, an' de same doctor come to see 'em whar 'ten' to de white folks when dey wuz po'ly. Dyar warn' no trouble nor nothin.' (10)

Though the Channings' place is a working plantation, there is no mention of farm labor. Page stresses instead the cordial relations between slaves and masters; the slaves we see are familiar and beloved servants, not semi-anonymous field laborers. At the center of this scene of domestic harmony, of the well-ordered household, sits the Big House. "De house" itself emanates care and sustenance, as if it were a maternal force nurturing its retainers. In return, the slaves feel pride and loyalty toward their masters. They are thrilled when an heir is produced ("De folks all hed holiday, jes' like in de Chris'mas") and, in royal fashion, Ole Marster presents the flannel-wrapped baby to a back-porch audience, who ritually tip their hats. This plantation is a well-ordered and benevolently ruled kingdom, serenely mixing feudal ceremony along with the squeamish Jeffersonian tradition of calling slaves "servants" or, as it is given here, "folks."

Young Channing determines to marry Lucy Chamberlin (the Juliet to his Romeo) and unite the two neighboring plantations. Instead, the lovers are separated by politically motivated feuding between their fathers. The political disorder and strife of the secession crisis are played out on a personal stage between the two families: the political is inscribed in personal terms so that in Page's economy a man is either a secessionist and a slanderer or a loyalist and a man of his word. Old Master Channing, a moderate Whig, runs for Congress and the Democrats run Colonel Chamberlin against him.[32] As in other New South fiction, the heroes (the Channings) are reluctant rebels, their ambivalence toward secession signaled by their allegiance to the Whig Party. Such a move was savvy of Page, since a Whig affiliation presented no potential offense to his readers, while the Democrats were still regarded by many northerners as the party of Rum, Romanism, and Rebellion.[33] Channing wins the election, implying that the voters of Old Virginia, like the Old Master himself, had moderate and loyal feelings toward the union.

In "Marse Chan," men with orderly and moderate political views (equated here with whiggism and unionism) demonstrate corresponding mastery of orderly and content households. Look to their attitudes about home and family, the narrative suggests; by their works you shall know them. From right attitudes about domestic order grow moderate and orderly political ideas. Not only do the Channings wish to keep the union (the American family) together, they—unlike the Chamberlins—work to keep the families of their slaves together: "Ole marster didn' like nobody to sell niggers, an' knowin' dat Cun'l Chahmb'lin wuz sellin' o' his, he writ an' offered to buy his M'ria an' all her chil'len, 'cause she hed married our Zeek'yel" (11). Here, the combination of the political and domestic orders is complete. Chamberlin balks at Channing's attempts to keep families together. Angry at losing the election to Channing, Chamberlin asks an exorbitant price for Maria. Before the transaction can be made, Chamberlin's slaves are seized for debt and auctioned, at which Chamberlin encourages another man to bid against Channing for Maria. The character of Chamberlin thus serves as an unsympathetic masculine figure against which the Channings, both father and son, are favorably compared.

Young Channing assumes responsibility for the management of the plantation household when the Old Master is blinded rescuing his slave (named Ham)[34] from a burning barn. Page carries the Channings' solicitude for their slaves very nearly to the last measure. Young Channing signals the sort of man and master he will be by nursing his injured father "jes' like a 'ooman," as Sam puts it (14). Sam also recalls how, as a child, Channing would not suffer little Sam to be beaten: "Stop, seh!" he warns his father: "he b'longs to me, an' ef you hit 'im another lick I'll set 'im free!" (15).

What are we to make of this display of tenderness, "jes' like a 'ooman," on Channing's part? The Civil War and Reconstruction era represented not only economic and constitutional challenges to the American people, but also, it is commonly argued, a crisis in gender as well.[35] The end of the century witnessed the questioning and redefinition of white manhood at a national level. Caroline Gebhard argues that white masculinity in plantation stories such as Page's functions in a complex manner, "enmeshed in a fin de siècle crisis of sexual definition, postwar race relations, and the emergence of a modern American nationalism." Thus, according to Gebhard, the white man in the plantation tale becomes the object of the homoerotic gaze, embodies elements of the camp, and represents interracial homosocial bonding, all "new ideological solutions to gender, race, and national identity."[36]

While the representations of white southern men in Page (and in Dixon as well) certainly share in some of these tensions, to my mind the greater significance of the figure of the white man in these texts is how they represent a "solution" to Progressive Era anxieties about white masculinity. Rather than an object around which elements of late-nineteenth-century gender anxieties can coalesce to solve problems of race, the white man in Page becomes an expansive subject omnivorously reworking masculinity for a white national audience. The domestic virtues of Old and Young Master Channing are set in high relief because of the absence of substantial female characters, who would in fact have been most responsible for the nursing, cooking, and other essentials of household management on a working plantation. Channing is thus both Ole Master and Ole Miss.

The crucibles of war and Reconstruction threw into relief the malleability of categories that in dominant cultural narratives often seemed natural and given. In "Marse Chan," Page recasts antebellum manhood for an era of emerging American nationalism and national masculinity. Consider the implications of Channing as both tender and domestic *and* manly and dutiful. On the one hand, this model of masculine sensibility is reminiscent of eighteenth-century men of feeling. But here Page also inverts the conventional Stowe-esque depiction of slave owners as violators of domestic order (through the splitting of slave families and with miscegenation), asserting instead that domestic virtues were central to antebellum (and by extension, contemporary) southern maleness. This womanly tenderness makes Channing a complete man, with his death in combat (the stage on which nineteenth-century manhood was taken to be most fully realized) signifying his impeccable maleness.

Having assumed his father's domestic duties, Marse Chan also takes up his role as a voice of political moderation. "Purty soon," recalls Sam, "Cun'l Chahmb'lin he went about ev'vywhar speakin' an' noratin' 'bout Ferginia ought to secede; an' Marse Chan he was picked up to talk agin' 'im. Dat wuz de way dey come to fight de duil" (16). Note that Sam attended these rallies and debates. He has nothing to say, though, about the issue at stake: southern independence and Yankee abolitionism. Page's representations of political oratory here say as much about the New South as the Old, of course. Page would have us disapprove of hot-headed sectionalism. But he takes as his hero a man who will give his life in a cause that would have split the Union. Page shows disdain for Chamberlin and his politics, while advancing through Channing the arguments that antebellum (and postbellum) southern culture was healthy and well ordered, with emphasis on a clear racial hierarchy and traditional gender roles. A "moderate" voice like Channing's (or Page's) serves the same racial and gender prerogatives as the more "radical" voices of Chamberlin.

"Marse Chan" also anticipates and attempts to defuse class tensions in the white South. According to Page, the origin of "Marse Chan" was "an old Confederate letter" shown to him by a friend that in many respects resembles the letter Anne writes to Channing, except that the principals in the "actual" letter are of a much lower social class:

> It was written . . . in a very illiterate hand, and my recollection is that it was from a girl in Georgia, one of the poor class . . . she wrote him that since he had gone off to war she had discovered that she loved him all the time—had loved him ever since she was a little girl and used to go to school with him at the old house in the woods and he had been so good to her. And now she wrote to say that if he would get a furlough and come home she would marry him. Then after she had signed her name, as though she feared this temptation would be too strong for him, she had added a post script, scrawled crookedly across the bottom of the little blue sheet. "Don't come without a furlough, for it you don't come honorably I wont marry you." . . . I observed that its date was only some two weeks previous to that of the battle in which her soldier was said to have fallen. I remember that I said as I handed it back to my friend, "The poor fellow got his furlough through a bullet. . . ."[37]

If this is in fact the genesis of "Marse Chan," what are we to make of Page's elevation of these characters to a higher station than they "actually" occupied? Is this an attempt by Page to deny that common white southerners are the proper material of romance and heroism? Though Page's elitist

   Manhood, Family, and White Identity

sensibilities are hard to deny, a subtler—or at least more literary— reading of this letter and its transformation in "Marse Chan" would recognize that such "found documents" serving as the nucleus of a narrative represent a very old and, by the nineteenth century, entirely transparent literary convention.[38] As for the letter itself, either Page has doctored the language of the Georgia girl, or she was not so "very illiterate" and low, after all. Page's own explanation of the social elevation of Channing and Anne runs thus: "I thought I could make [the story] more romantic if I placed my characters in a somewhat higher sphere, and besides I was more familiar with the latter." Here, I suggest, we approach the crux of the matter: Page sought to maximize sales. The inclusion of this "real" letter in the preface to the story serves as Page's assertion that whites of the "poor class" were loyal to the Confederacy and lived by the same code of personal honor that bound southerners of all ranks; that is, that class lines, or class consciousness, at least, should not disrupt the well-ordered white southern family.

Leaving aside the question of whether or not Channing represents a real Confederate lover, his end is entirely predictable in literary terms. Because of deaths in the company, Channing has been chosen by the rest of the men to lead the next assault. In the heat of the battle, the company threatens to break, but Channing seizes the drooping flag and exhorts the company to follow him. Faithful even under fire, Sam rides into battle with the cavalry. Having rallied his men, Channing sweeps the Yankees from the hilltop, but at the cost of his life. Sam finds him at the top of the hill, surrounded by dead and dying men, mortally wounded, but still holding the flag: "I tu'n him over an' call 'im, 'Marse Chan!' but 'twan' no use, he wuz done gone home, sho' nuff" (34).

Faithful until death and after, Sam takes up Channing, still clutching the flag, in his arms and "toted 'im back jes' like I did dat day when he wiz a baby, an' ole marster gin 'im to me in my arms, an' sez he could trus' me" (34). Traveling night and day, Sam brings Channing home. Continuing to serve as the emissary between the as-yet-unreconciled families, Sam rides to the Chamberlins' house to give them the news. Anne grows pale at Sam's appearance. Sam struggles for words, and finally says: "Marse Chan, he done got he furlough" (36).

The reconciliation among southerners that Page believed was enacted by the Civil War is reenacted in personal and familial terms by Channing's death in this story. Despite past tensions between the two families, Anne is received as Channing's bride by his mother. At the funeral, Anne hugs the coffin and kisses the body, and receives permission from the family to wear mourning for Channing. She walks with the family in the funeral procession and afterward moves in with the Channings as their daughter-in-law. This unconsummated yet immutable love and Channing's early death let the white woman remain forever pure and virginal, and the young man forever heroic, and perhaps virginal, too. Anne's assumption of a widow's weeds ensures that she will continue to pay tribute to Channing's heroism. Serving for a time as a nurse, she is broken by grief and illness, and dies just in time to avoid the disruption of emancipation (38). Sam is even more directly, then, the survivor of a dead order: his "principal" was killed in the war. Now, in the present, each of the white characters of Sam's narrative, having faded from the landscape, have joined Channing in taking on mythic status.[39]

In many respects contrived and entirely predictable, particularly for modern readers, "Marse Chan" does seem to have created the effect that Page desired. Some of the most eager consumers of Page's stories had only ten or fifteen years earlier been among slavery's most bitter critics. Among the readers of this "story of a faithful old Negro stricken by grief at the death of his master, who has fought for the Confederate cause" was Thomas Wentworth Higginson, "who had subsidized John Brown, served as colonel of a Negro regiment and had been present at the burning of Jacksonville," and who, some years later, was found weeping "over Page's *Marse Chan*."[40] Though Page's heroic white man may have died in battle, his image of heroic white masculinity did not, and in the end his image of a romantic and admirable white South won broad national applause.

Thomas Dixon: Stern White Mastery of the New South

"Can the Ethiopian change his color, or the Leopard his spots?" The title of Thomas Dixon's first novel, *The Leopard's Spots* (1903), drawn from *Jeremiah* 13:23, implies the question that the novel will ask about race relations in the Reconstruction-era South: Can African Americans live peacefully alongside Anglo-Saxons? With its reference to Kipling, the novel's subtitle, "A Romance of the White Man's Burden—1865–1900," suggests the pessimism of Dixon's answer. Dixon was not the only white southerner to imply that black Americans were inferior to whites, and that their moral inferiority particularly might manifest itself in assaults on the white home. What makes Dixon distinctive among Progressive Era narrators of white identity is his wildly successful refiguring of the domestic romance novel as a vehicle to advance arguments for a more ruthless policing of black men because of the danger they posed to whites throughout the region, and indeed throughout the nation. Dixon maintained that since the end of Reconstruction, black men were more licentious and dangerous than they had been under slavery, and that black political participation breached a wall between the political and the domestic, placing white America on a slippery slope toward black political and sexual domination. "By arguing that the assault of white women was a new feature of black activity after slavery," agrees Sandra Gunning, writers such as Dixon "could argue that black emancipation was tantamount to a breach of white national defenses."[41] The only sure guard against the rising tide of color was the white man; when Dixon wrote of the white man's common burden, it was in heavily gendered terms. The novel might well be read as a primer on white southern manhood for both a regional and national audience.

The Leopard's Spots was the first of Dixon's "Reconstruction trilogy," which also included *The Clansman: An Historical Romance of the Ku Klux Klan* (1905) and *The Traitor: A Story of the Fall of the Invisible Empire* (1907).[42] Phenomenally popular across the country, the trilogy secured Dixon's reputation as a best-selling author for New York's Doubleday, Page publishing house. With their broad stereotypes of vicious freedmen and unprincipled carpetbaggers, Dixon's novels brought to a wide national audience reinterpretations not only of the Civil War and Reconstruction, but cautionary tales about contemporary politics and race relations as well.

Thomas Dixon is now universally condemned as a "bad novelist."[43] One can certainly judge Dixon's work to be morally deficient and, moreover, socially harmful, except in the eyes of those who share Dixon's sensibilities. One thinks of the popularity of D. W. Griffith's landmark and cinematically groundbreaking film, *The Birth of a Nation* (1915), drawn from *The Clansman* and *The Leopard's Spots*. The revived Ku Klux Klan of the 1910s and 1920s drew their ritual and regalia from *The Clansman,* and *The Birth of a Nation* was used as a recruiting tool by the Klan in its various incarnations.[44] Yet Dixon's work is thought "bad" in another sense as well. "The first thing to be said in discussing Thomas Dixon Jr.'s novel *The Clansman,*" wrote Thomas D.

Clark in his introduction to the novel, "is that no person of critical judgment thinks of it as having artistic conception or literary craftsmanship."[45] To stress the literary demerits of Dixon's novels is to risk missing their importance. Dixon did not set out to write great novels, leaving aside the question of whether one was within his grasp. He wanted instead to write popular novels, ones that would move his readers to see, like his heroine Elsie Cameron, "how the cords which bound the Southerner to his soil were of the heart's red blood."[46]

Like Thomas Nelson Page's fiction, Dixon's is ultimately significant because his works refigured contemporary representations of family, race, and community in ways that drew upon and galvanized powerful nineteenth-century conceptions of the public and the private. "Paradoxically," argues critic James Kinney, "Dixon is among the most dated and most contemporary of southern writers. In genre an early nineteenth-century romancer, thematically Dixon argued for three interrelated beliefs still current in southern life: the need for racial purity, the sanctity of the family centered on a traditional wife and mother, and the evil of socialism."[47] Dixon's apparent datedness is in fact a vehicle for a powerful contemporary agenda: to complement contemporary narratives that asserted that the white South suffered under the indignities of Reconstruction, and that the common white experience of taming and ordering a savage race steeled them to offer firm guidance on racial matters to the rest of the nation.

Anyone reading Dixon sees that the black menace to white civilization and white women is a core concern.[48] Dixon's racist stereotypes of black men are well known. Yet one of the chief rhetorical effects of those racist stereotypes is less studied. Just as important, Dixon also used the popular form of the romance to craft and display a model of white manhood. In Dixon the depraved, half-civilized black man functions to set in relief that figure's opposite: the masterful, rational, patriotic white man, whose guardianship of the domestic protected the white home from the pollution threatened by black men. Again, Dixon was hardly alone in claiming that white women were under actual or potential assault by black men. Many contemporary white politicians explicitly made the connection between black aspiration for the ballot and for white women. But what remains insufficiently explored is the content and work of cautionary racist tales such as Dixon's. They posited the existence of a common white community equally threatened by black men's depravity, yet suggested that white southern men were equal to the task of meeting that threat.

Scholars employing psychoanalytical tools (notoriously difficult to use at such a historical remove) have sometimes ascribed the rhetorical effectiveness, or at least the prevalence of rape and assault narratives, to some trait in white psychology, either generally or in specific writers such as Dixon. Joel Williamson argues that Dixon "wrote *The Leopard's Spots* because he had a very deep emotional problem."[49] That Dixon was troubled may well be true, but it does not seem directly relevant to the impact of his fiction. And it is certainly tempting to pathologize white southern racism or to blame it on troubled men such as Dixon, but such an argument does not get one very far in dealing with race as a historically contingent phenomenon. We are dealing here less with Jungian white totems than with very skillfully wrought narratives of manhood and womanhood, of whiteness and blackness, which drew upon and fostered ideas of domesticity and sexuality in an era when ideas about these matters were being discussed and challenged in unfamiliar ways. The image of interracial sexual assault was and remains rhetorically effective and culturally powerful. At the turn of the twentieth century it was one of the white South's most galvanizing stories. Indeed, stories of the white home threatened by black men might be said to be one of the chief forces that conjured a white rhetorical community.

Dixon called writing *The Leopard's Spots* "the most important moral deed of my life."[50] Like his contemporary, James Vardaman, Dixon understood that the way to the nation's heart was through the home. *The Leopard's Spots* rewrites the political and social in terms of the domestic—in this case, the threatened white household. Throughout the novel, Dixon stresses the parallel between the well-ordered household and the well-ordered state. Good families make good citizens, and threats to the political order are also threats to the social order. Enemies of the South (and by extension, the nation) strike at marriage, morals, and the family early in their battle. Dixon's story, like Vardaman's speeches, exploits a common formula, which insisted that the racial discord surrounding African American emancipation and enfranchisement ultimately threatened white domestic life; the assault of white women by black men was inevitable. Dixon, like Vardaman, often claimed that he felt no malice toward blacks, denying that his novels were written in a spirit of hatred. "I have for the Negro race only pity and sympathy," said Dixon in a characteristic remark. "My books are hard reading for a Negro, and yet the Negroes, in denouncing them, are unwittingly denouncing one of their best friends."[51] Nevertheless, *The Leopard's Spots* is among the strongest literary evocations of interracial sexual assault, the specter that fired the imaginations of white southerners like no other issue.

Diane Roberts has provided a way to think about Dixon's assertion that black political rights led inexorably to the rape of white women without relying upon broad psycho-sexual explanations. Roberts notes the language of racism and its cultural effects: "the body, sexuality and race were the enmeshed elements which the white South fought to define and contain with the object of keeping all taint, all 'pollution,' even the smallest 'drop of ink' from the pristine whiteness it equated with goodness and order."[52] Dixon's fiction worked to persuade a national audience of the thrill and romance of the white South's having faced and mastered that challenge of ordering a savage race.

Dixon's provocative and sensationalist fiction flaunts such metaphorical, commonly unspoken meanings of readily apparent social power struggles. *The Leopard's Spots* provides a cohesive, heavily determined narrative to explain the racial rhetoric and isolated incidents that readers of this period found in daily papers, discussed with their families and neighbors, and that of course colored their political behavior. Considering the formulaic and predictable nature of Dixon's novel, we can safely disregard his claim in the preface that "The only serious liberty I have taken with history is to tone down the facts to make them credible in fiction" (vi). Yet, the narrative does capture a cultural reality that it orders and re-creates for its readers.

Dixon's novel retells Page's story of young love fighting against the obstacles of family disapproval and public disorder, and also provides a model of masterful white manhood in a near-contemporary setting. Charles Gaston, the hero of *The Leopard's Spots,* is the son of a Confederate soldier killed in the war. Gaston exhibits the traits that, according to Dixon, mark the southern version of "Anglo-Saxon" manhood and that make such a model of masculinity essential to meet the racial challenges faced by the turn-of-the-century American nation. Through iron will, natural oratorical gifts, an awareness of the threat to home and state posed by black men, and timely help from the white community around him, Gaston rises to become the governor of North Carolina and to marry the beautiful Sallie Worth, the daughter of General Worth, a wealthy cotton mill owner and power broker in the Democratic Party. As befits a long, nineteenth-century–style romance spanning thirty years, *The Leopard's Spots* contains multiple subplots that act upon the central story and complicate the overall narrative in ways that distinguish it sharply from Page's short story.

In his treatment of Reconstruction government and the Redemption of North Carolina by white Democrats, Dixon intertwined the domestic and the political, or perhaps more accurately, shows the permeability of the boundary between public and private, arguing that white Christian southern manhood is responsible for the security of both spheres. Gaston is modeled on Charles B. Aycock (1859–1912), Democratic governor of North Carolina from 1901 through 1905, "an ardent defender of white supremacy," who in 1898 "collaborated with Furnifold Simmons and Josephus Daniels in an inflammatory and racist campaign in defense of white supremacy, which returned the Democrats to control of the state legislature."[53] The political crisis of Gaston's young manhood is the 1890s Populist-Republican Fusion, which temporarily delivered a legislative majority to that alliance. This interparty/interracial alliance was a crisis for Dixon (and white Democrats generally) because the white South's sense of identity was, according to Democratic accounts, so tied to the Democratic Party and its fate. To Dixon, loyalty to the Democratic Party—"the white man's party" and "the party of our fathers," as it was commonly called—was the *sine qua non* of solid white manhood, of which Charles Gaston is a prime specimen. Dixon prepared his readers for this analysis of 1890s (practically contemporary) politics with two earlier volumes, the first set in the volatile Reconstruction period of 1865–70, and the second in the 1880s.

In Book One, "Legree's Regime," familiar political events of Reconstruction are combined with a cautionary tale about the dangers black men posed to white southern families. With the help of unprincipled white Reconstructionists, blacks take control of the political machinery of North Carolina and the rest of the South for the purpose of humiliating white men and making white women their own. The Republican ringleader who misleads the previously manageable blacks into mischief is Simon Legree, resurrected from Harriet Beecher Stowe's *Uncle Tom's Cabin* (1852), a novel whose popularity and cultural influence Dixon must have envied. Despite its postbellum setting, *The Leopard's Spots* seeks among other things to rebut

Stowe's representation of the South and southern manhood as hypocritical and illegitimate in its use of power. Instead, Dixon presented white families of the region as a common victim to, and the rest of the nation as a potential common victim to, misguided notions about the true character of black Americans.

Dixon's Legree is more than an opportunist who cynically advocates postwar racial equality. He is also a coward who "unmans" himself; when war came, he sold his slaves and "migrated nearer the border land, that he might avoid service in either army" (86). He moved nearer the gender border, too, to avoid service: "he shaved clean and dressed as a German emigrant woman" (86). With the end of the war, the changeling metamorphoses, this time into "a violent Union man," who claims to have been brutalized by the Rebels. He fools the ex-slaves, who "hang breathless upon his every word as the inspired Gospel of God" and rush to shake the hand "red with the blood of their race" (87). While for Dixon and his readership, "black blood" is polluting, here it serves to sanctify Legree in the eyes of the freedmen. Indeed, through his immersion in their blood, he further unmans himself in the eyes of a white audience. Not only is he an unprincipled cross-dresser, he is an honorary black man as well.

To discredit black political participation and to equate it with a common threat to white homes and families, Dixon pointed to what most white Americans by then considered the tragic era of Reconstruction; he also maintained that slavery, overseen by moderate yet masterful white men, was the only successful model for race relations the country had known. Dixon exploits fears of miscegenation to distinguish between "good" and "bad" whites, and "good" and "bad" blacks. One of Legree's political associates is an ex-slave, Tim Shelby. Shelby has armed the freedmen in preparation for the impending conflict over political and social control of North Carolina. Dixon represents him with the "blackest" stereotypical markers of race: Shelby is kinky-haired, big-lipped, and "when excited he had a way of wrinkling his scalp so as to lift his ears up and down like a mule" (89). Worst of all, from Dixon's point of view, Shelby is educated and eloquent, able to put into stirring words what Dixon implies lies at the root of black calls for civil rights. "We are done with race and colour lines," shouts one of Shelby's white companions as he launches into his reverie. Dixon shows just what the color line guards:

Our proud white aristocrats of the South . . . feel the coming power of the
Negro. They fear their Desdemonas may be fascinated again by an Othello!
Well, Othello's day has come at last. If he has dreamed dreams in the past,
his tongue dared not speak; the day is fast coming when he will put these
dreams into deeds, not words. . . . I say to my people now in the language of
the inspired word, "All things are yours." . . . We will drive the white man
out of this country . . . [and] will make this mighty South a more glorious
San Domingo. (90–93)

To guard against such a nightmarish scenario, Dixon suggests that
only an alliance of the recent (white) Civil War combatants can keep the
Othellos from the Desdemonas, and keep the South and America a white
man's country. Taking care not to alienate a northern reading audience, not
all Dixon's northerners are carpetbaggers; there exists in the novel the "gen-
uine Yankee soldier settler . . . who came because he loved its genial skies
and kindly people" (85). These northern men will sympathize with the plight
of a brave white South so ungenerously treated and, as Union veterans and
good Republicans, will be in a position to correct the excesses of political and
social Reconstruction. Just as important, they sympathize with the desire of
white southerners to protect home and family from a readily understandable
and commonly dreaded threat.

To achieve this white alliance, Dixon worked with tropes of division
and reunion, both familial and political. He worked toward not only a white
southern community but a white national family as well. On one hand,
threats to the family (in the Progressive-era South, conventionally represented as a black man assaulting a white woman) called for public action,
whether through lynching or Jim Crow legislation. On the other, because
the idealized family still carried heavy resonances of Victorian American domesticity, Dixon asserted that it lay beyond the "interference" of the state. By
extension, the South's reintegration into the American family would be on
just such terms: part of a community yet essentially self-ruling.

Dixon signaled the novel's reunifying work, especially its interest in pro-
moting a positive national image of white southern manhood, by opening with
the surrender of Lee. Admired by millions of Americans as one who counseled calm acceptance of Confederate defeat, and who promoted national

unity after the war, Lee had rapidly moved into the national pantheon. That Confederate defeat meant the rebirth of a nation is seen in the final letters to his family of the Lee-like Colonel Gaston, the news of whose death is brought home by the faithful black slave/servant, Nelse. The colonel's last thoughts are of home, not only his own, but in an almost unbelievably altruistic manner, northern homes as well: "how many hearts will ache and break in faraway homes because of the work I am about to do. I long to be at home again" (13). Writing to his son, Gaston explains his reasons for fighting: "I am not fighting to hold slaves in bondage. I am fighting for the inalienable rights of my people under the Constitution our fathers created" (14). Such rhetorical heavy-handedness should not be ascribed to Dixon's lack of skill as a novelist. Instead, such instruction to the reader helped Dixon create the audience that he wanted.

Dixon asserted the patriotic nature of the "right" kind of Confederate service. He noted that North Carolina ("the typical American Democracy") had seceded reluctantly, but with "a soul clear in the sense of tragic duty" (5). He tied the Civil War soldiers to those of the Revolutionary War generation, to stress again the South's place in winning American independence and to remove any stain of disloyalty from the Confederate soldier. The paeans to the new nation, the use of the Revolutionary generation, the ecumenical concern for the Union dead—these all enlist the sympathies of the reader and remove the taint of secessionism from the men of the Gaston family. Faithful Nelse, too, like Page's Sam, is a reconciliatory marker. Slavery, after all, could scarcely have been as brutal as Stowe painted it if Nelse feels such devotion to his "family" that he risks prison camp trying to cross into Confederate lines.

Juxtaposed against this picture of domestic harmony is a vision of a disordered South. "In every one of these soldiers' hearts, and over all the earth, hung the shadow of the freed Negro, transformed by the exigency of war from a Chattel . . . into a possible beast to be feared and guarded" (5). This racial disorder is but one of the evidences of an inverted world that returning Confederate soldiers would find; racial, economic, and domestic disorder are intertwined: "Grim chimneys marked the site of once fair homes" (4). A tattered soldier peers into the window of "a small deserted house." While he was away, his mother died, and his sister is now "a bad woman" who lives "in a little house down in the woods" (18). The soldier wishes he were dead. Following the conventions of Victorian melodrama, the soldier and the reader realize that death is preferable to sexual misconduct; there are indeed fates worse than death.

In contrast to Page's "Marse Chan," which treats the question of class by inviting the reader to admire, envy, and vicariously live in the world of a vanished aristocracy, *The Leopard's Spots* recognizes the existence of potential social class conflict in the South, only to defuse it immediately. Dixon showed how the entire white community worked together toward the common goals of reestablishing the well-ordered household and state. He asserted that the white South was unified; this was no "rich man's war and poor man's fight." Dixon's broad white community crossed regional, sectional, and even political boundaries. In Virginia, Tom Camp, a one-legged Confederate common soldier, meets a Union general: "I'm General Grant. Give my love to your folks. I've know what it was to be a poor white man down South myself once for awhile" (23). "If it had to be surrender," Camp replies, "I'm glad it was to such a man as you" (23). As did much of the rest of white America, Dixon presented Grant and Lee as equally admirable members of the American pantheon.

Tom, implies Dixon, is an example of the best of untutored Anglo-Saxon manhood—brave, home loving, religious—just the sort of man threatened by the problem of vicious, predatory black men. Tom has an instinctive hatred of blacks. The preacher remarks that "it's a funny thing to me that as good a Christian as you should hate a nigger so" (27). In his reply is Tom's single note of class-consciousness: "I always hated a nigger since I was knee-high. . . . We always felt like they was crowdin' us to death on them big plantations, and the little ones, too" (27). Tom does not blame the planters, note, but the slaves themselves, an unsubtle reminder from Dixon that to be antislavery is not to be pro-black. Here again the novel condemns the institution of slavery as politically divisive, but blames slaves rather than secessionist planters for the war. Tom says as much: "I had to leave my wife and baby and fight four years, all on account of their stinkin' hides . . . it seemed to me I could see their black ape-faces grinnin' and makin' fun of poor whites" (28–29). And again, Dixon makes the villain of the piece a figure that many white Americans were already prepared to despise.

In the novel, black men's interest in politics is always revolutionary, or disordering, therefore evil. Dixon shifts blame for black political organization onto Union Leaguers and camp followers; good blacks, according to the novel, show little natural interest in politics. Meeting a "burly negro" in a Federal uniform, drunk on whisky and power, one white character, the Reverend Durham, instantly understands the real meaning of Reconstruction: "this towering figure of the freed Negro had been growing more and more ominous . . . a veritable Black Death for the land and its people" (33). For black soldiers, the Federal service and the Federal uniform were signs of manly purposefulness.[54] So too were they for Dixon; all the more reason, then, to attempt to discredit black men's service and manhood. By putting these words into the mouth of a Christian minister, Dixon, himself a minister, of course, suggested a correspondence between southernness and Christianity in his idealized model of white manhood.

As the white male community moves to check this "Black Death," we see not only the power of Anglo-Saxons as a body, but their Hegelian ability to generate leaders of men to meet the challenges of the moment. Despite his homage to common men such as Tom Camp, Dixon's egalitarianism melts here in the face of his nineteenth-century romantic notion that there are great and natural leaders of men. Some white men are born to lead; war and revolution allow the superior man a chance to rise. In Hambright, North Carolina, the setting is grim: "people were restless and discouraged by the wild rumors . . . of coming confiscation, revolution and revenge" (63). Such a man for such an hour is General Daniel Worth, whose daughter the young hero, Gaston, will marry: "An expert in anthropology would have selected [Worth's] face from among a thousand as the typical man of the Caucasian race" (63). Even ex-slaves flock to him for advice. Worth was, of course, a loyalist: "I was a Whig in politics. I reckon I hated a Democrat as God hates sin. I was a Union man and fought Secession" (65). Worth sees on the horizon a prosperous region ("if the South is only let alone by the politicians"), but as with other men who wanted a New South, Worth would prefer the Old Negro: "Be honest, humble, patient, industrious and every white man in the South will be your friend" (66). Worth cautions the freedmen that freedom means neither social equality nor suffrage. He produces as evidence a letter that Lincoln wrote him just before the war as an appeal to southern unionists. Again, Dixon uses a racist critique of black vice not only to denigrate them, but also to craft a nationally appealing model of New South white manhood:

"The rank and file of the Negroes" are not pleased with Worth's message, for they had assumed that "freedom meant eternal rest, not work" (69), a belief conforming to the stereotypes surely held by many of the novel's readers.

General Worth's New South Creed was far more than a recipe for southern industrialization. Each of its major tenets, as historians have long noted, had clear implications for southern race relations as well. First, the South must turn away from one-crop agriculture and toward diversified economic development; slavery had forced the South into this pattern and its abolition was a blessing to the region. Second, the South could solve its race problems without outside interference, since white men knew blacks and would treat them equitably. Third, southerners bore no malice toward the victorious Union and, in fact, were the most patriotic Americans. As Henry Grady put it: "The South found her jewel in the toad's head of defeat. The shackles that had held her in narrow limitations fell forever when the shackles of the negro slave were broken."[55] Despite dissenters at the time and later, Grady's vision of a New South profoundly affected the course of twentieth-century southern history, providing a blueprint for regional politics, race relations, and efforts at industrial development.[56] In this context, Worth's sound politics and sound work ethic made him a figure of reliable white masculinity that a white national audience could admire.

For the present, the situation is grim: "The bonds that held society together were loosened. Government threatened to become organised crime instead of the organised virtue of the community" (94). What wars against the "virtue of the community" is the disorderly black man, particularly as encouraged by the Freedman's Bureau. "If the devil himself had devised an instrument for creating race antagonism and strife he could not have improved on this Bureau. . . . It was the supreme opportunity of army cooks, teamsters, fakirs and broken-down preachers who had turned insurance agents" (75). Blacks are at the same time responsible for and victims of this disorder. Freed from the gentle bonds of slavery, they regress, committing indiscriminate crimes against property, whites, and their own people. When Reverend Durham discovers an abandoned black child, he has the Freedmen's Bureau return him to his mother (his father having become "a drunken loafer"), who promptly "knock[s] him in the head and burn[s] the body, in a drunken orgy with dissolute companions" (94). This linking of alcohol and domestic tragedy was a staple of prohibition literature, both in Britain and America, and here again contrasts white order and self-mastery with a disordering black threat.

Dixon's novels and their adaptation in Griffith's *Birth of a Nation* made explicit the link between black drinking and criminal sexuality, and carried that message to a white national audience. Dixon, along with some white prohibitionists, argued that access to alcohol inflamed black passions and emboldened them to crimes a sober head would avoid.[57] At the same time, though, some white southerners maintained that blacks were not "reasonable men" and were, like children or animals, incapable of calculating the consequences of their acts. Further, if for white women rape was the fate worse than death, for the lustful black man, violation of the white woman was a prize worth storming the gates of hell; only the terrors of a brutal lynching could serve as sufficient deterrent or expiation. These two views of black criminality may seem incompatible: on the one hand, a cunning, subtle beast; on the other, a dumb, potentially ravenous brute unable to function within an Anglo-Saxon community based on obedience to law. But each stereotype held the same moral: blacks are dangerous and regressing, a matter of broad national interest because of their threat to the sanctity of white households.

Here, Dixon turns especially didactic, explaining to his audience that white southern manhood has the hard-won knowledge that the nation needs to order and regulate problems along the color line. While on a preaching tour of the northern states, the Reverend Durham encounters a great deal of sympathy for white southerners. Still, some misconceptions remain: "Your Negro question has already been settled," a Boston churchman tells Durham. "The nation has become a reality, not a name" (336). Durham corrects him, emphasizing the natural and necessary relationship between political solidarity and racial purity: "we haven't even faced the issues. Nationality demands solidarity. And you can never get solidarity in a nation of equal rights out of two hostile races that do not intermarry" (336). The South must be allowed to "save" itself, for the day will come when the South will save the nation:

> The ark of the covenant of American ideals rests to-day on the Appalachian
> Mountain range of the South. When your metropolitan mobs shall knock at
> the doors of your life and demand the reason of your existence, from these

        Manhood, Family, and White Identity

poverty-stricken homes, with their old-fashioned, perhaps medieval ideas, will come forth the fierce athletic sons and sweet-voiced daughters in whom the nation will find a new birth. (336–37)

Unable to answer such sweeping rhetoric, with its religious imagery and evocation of fears of immigration, mongrelization, class war, and the stereotype of the southern white as a racially purer strain of American, the deacon admits that the nation's racial experiment has failed: "To be frank with you," agrees the deacon, "I am on your side. I am tired of the Negro. I don't want to solve him" (339). By the turn of the twentieth century, many white Americans would answer with a resounding "Amen."

Readers of Dixon find his racist black stereotypes perhaps the most striking feature of his novels. Dixon's black world is consistently an inversion of his idealized white one. In contrast to the righteous Reverend Durham, black preachers during this period of social crisis "openly instructed their flocks to take what they needed from their white neighbors" (101). Such advice escalates racial tensions in town until violence erupts. Soon enough, the black terror reaches the white home: "A whole white family had been murdered in their home, the father, mother, and three children" (102). Five hundred white men gather in Hambright on the rumor of a "burning, pillaging and murdering . . . hoard of Negroes" (102). Nelse, true to form, remains loyal to his white folks; but then, Nelse and Eve, good, old-fashioned blacks, are the only black married couple in the novel. The intact, orderly black family essentially does not exist in Dixon's world.

A decade before Dixon wrote *The Leopard's Spots,* North Carolina had witnessed some of the most contested elections of the agrarian revolt. There was precious little white solidarity in North Carolina in the 1890s, certainly not the spectacle that Dixon paints of ex-Confederate soldiers looking to their ex-officers (that is, their natural leaders) for advice on politics and economics and order. By 1900 that picture had changed dramatically. The Wilmington riot of 1898 and the subsequent reassertion of Democratic control over the state signaled a rising tide of whiteness that soon erased the Populist/Republican challenge from North Carolina history.[58] Dixon stigmatized the Populists as reckless schemers, polluted by contact with blacks and the misguided notions of the North. The 1898 election in North Carolina, as well as Dixon's novels, demonstrates just how persuasive white men found narratives of white purity and black pollution, of order and violated domesticity; these narratives helped fuse a white coalition because they drew upon tropes of race, manhood, and domesticity that were current and broadly accepted by whites.[59] In the face of threats to his home and family ("fight us, and we will give this house and lot to a nigger") the common white man Tom Camp refuses a political alliance with blacks, remains loyal to the party of his fathers, and instinctively judges the Fusion Party disgusting because of the association with blacks it involves: "I ain't er nigger," he tells his wife, "and I don't flock with niggers" (107). Refusal to make a political alliance is presented here as a rejection of loathsome social equality.

No stereotype of corruption in Reconstruction government goes unmentioned. These men are not only publicly corrupt, but also privately depraved, with designs on spreading their mores throughout southern culture like cancer spreading through the body politic. Again, they serve to highlight the virtuous model of white southern men as represented by Gaston, Worth, and Durham. The new triumvirate ruling North Carolina are broadly painted and represent distinct stereotypes of particular vices: the governor is the unprincipled turncoat Amos Hogg, an ardent secessionist and partisan of John C. Calhoun until the Confederacy's fate became clear; the speaker of the house is the race- and gender-bending Legree; and the majority leader is the epitome of disorder, Tim Shelby, the educated black man given the reins of power. The legislators are an equally sorry lot: the ten white men among the 120 are draft dodgers and carpetbaggers.

Tellingly, the first assault of the men is upon marriage and the white home. Shelby introduces a bill on which he has been working secretly for months: "A Bill to be Entitled An Act to Relieve Married Woman from the Bonds of Matrimony when United to Felons, and to Define Felony." Anyone who served the Confederacy in any capacity, whether as soldier or public official, is *ipso facto* a felon and forever disfranchised; the bill annuls all marriages into which these men have entered, and prohibits either remarriage or cohabitation (114). "Four Carpet-bagger members of some education" rush aghast to Shelby's side, warning him that the state will not accept such a law (114). The legislators loot the state, seizing school funds, selling railroad bonds for ready cash, and installing a bar and brothel in the Capitol. After exhausting other funds, they levy a municipal tax of 25 percent in Hambright, threatening the homes of Tom Camp and Mrs. Gaston: in all, 2,320 homes in Campbell County come under the auctioneer's hammer for unpaid taxes

(119). Even Nelse and Eve fall prey: Nelse is beaten nearly to death by "bad niggers," and Eve realizes that the law will provide no remedy.

If the narrative has not been explicit enough about this corrupt government's assaults upon the home, the next episode raises the specter that will appear repeatedly to create the novel's most emotionally charged moments. Tom Camp decides that his sixteen-year-old daughter and the "gallant poor white," Hose Norman, will be married in Camp's house the night before it must be sold for taxes. But tragedy strikes on the wedding night as "a black shadow fell across the doorway" (125). A band of sixteen drunken black soldiers puts out the hearth fire (so blackness will cover the blacks in their black deed) and drags Annie into the woods. For Tom the situation calls for only one remedy. "Shoot, men! My God, shoot!" he urges Norman's friends. "There are things worse than death!" (126). Their bullets drive away the soldiers, but at the cost of Annie's life: "They laid her in the bed in the room that had been made sweet and tidy for the bride and groom. . . . Just where the blue veins crossed in her delicate temple there was a round hole from which a scarlet stream was running down her white throat" (127). Annie is the virgin daughter/wife, the two women in the eyes of the white South most precious and most threatened. The only blood that will stain the marriage bed is that from her delicate throat. All the men present agree with Camp that those who shot her "saved my little gal" (127).

It is the powerful and out-of-(white)-control black man who embodies the fears and secret desires of Dixon's world, who lives as a parasite upon the body politic and feeds mercilessly upon the bodies of individual white women. "The birth of a girl baby was sure to make a father restless," comments the narrator, "and when the baby looked up into his face one day with the soft life of a maiden he gave up his farm and moved into town" (202). This young girl is for Dixon a receptacle of all that makes the race distinctive, as well as the principal object of struggle between white men and black men in the novel. Regularly in *The Leopard's Spots* a black man attempts to or succeeds in defiling the bodily purity of a white woman. The defiled woman (or, if we extrapolate, the defiled culture) is then in a state of impure limbo, from which the white, upstanding, right-thinking men must free her by killing the beast and the beast within her.

The Leopard's Spots permeates these scenes of vampiric-style defilement and purification with Christian imagery, insisting (as Gaston does explicitly) upon the holiness of woman and the domestic sphere and the holy mission of righteous politics. Durham assures Tom that his dead-but-pure daughter has become the Christ of the white race: "Your child has not died in vain. A few things like this will be the trumpet of the God of our fathers that will call the sleeping manhood of the Anglo-Saxon race to life again" (128). Durham advises the local military commander to order the black troops out of town to save them from the righteous anger of the white men.

Here, in the South's darkest hour, Legree's forces seem poised to win the entire prize, symbolized by a "ringing order" from the commandant of District Two (the Carolinas), "permitting the marriage of Negroes to white women, and commanding its enforcement on every military post" (146). The scalawag Haley congratulates Legree supporter Tim Shelby, on this victory: "It's a great day, brother, for the world. There'll be no more color line" (146). Shelby agrees, and using a highly charged sexual metaphor, dismisses white objections: "Let 'em squirm. They're flat on their backs. We are on top, and we are going to stay on top. I expect to lead a fair white bride into my house before another year, and have poor white aristocrats to tend my lawn" (146–47). Scenes such as this one make the stakes abundantly clear: black aspiration to political participation and other civil rights is nothing less than the rape of the white South.

Dixon and other turn-of-the-century white southerners spoke and wrote as if black men were truly a threat to "their" white women and white homes. But did Dixon and others truly believe that black men threatened to turn the racial and gender prerogatives of white men on their head? A century later, Dixon's novels no longer carry the same popular weight. His novels no longer have the same galvanizing power to conjure white community. No mainstream voices defend Dixon and his views. In one sense, then, Dixon and his vision of white community are no more. He lost, and it is sometimes tempting to read back into his lost cause a sense that he knew his cause was shaky. Because most readers these days do not share Dixon's beliefs, it is easy to project our discomfort with racist narratives onto them and assume that at some level turn-of-the-century white southerners knew that they asserted an unjust cause, and thus faced a real crisis of gender.

Such anachronistic projections do Dixon's novels a disservice. A broad national audience was persuaded, moved, entertained, and inspired by what he wrote. In any case, the degree to which readers rationally calculated the odds of the black threat literally coming to pass is impossible to say. Narratives about monsters do more than act as forecasts, however. The hero has to slay the monster, and it is his story, too. The effect of the asserted threat is to elevate the relative prestige of white masculinity and to suggest that all white people are in this struggle together. Without a powerful threat against which to prevail, white manhood appears less lustrous. Dixon and other white supremacists' stories never failed to achieve proper resolution: the white man triumphs and the black man—no man at all—is punished. While Dixon may have imagined that black men might menace white women and the white household, he never wavered in his assertion that these things are legitimately the white man's to order, regulate, and control, and that the white community will survive the peril.

Dixon uses the example of Tim Shelby to bring that crisis to its crescendo. He shows that the leopard's spots cannot be educated out and that in the end white male supremacy will triumph; Shelby's inability to control his African lust—to regulate his passions like a man, that is—brings Legree's regime crashing down. Shelby advertises for a teacher, and Mollie Graham, with a blind mother and four siblings to support, applies for the position. She is forced to pay a social call on Shelby, who quizzes her acceptance of the new order: "The supreme law of the land has broken down every barrier of race and we are henceforth to be one people" (150). Shelby promises to give her the job and to excuse her rent if she will "Let me kiss you—once!" (150). In answer, she runs sobbing home to her mother. The next night, "two hundred white-robed silent men whose close-fitting hood disguises looked like the mail helmets of ancient knights" gathered outside Shelby's home, and the next morning his body is found hanging from the balcony of the courthouse (150). "His thick lips had been split with a sharp knife, and from his teeth hung this placard: 'The answer of the Anglo-Saxon race to Negro lips that dare pollute with words the womanhood of the South. K.K.K.'" (151). Dixon suggests that this white response was instinctual: this "Law and Order League was a spontaneous and resistless racial uprising of clansmen of highland origin. . . . This Invisible Empire of White Robed Anglo-Saxon Knights was simply the old answer of organized manhood to organized crime" (151–54). In this justification for murder we see how a firm adherence to traditional gender roles buttresses and rhetorically purifies the racialist attitudes of white supremacy and violence against African Americans. In the end, white manhood will stand as one and triumph.

Brought to solidarity by a righteous lynching, the white men of Independence rally together before the election to hear the politicians' speeches. "Are you a White Man or a Negro? . . . It was a White Man's Party, and against it stood in solid array the Black Man's Party" (161). The election is a simple "test of manhood": "Any man, black or white, who can be scared out of his ballot is not fit to have one. . . . The ballot is force" (163). Shifting the black stereotype from viciousness to buffoonery, the narrative suggests that blacks are so unfit for the vote that they mistake "elective franchise" for a government giveaway, and bring jugs and wheelbarrows to carry home their prizes. Blacks, the narrative implies, are not fit to enjoy the ballot because democracy is not in their blood, because they are not men. Voting—and political participation more broadly—is a gendered act in the novel, and disfranchisement emasculates the force that threatens patriarchal right. Preserving the ballot for white men feeds upon and perpetuates the assertion that white men are the only real men. Indeed, limiting the franchise to white men made the category of white masculinity politically and culturally meaningful. The blood of the real (white) men raised, Legree's forces are routed in the election. Off to New York, Legree becomes a Wall Street robber baron, to prey on the whole nation. Legree's flight marks the end of volume one as well as the symbolic end of the first phase of building the New South. The conflicts are not over, but with the outside agitators removed, the New South is now in the hands of white men.

Having established the basic lines of conflict, narrative strategies, and thematics of the novel, Dixon narrows his focus in volumes two and three so that the novel becomes the story of Charles Gaston's rise in politics and concurrent courtship of General Worth's daughter, Sallie. Though volumes two and three continue to feature race riots, interracial sexual assaults, and corrupt politicians, conflict here is symbolically reduced to a manageable competition between Gaston and his political and romantic rival, Allan Macleod. Dixon allows his novel to do what novels do best. As Nancy Armstrong has argued, the novel came into dominance as a literary genre and purveyor of cultural information as it "turned political information into the discourse of sexuality."[60] Nor is it a coincidence that the political and romantic subplots should be parallel. Just as the election of Charles Gaston as governor of North Carolina resolves the political strife and corruption represented in *The Leopard's Spots,* the marriage between Gaston and Sallie Worth resolves threats to the home and white womanhood, which the novel portrays as the greatest evil of the Reconstruction period.

In the context of his culture's struggle over the future of the race, young Charles Gaston becomes a man. His mother, horrified by the sight of blacks invading her home and preparing to bid on it, collapses and soon dies. Her dying charge to Gaston is to reclaim the home: "You will fight this battle out, and win back our home and bring your own bride here" (141). For Dixon, then, property, the ballot, and guardianship of white womanhood represent the fullest realization of white manhood. Thus complete, Gaston is prepared to seek his fortune.

Gaston's courtship of Sallie Worth is a conventional enough story of a jealous father convinced that Gaston is not good enough for his daughter, and of the young man's eventual, inevitable, triumph. Did Dixon include the romance simply to sell books? The Victorian Charles Reade who, like Dixon, wrote novels with social "purposes," commented to a friend that "The reader of fiction is narrow and self-indulgent. . . . He will read no story the basis of which is not sexual."[61] Yet *The Leopard's Spots* contains so many romances ending in marriage and is so teleologically destined toward marriage that to subordinate Gaston's romantic career to his more "important" (because more public, manly, or historical) political career is to misrepresent the interrelation the novel posits between the private and public spheres.

One solution is to read *The Leopard's Spots* as a "marriage plot novel," a predominantly nineteenth-century form in which (sometimes multiple) courtships and marriages are used to explore and ultimately resolve a variety of social and political concerns. Marriage works explicitly as the healer of political, social, and personal division. Of course it is "unrealistic" to suppose that a single marriage—or even a series of marriages—will solve the grave political and social dilemmas that Dixon's novel represents, but again, fiction such as Dixon's happily forgoes "realism" in pursuit of the "higher truths" found in the myths of race, home, manhood, and womanhood that the novel represents.

In one intriguing but minor subplot, the Gastons' ex-slave Nelse learns from the Freedman's Bureau that he and his wife Eve are not legally married, and that he must pay one dollar for a license and have the ceremony performed over again. He trifles with Eve, pretending that he might take his choice of young women. To his chagrin, however, she turns him out of the house and forces him to court her very formally before she agrees to the ceremony. Reinforcing the fundamental morality of these "old time" blacks (in implicit contrast, of course, to the younger generation), this episode implies that even these "simple darkies" realize the foolishness of the Bureau. The episode underscores the sanctity of the marriage bond: Nelse and Eve need no bureaucrat pursuing a license fee to certify that they are married.

A more sinister romance plot involves Gaston's rival, Allan MacLeod, and the wife of Reverend Durham. "In his tireless devotion to his work," Durham "had starved his wife's heart," so that MacLeod finds her vulnerable and "in a dangerous period of her mental development" (261). Just after the war, she had exercised her unfulfilled maternal energies in relief of the poor, but with the end of Reconstruction, this exertion was no longer necessary. "[S]he asked herself the question, 'Have I lived?' And she could not answer. She found herself asking the reasons for things long accepted as fixed and eternal. What was good, right, true?" (261–62). The narrator ties MacLeod's ambition to seduce Mrs. Durham to his ambition and his hatred of godly things, including Durham. MacLeod represents rationalism and the modern temper gone wrong; he also reinforces the confluence of sex, politics, and white Christian masculinity that pervades the novel. MacLeod's failure to seduce Mrs. Durham prefigures Gaston's ultimate success over him both politically and in pursuit of Sallie Worth. More than a plot device, this is an example of how the novel works constantly to reinforce the interdependence of lawful marriage and proper citizenship:

> With the Anglo-Saxon race guarding the door of marriage with fire and sword, the effort is being made to build a nation within a nation of two antagonistic races. No such thing had ever been done in the history of the human race, even under the development of the monarchical and aristocratic forms of society. How could it be done under the formulas of Democracy with Equality as the fundamental basis of law? And yet this was the programme of the age. (203)

The model of democracy Dixon invokes here is the Germanic association of equals that many scholars still saw as the historical antecedent of Anglo-American political institutions. There are distinctions of rank possible un-

    MANHOOD, FAMILY, AND WHITE IDENTITY

der this system, but they are natural, as the "natural selection" of Worth, Cameron, and Gaston demonstrates. Any poor boy of merit can rise to marry the daughter of the wealthiest man in this society of Anglo-Saxon equals. Any (white) boy can grow up to be governor. Gaston gets them both.

This neat arrangement, by which the most worthy man wins the most desirable woman and thus ensures the progress of the race, is threatened in a society where black men have equal political rights. For even if a black man were to become rich (by some subterfuge, Dixon would suggest), he would never have the "character," inherent in the white man's breast, necessary to win a virtuous woman. Any children produced by miscegenation would be evolutionarily unsound because racially inferior: "The Negro is the human donkey," insists the Reverend Durham. "You can train him, but you can't make of him a horse. Mate him with a horse, you lose the horse, and get a larger donkey called a mule, incapable of preserving his species" (464). It is precisely because human reproduction did not work that way that Dixon and other white men dreaded the notion of sexual contact between black men and white women.

Late in the novel, Dixon introduces a vital "shadow" marriage plot between a black man and a white woman that demonstrates this point. It involves the daughter of Boston congressman Everett Lowell and his political protégé, George Harris, the Harvard-educated son of Eliza Harris from *Uncle Tom's Cabin*. Seemingly modeled on Henry Cabot Lodge, Lowell has "a family tree five hundred years old" and is a longtime champion of the freedman. But, the narrator adds, Lowell "never confused his political theories about the rights of the African with his personal choice of associates or his pride in his Anglo-Saxon blood. With him politics was one thing, society another" (313). Instead, the text corrects Lowell by demonstrating that the political is the personal. White northern men (such as Lowell) are wrong, and white southern men (such as Dixon) are right. By educating Lowell on this point, the novel removes the last rational objection to black disfranchisement. Harris seeks to marry Lowell's daughter Helen, a "blonde beauty." Harris is "a familiar figure" in the home, where he uses the library. Harris is not one of Dixon's ape-like blacks: he is "handsome and almost white," and therefore so much the more dangerous.

Senator Lowell might well have taken warning from the words of Durham earlier in the novel:

When the white race begin to hobnob with the Negro and seek his favor they must grant him absolute equality. You cannot seek the Negro vote without asking him to your home sooner or later. If you ask him to your house, he will break bread with you at last. And if you seat him at your table, he has the right to ask your daughter's hand in marriage. (243–44)

This is precisely what Harris does. Lowell believes at first that the young man expects simply "some promotion in a governmental department at Washington" (394). Upon hearing what Harris desires, Lowell is repulsed: "Social rights are one thing, political rights another," he tells Harris (396). "If you are honest with yourself, you know it is not true," responds the younger man:

> Politics is but a manifestation of society. Society rests on the family. The family is the unit of civilisation. The right to love and wed where one loves is the badge of fellowship in the order of humanity. The man who is denied this right in any society is not a member of it. (396)

Of course, the irony here is that this rebuffed black man, too lowly to marry the beautiful Helen despite his education and cultivation, sees the truth about marriage and politics that this progressive senator hypocritically denies and that the white-supremacist heroes of the novel have been asserting for hundreds of pages. With such social "experiments" put firmly in their proper place, the novel proceeds to marry its hero and heroine in proper fashion.

The central marriage plot of *The Leopard's Spots* is complicated and delayed through two volumes by political differences between the general and Gaston, and by MacLeod's nearly successful attempts to befoul Gaston's name and have him imprisoned for election law violations. MacLeod, a power in the Republican Party, plays Satan to Gaston's Christ, offering him the world if he will switch his political allegiance. MacLeod reveals the Republican plans to ally with the Farmers' Alliance, and calls on Gaston to give up his irrational hatred of Republicans. Gaston responds that the black voter's menace to civilization (courtesy of his Republican champions) is reason enough for any red-blooded white southerner to hate Republicans:

The Republican party will stink in the South for a century, not because they
beat us in war, but because two years after the war, in profound peace, they
inaugurated a second war on the unarmed people of the South, butchering
the starving, the wounded, the women and children. Their attempt to establish with the bayonet an African barbarism on the ruins of Southern society
was a conspiracy against human progress. (196)

MacLeod reminds Gaston that the "black mob" is in truth ruled by whites.
Gaston answers: "Yes, but the black mob defines the limits within which you
live and have your being" (197). Obsession with blacks could shape a white
southerner's life. Dixon seems to be saying more here than even he realizes,
by showing us just how imprisoned within the language of race he and the
white South are. White manhood, in particular, is defined by that spectral
Other, the now politically and sexually powerful black man. For all of Dixon's
rhetoric about the danger of blacks and miscegenation poisoning the white
South, it is actually the presence of blacks that makes southern culture; there
is no whiteness without blackness.

Gaston recalls Durham's words: "The future of the world depends on the
future of this Republic. This Republic can have no future if racial lines are
broken. . . . Two thousand years look down upon this struggle, and two thousand years of the future bend low to catch the message of life or death" (200).
In contrast to those southerners who were happiest when the North paid
no attention to the South's attempts to manage its black population, Dixon
wishes for the entire country to see that the South has responded, minute-
man-like, to this new firebell in the night, and has shown the course that
history demands the rest of the country follow. Dixon is being disingenuous
here in asserting that the question of black versus white was the only substantive issue separating southern Democrats from Republicans. The tariff
was not meaningless, nor were the battles over currency and the banking
system. Dixon, though, will not allow that anything of substance separates
white southerners—if we are one people, then the only issue, the only question, must be whether blacks or whites will be allowed to rule.

In the end, of course, Gaston is rewarded for remaining true to the cause
with both the governor's mansion and Sallie to fill it. And lest we should once
again be tempted to see the marriage plot as a mere auxiliary to this political

conclusion, the final scene of the novel makes plain which is the better of Gaston's rewards. Asked to toast Governor Gaston and his wife at their inaugural ball, Reverend Durham "seemed to pay no attention to the Governor, but, turning to Sallie, he said: '[T]o her, the heroine who inspired Charles Gaston with power to mould a million wills in his, change the current of history, and become Governor of the Commonwealth—to her all honour, and praise, and homage'" (467–68). When Sallie asserts that she does not "'desire any part in public life'" except through her husband, Gaston's response, the final sentence of the novel, is characteristic: "And I had rather be the husband of such a woman than to be the ruler of the world" (468–69). In Dixon's world, white men could have both, and black men neither.

Conclusion

Reading *The Leopard's Spots,* or nearly any other work of Thomas Dixon's, helps us to recognize the vast difference in sensibility, and particularly in racial sensibility, between the early twentieth and early twenty-first centuries. It is impossible to conclude that Dixon was other than a rabid negrophobe, yet millions of readers devoured his novels or watched them transformed in *Birth of a Nation,* one of the seminal texts of American cinema. Thomas Nelson Page, on the other hand, now might appear (to those few who pay any attention to him) as a genteel racist, or perhaps just a dated but harmless apologist for old plantation days. Dixon wrote almost exclusively of the postbellum South, Page of the antebellum South. Dixon thought contemporary blacks were reverting to bestiality; Page showed blacks after the war opining that the old plantation days were the best they had known.

At the turn of the twentieth century, white American men fretted about the rising tide of color, as well as other perceived challenges to their racial and gender prerogatives.[62] Dixon and Page fashioned representations of masterful white southern manhood that proved appealing and reassuring, shorn as they were of reminders of antebellum tensions over secession and the moral quandary of slavery. In representing white southern men as loyal Americans and as benevolent yet stern masters of their households, regions, and racially inferior people, Dixon and Page provided a persuasive model of manhood for a broad white national audience. In the fiction of Dixon and Page, white southern men were transformed from rebels who threatened the

Union to the best guarantee of national (white) unity. Describing the 1890 Confederate veterans' parade at the dedication of Richmond's monument to Lee, Page wrote: "Only a thousand or two of old or aging men riding or tramping along through the dust of the street. . . . But they represented the spirit of the South; they represented the spirit which when honor was in question never counted the cost . . . the spirit that is the strongest guaranty to us to-day that the Union is and is to be."[63]

The nation, North and South, paid homage to the sanctity of (white) womanhood and something like what a later generation would call "family values," while worrying that those ideals might be under siege. Dixon, like Vardaman, might well have known that most lynchings of African Americans were not for attempted rape, but by declaring this galvanizing lie, they assumed the role of white male defender of pure white womanhood. The political payoff of such rhetoric was undeniable—in electoral and authorial popularity not only for James Vardaman and Dixon, but also for less overt racialists like John Sharp Williams and Page. The widely accepted narratives of domesticity and potential violation forged in those years had direct political implications for generations. To give one example, the solid southern delegations in the Senate filibustered proposed antilynching legislation in the 1920s and 1930s not by defending lynching *per se,* but rather by arguing that federal intervention in the South represented a violation of southern state autonomy—that is, the transgressing of a border as inviolable as a white lady.[64] White southern rhetoricians played a skillful game: on the one hand, with their invocations of pure womanhood and the embattled home, they stressed the similarities they were sure all white listeners shared; on the other, with their cautions to "outsiders" to stay out of southern affairs, they exercised one of the classic twentieth century white southern excuses—that is, people who did not understand southern culture (the "southern way of life") were attempting to legislate on topics whose intricacies they were not bred to know.

There is less ideological distance between Page and Dixon than one might suspect. Both Dixon and Page were Negro-obsessed men who were convinced that the fundamental problem of American life was the Negro and who offered damning critiques of contemporary blacks. Indeed, Page's critique is just as damning as Dixon's, for the old plantation, with its steadying and civilizing and domesticating power, is forever gone. Like Dixon, Page believed the South had the potential to teach the rest of the country how to deal with the problem. Writing of "the peril of contamination from the over-crowding of an inferior race," Page argued:

> The only thing that stands between the people of the North and the negro is the people of the South. The chief difficulty in the solution of the question exists in the different views held as to it by the two sections. Their ultimate interests are identical; their present interests are not very widely divergent. . . . [T]he white race has need to awake and bestir itself.[65]

Page could sound much like Dixon when representing a black character in-terested in Reconstruction-era politics or white women. In *Red Rock* (1898), "the negro, Moses" encounters a white woman, Ruth, who has lost her way in the woods: "A curious smirk was on his evil face. 'My Mistis,' he said, with a grin that showed his yellow teeth and horrible gums. . . . I will show you the way. Old Moses will show you de way. He-he-he.'"[66] Page was not only a writer of fiction, but also used his reputation to comment on the contem-porary South to the rest of the nation. Page remarked that "social equality" meant to the "ignorant and brutal young Negro" one thing: "the opportu-nity to enjoy, equally with white men, the privilege of cohabiting with white women." Neither Dixon nor Vardaman could have said it more plainly.

Page and Dixon are familiar subjects for southern historians. Tradi-tionally, most readings of the two have focused on the representations of African Americans in their work and their desire for goodwill between the (white) North and the (white) South. In his influential reading of Dixon, Joel Williamson writes that there "are two themes in *The Leopard's Spots:* na-tional unity and the retrogression of the American Negro."[67] Readings of Page have rightly examined his benevolent representations of plantation slavery. By the beginning of the twentieth century, writes Fred Hobson, Page's Old South, "a society simple, stable, and endowed with grace and charm—had become a romantic neverland for Americans North as well as South."[68] Both Page and Dixon saw blacks as an alien presence and considered white male unity across the Mason-Dixon Line as a natural American goal. Together, their narratives fashioned a model of masterful white masculinity, and by representing the white home as both sacred and threatened, provided an apology for the behavior, even violent excesses, of white southern men. Dixon's novels are a byword for turn-of-the-century racialist excess; Page's stories, when read, are studied as desiccated examples of a dead genre, the plantation apologia. Yet the representations of slavery and white manhood that both men provided live on and continue their work of definition and ordering. Most white people are glad that the North won the Civil War for the sake of the nation. As for slavery, the best that neo-Confederates can do is to argue that the Civil War was not caused by slavery. But still, many Americans think of the South—as represented for present-day tourists in the plantation homes of Natchez or the languid beauty of Savannah or Charleston—as a romantic landscape in which they imagine themselves wealthy masters and mistresses of lavish and well-ordered homes, surrounded by happy, obedient "servants."

In southern fiction as well as southern politics, white unity was built upon the rhetoric of every white man's mastery of his household and the control of black men. White audiences nationwide found such stories compelling. At home and abroad, white men accepted the "controlled use of force to further civilization, bring international order, and preserve the white race."[69] Assertions of white unity in the South were built upon a perceived and imagined black threat; other white Americans believed the stories white southerners told because those stories corresponded with what they believed about racial categories and political and domestic order. "The Negro," wrote Richard Wright in another context, "is America's metaphor."[70] The fiction of Page and Dixon used that metaphor to help build a broad pan-white community.

This New South fiction represents something more insidious than bad history. The "southerner" in turn-of-the-century southern discourse is always white, so this assurance that southern and white are one and the same seems to read African Americans out of southernness. But a center/periphery metaphor does not adequately represent the symbiotic relationship between whiteness and blackness, especially their mutual work in making the term "southern" meaningful. Rather than blackness being marginal in the making of southernness, then, here is a margin that defines the center: blackness in turn-of-the-century southern fiction, as in other racialized southern discourses, is the foil against which southernness and Americanness are defined. In Dixon and Page, the language of race is both overt and encoded.

Dixon especially is dogmatic and didactic on questions of race, manhood, womanhood, and power. The overtness and crudeness of that dogmatism is, of course, one reason that Dixon's reputation soured well before World War II. At the turn of the century, however, white audiences found the savagery of Dixon's black stereotypes and the now-embarrassing acquiescence of Page's stereotypical black southerners to be persuasive; their narratives of white identity were well received and paid them well. And Page's reputation as an essentially harmless if irrelevant writer endured, certainly into the 1950s and 1960s. Even today his work is typically not considered to be as venomous as that of Dixon. Yet his heroic, tragic, white southern men operated as an oblique critique of black southern masculinity and offered an implicit argument in favor of white male control of the South. The seemingly more benign language of race in Page's plantation fiction allows it to do much of its work of white community building out of the light of controversy. As custodians of antebellum homes have found, tourists today find little that is morally ambiguous about visiting such homes, now that the slaves are not in plain sight. In much the same way, the well-ordered home in the fiction of Dixon and especially Page serves as a commentary on black disorder, even when the black characters are not in sight.

Dominant voices in southern fiction did more, then, than provide crude dogmatism to underpin the emerging Jim Crow racial settlement; they provided a nationally persuasive definition of regional identity and masculinity that held southernness to be synonymous with whiteness, and with loyal support to the white American nation. During turn-of-the-century redefinitions of the American nation, the fruits of this definition of the South were tremendous. Blacks were excluded as rational actors; problematic aspects of the region's past were whitewashed. Because of its broad cultural dispersal through the seemingly apolitical medium of fiction, this definition of the South is not dead yet: one finds traces of it still in Old South nostalgia and neo-Confederate apologetics. It is also present in unconsciously racist forms. In popular usage, even much academic usage, the "southerner" is still assumed to be white. By presenting their fiction as sober, honest historical fact, Page and Dixon helped make it so.

3

"THE SOUTH IS A SINGLE, HOMOGENEOUS PEOPLE": CANONIZING SOUTHERN HISTORY AND LITERATURE

By the world at large we are held to have been an ignorant, illiterate, cruel, semi-barbarous section of the American people, sunk in brutality and vice, who have contributed nothing to the advancement of mankind; a race of slave-drivers, who, to perpetuate human slavery, conspired to destroy the Union, and plunged the country into war.

—Thomas Nelson Page, "The Want of a History of the Southern People"

Though we tend to praise the fact of community as a good thing (as in general we tend to praise unity or freedom as "good" things) its goodness is not a priori or absolute. If a community is a society which shares values, likings, and aversions, then the goodness of the community depends to some extent on what kind of values it shares. . . . the South, as an authentic community, has held to some values that surely were, and are, questionable.

—Cleanth Brooks, "Thematic Problems in Southern Literature"

"Much of what Dr. Page has said is correct," wrote Julian A. C. Chandler in his introduction to the twelve-volume history, *The South in the Building of the Nation* (1909). "No true history of the South has been written."[1] But if Thomas

Nelson Page and Chandler had cause to regret the absence of a "true history," it was not for want of effort by their fellow southerners. Even before Appomattox, white southerners were doggedly spilling ink to get the recently unfolded story right. Secession, war, and the shattering of the Confederacy struck writers of the immediate postwar years as their most pressing narrative problem—that is, the story most worth getting right. In a solemn tone common to these early efforts, clergyman and Confederate apologist R. L. Dabney wrote: "my purpose . . . is to lay this pious and filial defence upon the tomb of my murdered mother, Virginia."[2] But the great bulk of these histories and memoirs written during the 1860s and 1870s did not satisfy the next generation of white southerners, especially those who, like Julian Chandler, were academics. Overtly partisan and often narrowly construed, this first generation of Confederate apologetics would not meet the emerging professional historical standards of the 1880s and 1890s. Indeed, some early chroniclers of the Confederate experience realized that "an accepted history can never be written in the midst of the stormy events of which that history is composed, nor by the agents through whose efficiency they were wrought."[3] Further, these accounts had little appeal for lay audiences eager to move beyond contentious arguments over the legality of secession, the course of Confederate leadership, and the relative effectiveness of particular Confederate generals, and to reembrace an identity as patriotic Americans.[4]

The early works may have stretched up to 1,500 pages, as did Jefferson Davis's *Rise and Fall of the Confederate Government* (1881), but the task of these histories was simple: to assign praise or blame in what they hesitated to call the "Civil War." Whether apologetics (regional or personal) such as R. L. Dabney's *A Defense of Virginia and the South* (1867), Alfred Taylor Bledsoe's *Is Davis a Traitor?* (1866), or Joseph E. Johnston's *Narrative of Military Operations* (1874), or constitutional tours de force, such as Alexander Stephens's *Constitutional View of the Late War between the States* (1868), their efforts were not intended to be full histories of the South or of the war itself.[5] Instead, they were problem-oriented. Was secession constitutional? Was Johnston treated unfairly by Jefferson Davis? Should Davis have been clapped into irons in Fortress Monroe?[6]

But by the 1880s and 1890s a rich body of southern histories, as well as histories and anthologies of literature, began to emerge, both from professional scholars and the South's indefatigable host of amateurs. It is this generation that began to move toward the goal that Thomas Nelson Page articulated, that of producing full and ideologically satisfying examinations of the South's history and letters, of accomplishing what one turn-of-the-century scholar called the "difficult and important task of providing for a general history of the South."[7]

The studies of southern history and southern letters written in the 1880s and following years did not neglect the Civil War, of course, but they differed from the earlier accounts in one fundamental way. They began to fulfill the next generation's desire for full, sustained narratives of a distinct but fundamentally American South, a region that was unified, free of guilt over war and slavery, and confident in its mastery of contemporary challenges. By the end of the nineteenth century, the South as narrated by white southerners was a broad Anglo-Saxon family attempting to maintain order, whether over the new nation of the founding fathers, or later over a potentially disruptive black population, slave or free. Scholars, both within and outside the academy, helped make that White South. Their efforts, like other efforts to define a people or a community, were successful not because they were able to impose their narratives upon the region, but because their narratives "answered popular needs and complemented existing values," as Don Doyle argues of other nationalist projects.[8]

This chapter traces the efforts of white writers at the turn of the twentieth century to construct, in Page's words, the "true history," as certain white southerners saw it, of southern history and letters. One finds in these narratives remarkable similarities: the South is a distinct but fundamentally American region of the American nation; the region possesses an organic culture, the "southern way of life"; blacks (since the end of slavery) are potentially disruptive but generally satisfied, as they were under slavery, so long as they are under the strict management of white southern men, who know them and have their best interests at heart; and the South, having ordered its domestic affairs (that is, turned back the Populist challenge and begun a systematic course of disfranchisement and Jim Crow), was well prepared to assist the broader white nation in its turn-of-the-century attempt to solve the problem of the color line, at home and abroad. Finally, white southerners after the Civil War imagined themselves as essentially one people, "as a vast, extended kinship, a family writ large and one capable of protecting and benefiting family life."[9]

Like other white southerners, these turn-of-the-century writers were keenly conscious that the South's status within the nation was changing. New South prophets celebrated the region's emergence from the postwar wilderness. "No section of the country," went one representative account, "had added so many stars to the national flag, given so much territory to the Union, played so active a part in making the nation, and so long presided over its destinies as the South . . . she may again be ready to take in the Nation's councils the place, she so long held, of political primacy."[10] Scholars' definitions of southern literature and history not only assisted this renegotiation of the South's place in the nation, but also offered a reconceptualization of American national identity along regional rather than sectional lines. By emphasizing the South's long and stable history, and its role in the making of the United States, the new southern orthodoxy presented the South not as the disruptive section of American history, but as one region among a nation of regions. "The feeling that existed a few years ago with reference to the South," wrote one scholar in 1909, "is fast disappearing and the other sections of this country as well as the world at large are realizing that the South is not such a section as she has been represented to be . . . the Southern people have figured in more ways than one in the history of America."[11]

Discovering Southern Letters

The years 1895 through 1915 witnessed an explosion of interest in southern writing, with the publication of more than a dozen major histories and anthologies of southern literature, including such works as the seventeen-volume *Library of Southern Literature*.[12] Literary critic Arlin Turner asked in 1975: "How do we account for the number of books on southern literature published early in the present century?"[13] While the motivations of individual authors are unrecoverable, certain things seem clear. Turn-of-the-century white southerners claimed that they were shaping a previously undiscerned subject; they felt part of a conscious, regionwide project to get the story right—for most of them, right in terms of professional standards of scholarship as well as regional pride.[14] For instance, William Malone Baskervill, chair of English at Vanderbilt University, wrote in 1897 that since the Civil War, southern writers had been "conspicuous contributors to the nation's literature." Baskervill hoped that his *Southern Writers: Biographical and Critical Studies* (1897 and 1902) would "secure in the nation at large a

   "The South Is a Single, Homogeneous People"

just estimate of the South's latest contribution to the common storehouse of American literature" (1:iii, v). Expressing sentiments that could stand as the thesis of a host of studies of southern literature written at the turn of the twentieth century, Baskervill argued that the South was both distinctive and American, an equal partner in the American nation and a party to its continuing reevaluation and reinscription.[15]

From the 1890s through the First World War, scholars and the reading public defined a canon of American literature.[16] The consequences of this project were enormous, and have rightly drawn much recent scholarly attention. In his study of the creation of American literature as a discipline, David Shumway argues that "the discipline's most significant achievement was to secure for Americans a belief in their success as a culture."[17] But the "Americanization" of the curriculum did not proceed without loud complaints from that era's traditionalists. Classics departments (largely departments of philology) fought a fierce rearguard action against the introduction of English and, especially, American literature into American college classrooms. The study of the English language itself became a cause for alarm, as purists complained that the nineteenth-century emphasis on rhetoric was being abandoned in favor of English composition.[18] Composition, modernizers argued, was more useful than rhetoric—an especially important justification in an age of growing efficiency concerns, which ultimately prompted the development of a lean, business-friendly compositional voice.

This interest in teaching American literature and language also grew out of late-nineteenth-century anxieties over the "New Immigration" from eastern and southern Europe and its impact on what most middle-class white Americans would later unproblematically call the American character. The efforts at canon building occurred during a period when "native" white Americans, particularly in the culturally dominant Northeast, were giving renewed attention to the question of who could become an American—a degree of attention to cultural assimilation not seen since the 1840s and 1850s. The explosion of canon building, then, both North and South, as an adjunct to this project of asserting and disseminating a national culture, comes as no surprise, nor does the southern texts' emphasis on the fundamental Americanness of southern letters.[19]

"Whatever in our literature is distinctly Southern . . . must be distinctly American," argued Joel Chandler Harris, the father of Uncle Remus, in introducing Jennie Thornley Clarke's anthology of southern poetry, *Songs of the South* (1896). Harris's argument is representative of many turn-of-the-century arguments about southern letters. Southern writers merit attention, so the argument goes, not simply because they are southern, but because what is southern cannot help but be American to the marrow. Characterizing pride in the South's literary achievements as a "healthy provinciality," Harris expressed confidence that the anthology would "meet with a cordial reception in all parts of the country." Harris was certain that the nation was ready to appreciate southern literature, which, he was quick to add, was a vital part of a broader American tradition.[20] In the past, Americans might have developed "different aims and views," but as (white) Americans they were "people of the same race and blood," sharing, among other traits, a "spirit of good humor," and thus a common culture, albeit one with regional variegation.[21]

In the immediate post–Civil War decades, white southerners discovered that they had a literary tradition worthy not only of regional piety but also of national attention, and acted upon this discovery.[22] They published anthologies and histories of southern letters, created college courses and reading circles, and recovered what they considered a tradition fundamentally American but distinctly southern.[23] The arrangement and rhetoric of the critical texts from this period is revealing. Their arguments for a "southern culture" often betray ambivalences over the South's social and political place within the reconstructed Union, not least of which were lingering concerns about the degree to which the South's fundamental Americanness nevertheless carried special concerns and conditions that needed to be met. For example, the B. F. Johnson Publishing Company advertised its line of "Johnson's English Classics" (including works by Shakespeare, Milton, Walter Scott, Pope, and Tennyson) as "a set of books which, without sectional bias, will answer especially to Southern needs."[24] How Shakespeare or Milton might be sectionally biased, or how such bias might be addressed, the company does not say.

Within the same work one often finds both defensive pride about the value and uniqueness of southern culture and a wish to emphasize the Americanness of the region. In *The Literature of the South* (1910), for instance, Montrose J. Moses asserted that the aim of his work was "to escape the stigma of sectionalism." "The South per se," he continued,

Retains its individuality—but its significance, as part of the nation, should have a wider understanding. For it will be found that the South has contributed to American literature. . . . The literature of the South is a literature of a people, and those people are Americans as well as Southerners.[25]

Along with these assertions of the southerner as American came arguments that the South was unique and pure—one broad white family. As Charles Kent wrote in introducing the *Library of Southern Literature,* "little has been made of state lines, for the South is a single, homogeneous people." Scholars such as Moses stressed the role of the South in the building of the nation, and hailed a New South: "A new day has dawned, and with it a new literature marked by new energy, new freedom, and self-analysis, and descriptive power. Democracy has at last made up its mind to care for its children with persistence and intelligence."[26] Gaines Foster has written of the latter project:

> If seventeen volumes and 8,451 pages written by 527 men can have a thesis, that of the *Library of Southern Literature* was: The South has made great contributions to the creation of the United States and its literature. The Civil War remains the central event of the South's history, but this need not lessen the positive contributions the South has made nor even prevent the reconciliation of the sections.[27]

These early efforts at creating a canon of southern literature have drawn relatively little attention from critics who often dismiss them as evidence of misplaced and unfounded southern chauvinism; Michael O'Brien has characterized such "compendia" as the *Library of Southern Literature* as "arid filiopietism."[28]

But these works merit closer attention. The canonization of southern literature is terrain where visions of the South were weighed, reconciled, and codified. These works also show southern scholars and a southern reading audience articulating their relation to the rest of the nation in the post-Reconstruction period of compromise and goodwill among white Americans. These texts enlist such writers as George Washington, John James Audubon, and Henry W. Grady to show both the long tradition of southern letters and the South's formative role in the making of American culture. Needless to say, the "self-analysis" and "descriptive power" of such African American writers as Charles W. Chesnutt and W. E. B. Du Bois, for instance, both critics of turn-of-the-century narratives of a white South, are excluded from the canon. One black writer is sometimes included—Booker T. Washington, lauded by the *Library of Southern Literature* for "echew[ing] offensive partisan politics." Washington "commands recognition on the ground of meritorious service and of high character."[29]

Selections in the *Library of Southern Literature* made little mention of antebellum debates over slavery or Reconstruction, both subjects that might have tempered the praise the editors expected the collection to gain throughout the nation or the reception they trusted it would receive in (white) southern homes throughout the region.[30] Many of the turn-of-the-century anthologies and histories of southern literature such as the *Library of Southern Literature* shared two themes. First, while it was essential that southerners must recognize their neglected tradition, the project could not have full value unless it caught the national eye—that is, unless their efforts were approved and certified by "outsiders." At the same time, the critics insisted that the only valid definitions of the South were those put forward by white southerners themselves—they insisted that the nation accept the South on the terms they offered.

Few southerners were more concerned than Mildred Lewis Rutherford with making sure that the South was correctly portrayed as patriotic, honorable, and sound. A member of the United Daughters of the Confederacy, Rutherford led efforts to censor schoolbooks, erect memorials to the Confederate dead, and see to it that southern states recognized the Lost Cause with official holidays.[31] At the same time, Rutherford claimed, as did many students of southern history and letters, that her task would aid in sectional reconciliation: "Patriotic men and women of the North as well as of the South . . . are demanding true history, and our sectional differences will disappear when we succeed in getting down to the truth of history." History, truth, white solidarity and patriotism—both southern and American patriotism— were for Rutherford easily compatible, as long as one accepted the terms of definition she offered.

One of Rutherford's contributions to the literary memorialization of Dixie, *The South in History and Literature* (1906), provides 866 pages of biographical sketches and some excerpts from southern writers ranging chronologically from "The Settlement of Jamestown, 1607, to Living Writers" (i).[32] Rutherford, chair of literature at Athens, Georgia's, Lucy Cobb Institute, like many of the students of southern literature, saw her work as a monument to the greatness of southern letters, and a spur to other scholars to rescue many of the lesser-known figures, especially contemporary writers, from undeserved neglect. "The South," she explained, "has never realized the importance of preserving its records either in history or literature." Rutherford was conscious of the work others were performing in shaping a new canon of southern as well as American literature. She was particularly taken with the work of Thomas Nelson Page, commending him as influential in her own work, not only through his fiction but also for his efforts to recover the South's neglected literature. She affirms his argument that "[the South] has been left behind in the race for literary honors" (xxxv), and applauds his work in southern history (particularly *The Old South*) for "calling attention to misrepresentations of many of her [the South's] institutions" (xxvii).

In part, Rutherford saw her task as gathering source material for a larger, cooperative regionwide mapping of southern culture. Comparing her efforts with those of contemporary state historical societies, which were not only to preserve current records but "search for any record of past history," Rutherford expressed confidence that the South was awakening from its neglectful slumber: "the day is not far off when the South will not only realize more fully her own greatness, but will take a laudable pride in having other sections recognize it" (xxxv). Rutherford gets close here to expressing the instrumental value of these definitions of southern culture. Not only will the South benefit from having its culture recognized and celebrated internally (that is, self-knowledge will bring health and happiness), but that there are clearly gains to be made in the eyes of the nation as a whole by fostering a particular vision of homogeneous white southern culture.

The South needed to assert its cultural integrity, first by getting its own house in order. Only then could the South "stand up" to New England. And the metaphors Rutherford used, of gathering, collecting, and building, all unmistakably suggest a spatial conception of the project. The South will have more "room" if the cultural hegemony of New England is broken, if only by disproving its claim to be the only cultural section of the country, or rather, the country's culture. There is literally a suggestion here, as in *The Library of Southern Literature,* that the sheer bulk of the project will command cognitive as well as shelf space, and will lead to an altered conception of the United States. Indeed, Rutherford's as well as other anthologies seem in part prompted by fears that the South was in danger of losing its distinctiveness. To insist upon southern distinctiveness in the post–Civil War era, with industrialization and all the other potentially homogenizing forces of modernity at work, suggests a degree of cultural anxiety. One starts to insist upon distinctiveness and individuality when one begins to doubt it.

Like most of the other writers under consideration here, Rutherford offers no explicit definition of "the South," nor does she offer evidence of self-conscious southern identity, let alone strong proto-national consciousness, on the part of the early writers she includes. Instead, she simply asserts the existence of a long tradition of what she unproblematically calls southern letters. Rutherford's strategy is to enlist as the keystone of this southern canon a writer whose "great" status would seem to involve no special pleading or regional prejudice. As literary critics of the post–World War II generation anchored the South's claims to literary greatness to William Faulkner, Rutherford chose Edgar Allan Poe.[33] "It has been stated that no literature of any value came from the South before 1860," argued Rutherford. "Surely those making this statement forget that [Poe] lived before that time" (3). Rutherford plunges into her defense of southern letters by citing authorities who testify to Poe's greatness, begging entirely the question of his southernness. Poe is for Rutherford clearly the region's literary heavyweight, and she proceeds to clear a path before her by using Poe as her juggernaut: "there is not a question as to his poetic merit or his ability as a prose writer, and critics North and South accord this" (3). Finding in his poetry only one lack— "faith"—Rutherford concludes, without sensing the apparent contradiction, that for all his representative southernness, Poe was *sui generis.*

Running through a series of southern writers of the Chesapeake, the Carolinas, and the Old Southwest, including Francis Scott Key, Edward Pinckney, John James Audubon, the historians Parson Weems and Henry Lee, Francis Goulding (author of *Young Marooners,* the "Robinson Crusoe of America"), John C. Calhoun, Henry Clay, and the southwestern humorists, Rutherford mixes chronology, state, and genre to make the case for an active literary movement within the antebellum South. After this initial whirlwind, Rutherford fleshes out the development of the southern literary tradition. In her list of America's literary firsts she cites John Smith's *History of Virginia* ("from a member of the Jamestown colony, and not the Plymouth

Rock colony"); the "first contribution to American literature," the "first book really written on American soil" ("Whittaker's Good News"); and "the first book to come from a printing-press in America" (7–8). After these assertions Rutherford's argument loses force; she adopts a near-pleading, semiapologetic tone: "The people of the South before the War Between the States were literary and the love of letters was always just as keen in Southern States as it was in the New England States, and there were really just as many highly educated men" (8).[34]

Rutherford's is one of the few studies to find a place for black southerners other than as quaint objects for writers of local color fiction. Indeed, Rutherford comes perhaps closer than any other writer considered in this chapter to finding evidence that elemental features of southern life were not merely white creations. But the role assigned to black southerners is that of a cultural drag and intellectual poison: "[Among whites in the Old South,] many careless ways of speaking and writing did creep in, for contact with the negro mammy could not but affect the speech of the Southern child without a consciousness on the part of the child or its mother that such was the case" (8).[35]

The South is unrecognized as a hotbed of American letters, Rutherford continues, not because of a lack of talented writers, but because the region has not recognized and nurtured the talent in its midst. New England, on the other hand, has fostered its reputation as the home of American letters with great care, the implication being that that region's reputation is inflated by a passion for collecting rather than celebration of real merit. The South, she argues, has not been vigilant in preserving its own records, or careful in overseeing the way American history and literature is taught to its children:

> There is not a child of any age but can tell, without a moment's hesitation, the name of the *Mayflower,* the vessel which brought over the Pilgrim Fathers, but where can be found a child in a thousand that can call the names *Discovery, Goodspeed,* and *Susan Constant,* the vessels which brought the Jamestown colony. . . . Children at the South are really growing . . . believing that everything good and great came from the North, and this will continue to be so as long as parents allow their children to be taught from text-books that present only one side of the history of our land. (9)

At the turn of the twentieth century and for generations afterward, white southerners like Rutherford continued to monitor textbooks, seeking to ensure that the South and nation they wished the weight of evidence to reveal—white, Christian, and triumphant—was the one represented.

If Rutherford's efforts at compilation and censorship sought to swell the ranks and guard the purity of the southern literary canon in order to compel recognition by a broad national audience, other scholars were more concerned with the sources of the tradition and its relation to the larger, emerging canon of American literature.[36] Unlike Rutherford and her fellow antiquarian compilers, some critics thought of southern literature not in spatial but in organic terms. (In examining poetry anthologies, Rutherford unhappily noted that Walt Whitman received more pages than Henry Timrod, for instance.) If Rutherford saw the landscape of American literature as unnaturally—artificially, even—devoid of southern growth, other critics argued that an American literature could be sound and strong and at the same time exhibit significant regional variation. Because southern literature was but one species of the genus American, so the argument went, a vital American nationalism was abetted by, and indeed grew out of, vital American regionalisms.

In his *History of Southern Literature* (1906), Carl Holliday begins with a ringing declaration of southern literary independence:

> When, in the development of a nation, the extent of territory inhabited by that people becomes so great as to preclude a mutual understanding of the diverse customs and feelings of the various sections, it is but natural and indeed necessary that such a commonwealth should have more than one distinct type of literature. (13)[37]

It is not a cordoning-off of southern letters Holliday desires so much as a redefinition of American literature itself. Making a comparison that signals his conception of the South's place in the nation, Holliday argues that the literatures within the British Empire were undergoing the same transformation (spinning off into newly constituent parts in a way that irrevocably transforms the whole) as the literatures of the similarly far-flung American nation. In a more daring juxtaposition, he notes the presence of vital regional differences within other national literatures, pointing out differences between French literature and Provencal literature, a comparison suggestive of Provencal culture's organic rootedness, if not the potential for political fragmentation.

For Holliday and other like-minded students of southern literature, southern literature's distinctiveness was geographically determined. It proceeded almost literally from the conditions in which it was produced. Such assertions were typical of other literary nationalisms of the period. While scholars of Racine or Shakespeare or Goethe certainly stressed the universality of their nation's literary giants, they gave increasing attention to the particular conditions under which their literatures were produced. English, French, Irish, or Russian literature was very much seen by nineteenth-century scholars as growing out of the national soil, or soul. The British romantics were tied to certain regional settings, the Brontës to a narrow neighborhood. Southern literature, or the claims for it, was not different in that way. Just as contemporary historians and social scientists were arguing what later generations would see as geographical determinism, southern literary critics were convinced that their subject's emergence began as soon as American peoples settled different parts of the continent.

These formulations of the South did not see a self-conscious South emerging only as a result of the Missouri Compromise, abolitionism, Confederate defeat, or some other outside stimulus. The conditions for an organic southernness, they argued, were there from the beginning. And while their genealogies of cavalier arrayed against Puritan stock strike us as inaccurate and inadequate, we should bear in mind that many white southerners believed these things, or at least acted as if they did, and offered them as serious explanations of who they were and how their region had developed.[38]

Holliday stands as an example of this attempt literally to link southern literature and the land itself. If southernness inheres in the land, its existence in southern literature and elsewhere is beyond cavil. The "writings of this section," Holliday argues, "Are not mere disconnected efforts of isolated thinkers, but, rather, the natural, logical, and continuous productions of a people differing so materially in views and sentiments from their neighbors on the North that even civil war was necessary to prevent their becoming separate" (14).

The self-conscious formation of a national literary canon in the late-nineteenth century allowed southern scholars an opening for their claims that there was not one American tradition, unassailable because of its antiquity. It was clear that American literature dated from no earlier than the seventeenth century, and two and a half centuries was not long, compared with European claims to one thousand years of British, French, or German literature. In this context of emerging and competing definitions of regional and national culture, white southerners claimed that their regional tradition was organic, a thing healthy in itself.

But employing organic metaphors for southern and American letters could be complicated and at times contradictory. For Holliday, for instance, national or regional literature could be at the same time organic and self-consciously constructed. "American literature," writes Holliday, "had a conscious birth . . . it *sprang* into existence" (15). "In character it was not a pure growth of the native soil, and it had not and never has had, as a whole, the national originality, the unmistakable native note, such as is found in the writings of France or Germany or England" (16). Holliday's language is steeped in botanical tropes. His awareness of the recent invention of American literature is by no means an admission that it is inferior to the European tradition. Holliday and his contemporaries well understood that "pure" strains are sometime weak—hybrids are more hearty, are human engineered, and less subject to atrophy and blight. Such a reading does not seem far-fetched given the era's fascination with the promise of science and social science to engineer better things, including human beings.

How did Holliday reconcile this awareness of constructedness and the need for nurture with the concerns for organicism that he also displays? Was his a self-consciously rhetorical posture, a canny awareness of the contingency of all canons? Perhaps so. Indeed, Holliday, Rutherford, Page, and the other students of southern literature were aware that they were constructing a counternarrative of American letters. On what basis did they make this claim, if not on the basis that an organic, vital tradition was being denied or obscured?[39] They asserted that their region had produced a distinctive literature, in some ways the first American literature, and that it had been both neglected and denied, a situation they were determined to remedy, both at "home" and "abroad."

Holliday and other contemporary scholars showed recognition, self-consciousness even, that their subject was one that not everyone recognized as legitimate. "It has sometimes been doubted," Holliday remarks, "whether that district commonly known as 'the South' has produced literature so different in its fundamental conception and growth as to deserve separate attention. They alone doubt whose knowledge of the subject is limited" (13). And by "they" Holliday meant not only the scholarly establishment but the "reading public" as well. Like Rutherford, Holliday argued that it is the South itself, not the North, that is to blame for this critical neglect of its literature. The North "has been busy extolling its own representative writings," while the South, "because of its genial carelessness and procrastination before the Civil War and its poverty since that conflict, has suffered the critical spirit to lie dormant" (13). Holliday, then, saw his task not as piling on author after author in an attempt to force recognition of the South's letters by a national audience, but as developing in the region what he saw in New England: a "just yet friendly criticism" (14). Without it, the South has allowed many talented writers to "go into oblivion" who, in the North, would have been "encouraged" into "geniuses of high rank" (14).

In sympathy with Holliday's wish to develop a "just yet friendly criticism" in the South, some students of southern literature were as interested in assessing the state of southern letters and developing a critical voice within the region as they were in compiling massive anthologies. One of the most notable of this latter type was William Peterfield Trent, who developed a reputation among many white southerners as the New South's most prominent critic of the Old South. Trent edited his own collection, *Southern Writers* (1905), which in 1907 John Bell Henneman, dean of the College of Arts and Sciences at the University of the South and later editor of the *Sewanee Review,* called "the best single volume on the subject," and lauded Trent as "distinctly a contribution of the New South to the New Nation."[40] Like many southern scholars of his generation, Trent was a student of Herbert Baxter Adams at Johns Hopkins University.[41] An indefatigable worker, Trent founded the *Sewanee Review* (1892) and wrote voluminously, including biographies of William Gilmore Simms (1892) and Robert E. Lee (1899). His biography of Simms drew a firestorm of criticism, as Trent, from his seat at the University of the South, a guardian of the Lost Cause, characterized the society of the Old South as "a life that choked all thought and investigation that did not tend to conserve existing institutions and opinions."[42] The administration backed Trent against thundering editorials from the *Charleston News and Courier* and other southern newspapers. But Trent never again found the South congenial, and left in August 1900 for a position at Columbia University, where he became a well-respected authority on American as well as southern literature.[43] Looking back on what prompted him to leave the South, Trent blamed "shallow thinking on political matters, provincialism of taste & sentiments."[44] Reviewing contemporary southern literature, Trent remarked: "Of careful analysis of social conditions, of profound study and comprehension of the principles of human action, and of serene, self-contained art there are still few traces in the Southern literature of the present generation."[45]

Yet when, eight years after announcing that severe judgment of southern literature—of southern thought, really—Trent came to edit his own collection, he gave a measured, somewhat affectionate account of southern literature.[46] While not surrendering his critical faculties, and in fact including such evidences of the "careful analysis of social conditions" that he had earlier missed (the work of such New South reformers as Walter Hines Page), Trent produced a work that was yet another assertion of southern distinctiveness. Expressing the hope that his *Southern Writers* "will not, I trust, be regarded as a sectional product in the unpleasant sense of that term," Trent adopted a quasi-apologetic tone common in many southern literary histories. Admitting that "the South has never been prolific of books and writers," Trent maintained that "its people have contributed a larger and a better share to the national letters than is generally admitted."[47]

Perhaps to be expected in a volume by a white southerner of his generation, but significant coming from a Columbia University professor, Trent included a glowing assessment of the literary gifts of Robert E. Lee, asserting that "[Lee] may be legitimately included in a volume like the present for the reason that prompts one to admit Washington"—which he did. Trent included nine selections from Lee, a man whose "character was so lofty that it made whatever he did and whatever he wrote worthy of admiration." After all, Lee was no longer merely a southern hero: "his noble character . . . and brilliant genius . . . are being more and more acknowledged throughout the rest of America and throughout the world." Many agreed with Trent, of course, on the national role Lee was beginning to play: "All the forces of enlightenment that are now remaking Southern civilization should claim [Lee] as the champion of nationalism rather than sectionalism, of reason rather than passion, of fairness rather than prejudice, of progress rather than reaction, of constructive work rather than futile obstruction."[48]

But not to be explained away so quickly is Trent's treatment of John C. Calhoun, a man not yet so warmly regarded by Yankees. Earlier, Trent had not treated Calhoun with what many South Carolinians considered proper respect. Now, Trent defended Calhoun: "As a man he was above reproach; as a statesman full of courage and resources; as an orator dignified, impressive, and not lacking in deep passion; as a writer clear and cogent; as a political theorist weighty and acute."[49] What is significant here is Trent's failure to characterize Calhoun as an exponent of political sectionalism—indeed, as the intellectual godfather of secession. Instead, Trent sees Calhoun merely as an indigenous southern growth, shorn of any troubling questions about the terms of American union. His presence in southern letters, according to Trent, does indeed signify a difference between American regions, but not one that any longer need have the kind of overt political implications that any reading of Calhoun's work undeniably raises.

Some southern literary critics, anxious to avoid the appearance of special pleading in favor of an inferior product, adopted a "less is more" strategy, concentrating on a handful of southern greats. Such an approach is found in Montrose Moses's *The Literature of the South* (1910), which might well be responding directly to the vast bulk of the seventeen-volume *Library of Southern Literature*. Moses writes: "Many of the Southern manuals and estimates reveal too generous an inclination to include within their pages the names of those whom sentiment conjured up beyond the real measure of their importance."[50] True to his word, Moses highlights such writers as William Gilmore Simms, Edgar Allan Poe, George Washington Cable, and Ellen Glasgow, none of whom scholars would find unfamiliar today, anthologized as they are in American as well as southern literature texts. More interesting is a subtext running throughout Moses's work: a dispassionate, almost anthropological reading of the South as the site of a separate, organic culture, somewhat like Holliday's formulation: "Only within very recent years," writes Moses, "has a comparative method been adopted, wherewith the South has been made to recognize that its literature, as an expression of life, possessed an organism of its own." In assessing Glasgow's work, Moses bemoans her *Ancient Law* and *The Romance of a Plain Man* as "morbid," because of a method Glasgow "undoubtedly adopted after saturating herself in foreign literature of a neurotic type." In his advice to southern writers, one clearly sees his vision of a distinct South: "The Southerner is therefore much more healthy when content to apply a culture, which is absorbed rather than outwardly assumed, to a soil of which he is part, by tradition and training."[51]

Finally, it is worth noting that as we saw with William Trent's efforts at biography and Thomas Nelson Page's work on history, fiction, and studies of race relations, the distinction between historian, literary critic, and popular author did not seem to trouble these authors. The "Southern Fiction" volume of the Southern Historical Society's multivolume *The South in the Building of the Nation* is representative, too, of turn-of-the-century attempts to define a canon of southern letters by asserting the subject's unity and distinctiveness. Edited by Edwin Mims, professor of English at the University of North Carolina, the 444-page volume contains a fifty-four–page general introduction by Mims, followed by selections from and brief commentary on eighteen southern writers ranging chronologically from Edgar Allan Poe and William Gilmore Simms to Grace King and Frances Little.[52] Intended "not for schoolchildren nor specialists, but for the general reader" (x), the volume aimed not at encyclopedic thoroughness of coverage, as with the *Library of Southern Literature,* but at providing readable excerpts from representative authors of the nineteenth and early twentieth centuries.

Mims's principles of selection for inclusion in the volume were: 1) that the selections "have an absolute value from the standpoint of pure fiction"; 2) that "they serve also as an interpretation of various phases of southern life"; and 3) that a "certain unity" has been satisfied, one that "suggests the main tendencies of Southern fiction and the characteristics of some distinct groups of writers" (ix). The second principle is suggestive, for Mims recognizes literature's value in the study of a culture on a basis other than the "absolute value from the standpoint of pure fiction." Like William Trent, Mims could be highly critical of what he saw as the intellectual sterility of many antebellum southern writers:

> Most of them wrote carelessly, even slovenly. Furthermore, the absence of anything like a literary center was a hindrance; there was little of the influence of one writer on another. Slavery, and the feudal system that perpetuated thereby, militated against purely literary work.[53]

But in the end, Mims, like other anthologists of the period, finds for southern literature both a distinct character and an indisputable Americanness: "The Introduction attempts to give some idea of the main tendencies of Southern fiction—tendencies that are found to be those of American fiction as well" (x).

Mims demonstrates in his ambivalent treatment of Edgar Allan Poe some of the difficulties of building a southern American canon for a post–Civil War nation. Were southern writers to be valued because they were distinctly southern or because of their essential Americanness? In assessing Poe, Mims notes the tendency of earlier scholarship to see Poe as "existing in a cosmopolitan limbo, denationalized, almost dehumanized," and observes that the latest work stresses his connectedness, his rootedness, in a tradition, whether southern, American, or international. Mims follows these lines, albeit cautiously, in stressing Poe's life in Richmond with a family "in close touch with the best elements of Southern life" and calling attention to his (brief) attendance at the University of Virginia (xi). Mims includes University of Virginia President Edward A. Alderman's celebration of Poe that, somewhat embarrassingly, is equally an ode to his university:

> And then, as now beauty dwelt upon the venerable hills encircling the horizon, and the university itself lay new and chaste in its simple lines upon the young lawn. I venture to think sometimes that when our poet wrote those stateliest lines of his—To the glory that was Greece, And the grandeur that was Rome—perhaps there flashed into his mind's eye the vision of the Rotunda upon some such night as this, with its soaring columns whitened by the starlight and vying with the beauty and witchery of the white winter around us. (xii)

Mims's picture of the southern Poe is fleshed out by such details as John Pendleton Kennedy's discovery of Poe in Baltimore and Poe's editorship of "the most distinctly Southern magazine, the *Southern Literary Messenger*" (xii). He quotes G. E. Woodberry: "No one meeting him [Poe] could have failed to recognize him as a Southerner . . . always homesick for the place that he well knew would know him no more though he were to return to it." Warming to his task, Mims finds in Poe's critical writings the best indication of his "Southern bent of mind." But in the end, Mims is restrained, finding in those who push too hard for Poe's debt to the South "a note of special pleading."

Like Mims on Poe, students of southern writing at the turn of the twenti-eth century claimed both a distinctive, organic southern cultural tradition and an essential Americanness for southern letters. These claims were grounded in assertions of white community, both in the region and the nation at large. The construction of a tidy white canon of southern letters grounded white southerners' racialism in a broad national project. To the degree that such claims spoke to the era's racialist and reconciliatory nationalist needs, these scholars' arguments were accepted by a white national audience.

Making Southern History

At the turn of the twentieth century, amateur and professional historians of the American South asked some of the same questions as Mims, Page, Trent, and Rutherford about racial order, southern communities, and the relation between the South and the rest of the nation.[54] Their work was a chapter in the development of what historian Richard Gray calls "the Southern argu-ment . . . ideas of a distinct local identity, a peculiar character and a special destiny." Like authors of fiction and scholars of southern literature, histo-rians were engaged in "reimagining and remaking their place in the act of seeing and describing it."[55] The stories they told were of the white South as an orderly, patriarchal land, one that had shaped the American republic, and was shaped by masterful, benevolent white male authority. Contemporary black scholars such as W. E. B. Du Bois recognized that much of the history these white scholars produced distorted the past and present, or at least of-fered a picture of slavery, war, and Reconstruction in which black history and black aspirations did not particularly matter.[56] But the bulk of this history of a distinctive but integral white South with a common white experience was warmly received, both in the South and in the nation at large. This work helped cast academic legitimacy over the narratives of white southern iden-tity present in contemporary southern fiction, political rhetoric, and pub-lic space. In a very real sense, then, white historians helped craft a sense of broad white southern identity.

Professional, academically trained historians were responsible for much of this shaping of contemporary understandings of the South's history—in the South, of course, but also in the North, under William A. Dunning at Columbia University and later William E. Dodd at the University of Chicago,

   "The South Is a Single, Homogeneous People"

and on the "border," at Baltimore's Johns Hopkins University. Johns Hopkins President Daniel Coit Gilman asserted that the southern states' "educational history for the past quarter of a century has been largely that of the Johns Hopkins University."[57] Indeed, throughout the twentieth century, Columbia, Chicago, and Johns Hopkins would remain leading centers for the study of the American South, very often employing southern-born historians to teach the region's history.

In the late-nineteenth century, southern colleges and universities, following the lead of Herbert Baxter Adams at Johns Hopkins, began offering courses in southern history and encouraged the collection of primary source material. Historians at the turn of the century produced a great deal of work exploring the South's past, all with implicit definitions of the South and its place in the broader American nation. In scope and tone, much of this work resembles the contemporary efforts at defining a canon of southern literature. The Southern Historical Publication Society began in 1909 the publication of a twelve-volume history, *The South in the Building of the Nation*. With a range of authors including academic historians Ulrich B. Phillips, Walter Lynwood Fleming, and Charles W. Ramsdell, the project was intended to "rectify the misconceptions of many Northerners, placing the South in its true position with reference to the rest of the nation."[58]

At the same time, groups such as the Southern History Association (founded in 1896) brought together professional and amateur students of the South in their efforts to establish state historical societies and encourage scholarship, all along orthodox lines. Formed in Washington, with its members drawn from the ranks of academia, journalism, and government, the association aimed to "study all the Southern States from the beginning." One of their first tasks, members of the association decided, was the systematic collection of state records and documents. General M. C. Butler, one of the founders, agreed; he "regretted the backwardness of the Southern people in preserving their records, and instanced how far they were behind New England."[59] This consciousness of "how far they were behind New England" was a central theme of southern academic life and historical study in the three decades following the end of Reconstruction. Despite their claim "that this association shall [not] be purely sectional" (41), their first president was former Confederate General Jubal Early, and book reviews in their *Tracts* contained such revealing statements of regional sensitivity as "The author evidently sees only through the *bluest* of spectacles" (111), and "Let us unite in making the discussion full, thorough, and a complete vindication of our long slandered people" (110).[60]

White academic and professional historians were not the only people attempting to shape historical discourse. As one contemporary noted, "so many valuable investigations have been pursued by state, national, and private organizations, and by individuals."[61] Nonacademic but keenly interested organizations such as the United Daughters of the Confederacy shaped the content of history courses and textbooks, even decades after the close of the Civil War.[62] The early twentieth century witnessed a continued outpouring of Confederate memoirs, reminiscences, and other publications, printed by mainstream publishing houses, state historical societies, and quasi-academic organizations such as the Southern Historical Society. Also outside the mainstream academy, but taking a radically different view than the Lost Cause acolytes, were African American historians such as George Washington Williams, Carter G. Woodson, and W. E. B. Du Bois, as they contested the narratives of a white South and a white nation that white scholars were constructing. But outside the world of black colleges and universities, the work of Williams, Woodson, and Du Bois was not well known.[63]

The first generation of professional historians of the South, trained in seminars at Johns Hopkins, Chicago, Columbia, and Michigan, among other universities, believed that their work contributed to the emergence of a mature American historiography for a nation then beginning to cut a figure on the world stage. In an era when England, France, and Germany produced staggering collections of primary source material and scores of studies tracing the evolution of their nations' cultures and institutions over the centuries, American scholars also were eager to trace the rise of the American nation, using the latest German-imported methods of scientific, "objective" historiography. Even critical voices such as Du Bois shared the conviction that the American historical profession was correct in looking to "the general principles laid down in German universities."[64] Likewise, students of Dunning and Dodd intended to move beyond earlier filiopietistic treatments of the South's past at the hands of Confederate veterans and other guardians of the Lost Cause.[65] At the same time, however, their narratives of the South's past complemented other visions of the South's past being crafted outside the academy; both helped to shape emerging definitions of a white South.

　　　"The South Is a Single, Homogeneous People"

There was no simple professional/amateur distinction at work in the development of southern historiography, let alone an easy triumph of truth over error, or error over truth. Though most professional southern historians pursued, in good faith, models of objectivity, their stories of the South's past were not so far removed from the efforts of Confederate veterans and the United Daughters of the Confederacy as they might have imagined. The latter groups were, of course, mainly interested in keeping alive a heroic view of the South's part in the Civil War and in keeping a sharp eye on how the South's past was taught in southern schools. Further complicating the simple dichotomy of academic historians and unreconstructed rebels are such men as Thomas Nelson Page, with his undisguised literariness but adoption of the forms of scholarship. Any sharp distinction between Page and academic historians is likely to be more misleading than useful. His picture of slavery and the antebellum South was, after all, more widely read than the work of any southern historian. Indeed, in *The South in the Building of the Nation*, Edwin Mims maintained that writers such as Thomas Nelson Page had been "among the prime forces in revealing the South to the nation and the nation to the South, thus furthering one of the most important tasks of the present generation—the promotion of a real national spirit."[66]

More important, at a fundamental level practically all white southern historians, amateur or professional, increasingly agreed on a number of basic proposals that inexorably shaped the narratives they spun of secession, war, and reunion: the Civil War was a white man's affair, the Confederate struggle had been honorable if ill-advised, and questions of the morality of slavery and blacks' roles in emancipation were not worth asking. This emerging canonical view of the South's past was a project that fell on increasingly receptive ears in the North as well as the South. As Peter Novick argues:

> The near unanimous racism of northern historians—not, of course, peculiar to them, made possible a *negotiated settlement* of sectional differences in the interpretation of the Civil War and Reconstruction [emphasis mine]. By the 1880s and 1890s many southerners were, in varying degrees, willing to concede that secession had been unconstitutional, and that slavery . . . had been wrong. . . . In the extended negotiation of a consensus on slavery, southerners managed to achieve a certain moral ascendancy. . . . Southerners saw themselves, and did their best to get their northern colleagues to see

them, as wounded victims of northern lies and calumnies, which they were valiantly trying to correct.[67]

At the turn of the twentieth century, white historians of the American South crafted a portrait of the region's past that remained intact for nearly half a century; parts of it still prove remarkably tenacious. Southern historians argued that the region played an integral part in winning American independence from Britain, in creating the new government, and in providing political leadership for the new republic. At the same time, they maintained, the Old South produced a distinct culture and society, one in which whites were bound in a mutually satisfying organic community and in which blacks were contented in a benign slavery overseen by masters who understood them instinctively. As for the Civil War, they argued that the South had fought not to preserve slavery, but out of an understandable if perhaps misguided notion of their rights as Americans. Finally, national reconciliation was complete, and the New South was a modernizing region eager to rejoin the national march toward progress. The city of Richmond, one contemporary account noted, boasted not only statues of Lee, Jackson, and other Confederates, but also statues to "perpetuate the memory of colonial, Revolutionary and national leaders."[68]

These elements of what we might call the Compromise of the 1890s are inseparable; each of these pieces needed the others to be complete and satisfying. Taken together, they present an interlocking and complementary picture of the southern and American past. This emerging vision of the South was advanced and believed not only by white southerners, but by the historical profession and the white general public at large, with consequences not only for twentieth-century American historiography but for public policy and the larger culture as well. A pivotal and absolutely essential element of the emerging narratives of a white South in a white nation, and the white southern contribution to the "compromise," was a rhetorical silencing of the guns, the strange absence of an "unreconstructed" historiography.[69] As did southern politicians and writers of fiction, southern historians by the 1890s gave up any lingering celebration of secession or any hostile or aggrieved tone over the failure of the Confederacy to win independence.[70] The impulse of southern historiography was in fact toward national reconciliation. In so moving, the white South gained more than it lost in renouncing the moribund doctrine of secession and the unattainable hopes of separate political or economic existence. In exchange for the white southern agreement that the Lost Cause was truly lost (or that might made right, in some white southerners' estimation), the South gained a face-saving portrait of the rest of its past, and an implicit agreement that no large-scale task of reconstruction remained to be undertaken, at least by the North. At the same time, historians' emerging view of the relationship between the South and the rest of the nation provided a reimagining of the American nation as a union of organic regions, and along with that assumption came a rationale for a real, substantial degree of "home rule," especially on the "Negro Question."

How did southern historians manage to find a rhetoric and narrative that satisfied at the same time their professional judgment, the approval of their northern colleagues, and the broad acceptance of the white South? The Compromise of the 1890s was a brilliant settlement that managed at the same time to redefine both Americanness and southernness. Many factors allowed this reimagining of the nation's history: the post-Reconstruction rush to figure out the terms of sectional reconciliation and the meaning of American citizenship and nationality; the struggle to define the mission of the American nation in the world; and the typical fin de siècle summing up of the century's meaning.

In this brew of redefinition, the white South had a ripe chance for a defining seat around a national table, the contours of which were still being decided. The picture they provided proved satisfying to white southerners eager to regain a measure of national power and freedom from federal "interference," it provided rich and soothing materials for writers of southern fiction to draw upon, and in an era of international imperialism, provided a picture of black Americans that confirmed racial prejudice and flattered white notions that they were innately and uniquely fit to frame and administer governments.

White southerners were proprietary of their history, and often claimed that the South's past had to be written by southerners—people who instinctively and innately understood the land and its people. John Bell Henneman wrote: "Our history is being chiefly written in New England . . . do we then wonder that works so produced seem to us often to contain much that is twisted and wrenched, or even at times vindictive?"[71] "Because they have not been reared under Southern conditions," one scholar explained, northerners "have been biased by the environments of their youth and by their residence without being aware of the fact." In their judgment, even sympathetic historians such as James Ford Rhodes, who shared many white southerners' judgments of the intellectual inferiority of blacks, could not overcome the handicap of northern birth and residence to enter into the bone-deep understanding that southern-born and -bred white men could muster for the task. "Since it is the function of the historian not only to narrate facts but to interpret them," went one statement of this point of view, "the writers [of *The South in the Building of the Nation*] have been selected from scholars who, because of their thorough familiarity with the historic traditions, sentiments and facts of the South, are best qualified to write its history."[72]

Clearly unfit for the task were historians like Albert Bushnell Hart at Harvard, with his pride in his abolitionist forebears, willingness to oversee the graduate work of W. E. B. Du Bois, and general reputation as perhaps the most famous white historian sympathetic to the African American struggle. Hart, wrote one scholar, was not "able to view the life of the South through the same lens as a [white] Southerner." But Hart recognized that differences over the treatment of black Americans were not enough to prevent national reconciliation: "The North and South still have different ideals as to the negro race, but they are united by personal relationship, commerce, and common standards."[73] And many white southerners were aware that the historiographical tide was turning their way. Charles W. Kent wrote of the University of Chicago's Eduard Hermann von Holst, the first chair of the history department and author of a critical biography of John C. Calhoun:

> there are signs that the Von Holst school of historical criticism, foreign in its origin and foreign to our ideals of free thought, free speech, free institutions and free enjoyment of all the immunities and privileges of citizens, freedom to admire all men of heroic mould and saintly lives, freedom to claim all greatness, whether it served our narrower purpose or not—is losing somewhat its prestige and the wiser and gentler spirits of our day admire sometimes where they cannot approve and proudly acclaim what they have not always loved.[74]

As the historical profession came to accept the white South's version of the region's past, southern historians could afford to strike a more conciliatory, nationalistic tone. In a history of the South's economy published in 1910, Johns Hopkins historian James Ballagh explained that the work's "spirit" was "national and not sectional." Ballagh continued:

> The remarkable debt that the North and West owe to the South for an important element of their population and development, and the no less striking one that the South owes to the Northerners and the Westerners who came within her borders and aided so materially in shaping her destinies both before and since the war, should be but the evidence and earnest of the larger Americanism that knows no boundary of sectional feeling and prejudice, but is impelled by a common patriotic and business purpose.[75]

The profession's accommodation of white southern sensitivities might seem remarkable given that one hundred years ago historians advanced an ideal of objectivity, of arranging the facts and letting them speak for themselves. On the other hand, the bulk of historians of that era perhaps felt that black inferiority was one of those self-spoken facts. In any case, the white South largely got what it wanted: a historiography that told the stories they longed to hear. The argument that only a (white) southerner can really understand the South became central to the narratives southerners told about themselves, and it is certainly not dead yet in the twenty-first century. Woodrow Wilson famously declared that "the only place in the country, the only place in the world, where nothing has to be explained to me is the South."[76] By extension, his remark clearly suggests that no one not born in the South can ever enter into this deep sympathy and understanding of the region. White southerners, on the other hand, argued (and many believed) that they could understand and control African Americans, while no one else in the country could tell them a thing on the subject. It was well into the 1930s and 1940s before some white southerners, such as the Mississippian David Cohn, would admit that while blacks lived in close proximity to whites, southern whites had absolutely no notion of black life and black aspirations.[77] But at the turn of the twentieth century, few audible voices contradicted the soothing stories white southern historians told about race, region, order, and tradition.

Making the Nation

Southern historians looked to colonial America and the early republic to stake their claims for the South's deep and fundamental Americanness. Or, rather, to invert C. Vann Woodward's argument that the South was American before it was southern, many of these historians (including the belletristic Thomas Nelson Page) argued that America was southern before it was American. And the state of Virginia usually received first billing in this particular narrative of American origins. "'Virginia' was three hundred years ago the term applied to all the practically unknown land which is now the United States."[78] These accounts also suggest that from earliest settlement, whites (southern and American) constituted one broad family engaged in a common purpose of conquest, community building, and progress. It was in Virginia that "the first great struggle of the white race was begun . . . many years before the 'Pilgrim Fathers' first sighted Plymouth Rock. . . . The 'cradle of liberty for this Continent' was first tenanted and rocked there to lull the cries of the 'child of freedom.'"[79] "In the Revolutionary War Virginia took a prominent part. . . . In the formation of the Union she was equally as prominent." In the annals of American higher education, "No college has higher claims upon the Nation" [than William and Mary]. And in the framing of the Constitution, wrote one scholar, "the Virginia contest was the only real debate over the whole Constitution."[80]

The stories of the South's and America's colonial past were rarely formulated so bluntly as a recitation of southern "firsts"—that was generally the task of state and local antiquarians, as well as the Daughters of the American Revolution and United Daughters of the Confederacy. Southern historians after 1890 seemed more concerned to decenter New England than to replace New England with the Chesapeake. They wanted to preserve an American narrative, one of progress and stability, but one that allowed the South an honored place in the tale. To many northerners, what southerners called the War Between the States was still viewed as the War of the Rebellion. Few white southerners, no matter how they felt about the wisdom of secession, were able to stomach charges of treason. During the war, Confederates made much of the fact that the American Revolutionaries were called treasonous rebels. Likewise, this later generation of historians enjoyed reminding Americans of this fact, too, thereby taking some of the sting out of the word "rebel." Also, historians occasionally took direct shots at the New

 "The South Is a Single, Homogeneous People"

Englanders, or "Pharisees," as Ulrich B. Phillips termed them. According to Phillips, "the Puritans particularly were accustomed to give thanks to God at the conclusion of a successful slave-trading voyage." Shady businessmen as well as hypocrites, the "deacons in Massachusetts when sending their ships to Guinea would advise their skippers to water the rum and give short measure when buying slaves with it."[81]

At the turn of the twentieth century, American historians told the story of the nation's past as an unproblematic rise of America to greatness. "Anthropomorphized into a being with personal traits and lofty purposes," as one recent assessment puts it, "the nation walked away with the principal part in the historical drama of the United States that was taught to successive generations of students."[82] For some historians of Virginia, this anthropomorphizing invited comparisons of the state not only to a parent, but also to a creation deity. In discussing Virginia's surrender of its western land claims to the new nation, one account argued that "for the sake of peace, and that a closer union of the thirteen states, Virginia gave to the United States" an "area six times larger than the present state . . . in equally as great-hearted a manner, [she] gave consent for a large slice [Kentucky] to be taken from her side."[83] A multivolume history of the South was organized along these same organic lines: "Virginia and the states formed from her original territory: Maryland, Kentucky, West Virginia, North Carolina, South Carolina, and Tennessee," and "Georgia and the states formed from its original territory: Alabama and Mississippi."[84] Such a creation story asserted a literal kinship of the white South.

By no means did southern historians attempt to elevate their region by denigrating the broader national history. They merely wished for a retooling of the narrative. In practically all nineteenth-century American histories, the story of the colonial period and indeed overwhelmingly, the dominant narrative of the nation's past, was the story of New England. The majority of the leading Americanists of the period looked to the colonial past (with special interest on transatlantic institutional and intellectual ties) and the early republic with an eye toward showing their evolution into the contemporary American nation. Turn-of-the-century histories are filled with arguments for organic growth and development of states and governments. "The American Senates, like all other great institutions," argued Franklin Riley, "are not the products of invention but of growth; a growth, too, which required more than a century to mature." Similarly, another historian asserted that the "colonial history of Connecticut . . . is the portrayal of a steady and uniform growth."[85] Southern historians insisted that their story too was the American story.

Southern historians worked mightily to argue that the South was not a secessionist aberration, but rather as deeply American as the rest of the nation. They began by stressing the centrality of Virginia in the saga of what Woodrow Wilson called "this self-helping race of Englishmen" in America.[86] Similarly, the framers of the Constitution of 1787, wrote one historian, were "men of similar mental habits, being of one race and language fused into coherence by the joint struggle of war."[87] Southern historians argued that there was a need for "a judicious and unimpassioned account of the important and honorable part the South has contributed to the history and wealth of the nation."[88] Typically, these historians blamed not a New England cabal for this imbalance, but the neglect of southern history by the region's own people. "The geography, industries and resources of Virginia have been greatly neglected," wrote the authors of one geography textbook.[89] And in his edition of the letters of Richard Henry Lee, Johns Hopkins historian James Curtis Ballagh lamented that despite Lee's "contemporary fame as an orator and statesman" and historical significance, "his services and name have been almost forgotten by the public."[90] The majority of these historians congratulated the New Englanders on their pious attention to their past, maintaining that it was only natural for Americans to take an interest in the country's national life and their region's part in it. They increasingly insisted too, however, that the story of the American nation was a story of organic and related regions, and not simply New England.

As late as 1935, E. Merton Coulter, as the first president of the Southern Historical Association, agreed that the South "has permitted its history to lie unworked and many of its major figures and movements remain to this day 'unhonored and unsung.'" Coulter opined that the South's neglect of its history owed at least in part to the predominance of its Scots-Irish population, well known to be "individualistic and greatly lacking in self-consciousness," in contrast to the New Englander, who was introspective and made himself "busy not only with his own affairs but also with the affairs of others."[91] However broad and unconvincing as most historians now find such racialist speculations on regional character, Coulter's remarks at least suggest how deeply rooted and long-lived were notions of southern distinctiveness and turn-of-the-century regional stereotypes within the profession.

Southern historians saw their audience not only as other historians, but also the general public. They were aware of the public stakes and the political payoff of substituting an honorable version of the South's past for the relative neglect they believed it then enjoyed in dominant American narratives. White southerners paid careful attention to the way history was written and taught because they well understood that history textbooks have consequences. "School children in all parts of the country know of the *Mayflower*, but few know of the *Discovery*, the *Godspeed* and the *Susan Constant*," lamented Julian A. C. Chandler in *The South in the Building of the Nation*.[92] "Few will remember that Virginia was a colony of eleven plantations with a Representative Assembly making laws for the government of the Colony, planning for a college, asserting the rights of British subjects before the Pilgrims had landed at Plymouth." Here were the crucial elements for an argument that the roots of American order and culture were to be found in Virginia and, by extension, the South. The passion and genius for self-government, the respect for education and culture, and the unalienable conviction that they were free men who must have a free man's due—in some combination, these elements provided the rhetorical building blocks for the broader story of the South's past that southern historians enjoyed telling. The best apologia and defense of the South's nineteenth-century actions was solid historical proof that the South acted not out of spite or malice, but instead out of obedience to an American history older than any of its critics. And in the end, they were not above pointing out the cruel truth that "the Pilgrims who sailed in the *Mayflower* were searching for Virginia but were unexpectedly driven to the bleak coasts of New England."[93]

Especially when the historians were Virginians, reflections on America's colonial past could prove especially satisfying. "No page of the History of the Race," wrote Thomas Nelson Page in his history of "The Antient Dominion," "will better repay patient study; for none shines with more heroic deeds, or more sublime fortitude and endeavor."[94] He continued:

> Her History belongs not to the present Virginia alone. She brought forth in
> time a new Civilization where Character and Courtesy went hand in hand;
> where the goal ever set before the eye was Honor, and where the distinguishing

marks of the life were Simplicity and Sincerity. It was by no mere accident that Washington, Madison, Marshall, Henry, Mason and their like came from Tidewater and Piedmont, Virginia. They were the product of her distinctive Civilization, and were not uncommon types of the Character she has given to her Children.[95]

Note the rhetorical elements within this fulsome praise of Virginia: the fanciful elements, the look to the Enlightenment past, the racial stock theory of history. Page's history is in fact history written like a historical novel, with all the novel's power to disarm skeptical analysis. Assertions of the impeccable Americanness of the South could take other forms, of course, than the piling on of evidence and demanding of respectful admiration, as Page does. Many southerners were not above flattering a national audience. In his *Southern Statesmen of the Old Regime* (1897), delivered as lectures at the University of Wisconsin, William P. Trent praised the city and the university: "Madison is a very paradise for lecturers; it is also one of the least sectional and biased places I have ever known. . . . I did not encounter a single critic who was not as liberal and magnanimous as a true American ought to be."[96] By the turn of the twentieth century, few mainstream historical accounts took issue with white southern historians' claim that their region was truly American, and few white southerners seemed vexed still to be part of the United States. In less than a generation after the Civil War, the mainstream white southern view of the region's and the nation's past was well established in southern state universities as well as national research universities.

Explaining Slavery

At the same time that southern historians offered narratives of the essential Americanness of the South, they also provided narratives of slavery that absolved the South of any sin associated with the region's peculiar institution. The period's emerging "scientific" historiography of slavery effaced questions of morality with "objective" understandings of black inferiority and blacks' need for order, regulation, and management. The first studies of American slavery employing techniques of German-influenced scientific historical scholarship were produced at Johns Hopkins University and published in the university's *Studies* series beginning in 1883.[97] Mostly the products of young scholars (at least seven were doctoral dissertations), the *Studies* of slavery attempted to approach the subject dispassionately—free of the rancor that had in their view marred earlier work in the field.[98] "Objective views of the local character of slavery," wrote one Hopkins scholar, "are prerequisite to its true history in this country."[99] Guided through seminars by Göttingen-trained Herbert Baxter Adams and others, the students at Johns Hopkins examined a wealth of primary source materials, including books, manuscripts, and newspapers, which the university eagerly sought to acquire.[100]

The *Studies* departed from earlier work in that they avoided discussion of the morality of slavery or its political consequences; instead, the monographs examined such topics as the beginnings of slavery in America or its operation in various states. The works produced at Johns Hopkins were highly influential, largely because they were seen in the profession as avoiding the "partisan excesses" of past neo-abolitionists and southern apologists. Nearly one hundred years later, one scholar wrote: "These studies do not attempt to defend or condemn the institution of slavery. They are objective discussions of the history of slavery."[101] Along with the efforts of William A. Dunning at Columbia, the Hopkins *Studies* helped make the study of southern history a legitimate scholarly activity. The *Studies* contributors mirrored the mood of the nation. The North and South were moving toward national reconciliation. Historiography, by avoiding recriminations and concentrating on less tender areas than the morality of slavery, proved to be another field of common endeavor and indeed another area in which the white South's version of the story became part of the broad national narrative.

Those at Johns Hopkins were proud of the results achieved there. Near the end of his life, Adams remarked of his department that "Yale and Harvard have followed in its lead."[102] But the Johns Hopkins historians' attempts to remain dispassionate and their refusal to engage in what they saw as partisan debate have not worn well over time. By the 1950s, the work of Kenneth Stampp and other historians made the blind spots of the Hopkins *Studies* apparent. In assessing the Hopkins work, Stanley Elkins found that in striving too hard to approach scientific objectivity, much of the work appears uninterested rather than disinterested; Elkins ultimately dismissed their efforts.[103] While Elkins was correct that the studies were badly dated and incomplete, it is important to remember how influential they were in their day. The Hopkins work was significant, both as models other scholars followed and in classrooms throughout the South and the rest of the nation, where many of the Hopkins graduate students eventually landed. Finally, their quest for neutrality in assessing slavery served mainly as a not-so-subtle ether to lull such qualms as remained over the South's peculiar institution; though they certainly made no attempt to defend slavery, many of their statements about the institution drew from and reiterated contemporary assessments not only of African American character but also of the essentially benign mastery white men exercised over the South and an inferior race.

The Hopkins *Studies* authors shared the era's prejudices against African Americans, a fact that should hardly come as a surprise. For instance, in his study of slavery in North Carolina, John Spencer Bassett characterized the love of whiskey as an African American "race trait": "all of them, men, women, and children, liked it." Bassett's portrait of slave life confirmed many contemporary judgments that white men were benevolent masters and that slaves showed limited capacity to regulate their own households: "The negroes were contented and happy among themselves, if left alone by outside influences." Bassett continues: "Under the care of the owner the slave's health was good, much better than it is now. Slave mothers frequently neglected their children, while for the children of the whites they manifested great affection." The latter statement is at once a harsh assessment of black family life and a scholarly iteration of the mammy myth that became so tenacious in the post-Reconstruction South.

James Ballagh's study of slavery in Virginia paints a particularly rosy picture of the institution. The "cheerful," "polite" slaves engaged in much "dancing, laughing, singing and banjo-playing." Enslaved "wives and mothers," argues Ballagh, "were at greater liberty than they are today." Skilled slave laborers enjoyed "much free time." Unbelievably, "custom" and "right" ensured the slaves' "right to private property" and "right to education." There was "no disposition to keep down deserving intelligence and morality wherever disclosed." The slaves' "manners were . . . those of a person accustomed to liberty by the reign of law and order." "In truth," concludes Ballagh, "the slave was not a slave, he was a servant . . . a retainer, a member of the family, a friend." While the casual racism of this assessment makes for hard reading today, it is vital to note that Ballagh advances an argument not only about slaves, but also about their owners. As in Thomas Nelson Page's Virginia, the content, well-mannered slave of James Ballagh's Old Dominion is a not-so-oblique testimony to white patriarchal authority. Even the "field hand learned to improve his manners from the example of the whites." The "mass of negroes were not neglected, either socially or morally, as the antebellum type—now all too rapidly fading away—is an eloquent witness."[104] It is difficult to differentiate that scholarly judgment of slavery from the one found in the fiction of Ballagh's contemporary, Thomas Nelson Page.

But even so, it is a mistake to characterize the Hopkins slavery studies as mere apologies for the South's peculiar institution. In assessing the end of slavery, John Bassett directly refutes the myth of the Civil War–era loyal slave, arguing that the "quietude of the slaves has been attributed to their good nature. . . . They did not remain quiet because they loved slavery. They had small opportunity for rebellion." Though Bassett may overstate the slaves' "quietude," he did recognize their aspirations for freedom and "desperate courage" in combat.[105]

By the early twentieth century, however, scholarly interpretations of slavery, like other aspects of American race relations, took a harder turn. Reminiscent of the antebellum defense of slavery as a positive good rather than a necessary evil, some white scholars turned to slavery and saw not a regrettable institution but instead read slavery as a benevolent training school for benighted Africans, whose "genius was imitative," as one scholar wrote. This interpretation reached its apogee in the work of Ulrich B. Phillips. Before the revisionist work of Kenneth Stampp in the 1950s and Eugene Genovese in the 1960s, Phillips stood as the twentieth century's most influential historian of slavery.[106] The son of an old Georgia family, Phillips deeply admired the values of the antebellum planter class. Yet he strove to maintain an air of scholarly detachment. He brushed aside attempts by the Virginia Daughters of the Confederacy to "revive the waning passions of the Lost Cause."[107] Even so, Phillips's voice is distinctively and unrepentantly that of a white southerner.

Other than black historians, few questioned the basic soundness of Phillips's interpretations. His work was completed by 1930, but the questions Phillips raised were the basis for nearly all subsequent research in the field for the next generation. His methodology and ideology were under fire within the profession by the 1950s. But Phillips set the tone for a generation of scholarship, one that lingered in school textbooks into the 1960s and 1970s. While *American Negro Slavery* (1918) and *Life and Labor in the Old*

South (1929) are little read today, Phillips once enjoyed a towering reputation within the profession and influenced generations of American historians.

In assessing the plantation South, Phillips describes a world characterized by "mildness," in which the slaves enjoyed "crude [material] comfort," while the benevolent masters practiced "liberalism and profit-sharing." The overall picture is one of order, ease, and plenty, an implicit rebuke not only to white abolitionists' accounts, but also to African Americans' memories of the institution. At hog killing time, the plantation seems almost a carnival: "spare ribs and backbone, jowl and feet, souse and sausage, liver and chitterlings greased every mouth on the plantation." The "darkies," as Phillips calls them, are as content as any slaves found in postwar fiction. Even the occasional trace of moral ambiguity to be found in Thomas Nelson Page is absent here. While Phillips does admit the occasional "injustice" or "oppression," he undercuts such admissions by inviting the reader to contemplate "the considerate and cordial, courteous and charming men and women, white and black, which that picturesque life in its best phases produced."[108]

Phillips's African Americans are charming and ingratiating, though at root children. This infantilizing of Africans and African Americans deeply informs all of Phillips's work on slavery, for if the slaves were children, what better for them than loving, concerned—if sometimes chastening—fathers? Phillips writes: "If anyone in the twentieth century wants to see the old-fashioned prime negro at his best, let him take a Mississippi steamboat and watch the roustabouts at work—those chaffing and chattering, singing and swinging, lusty and willing freight handlers."[109] As in the fiction of Thomas Nelson Page, Phillips manages here to deny African Americans any claim to moral complexity, and also to imply a continuity of some essential Negroness from slavery into freedom.

Phillips's reading of slavery, unabashedly racist though it certainly is, stood squarely within larger American historiographical narratives and traditions. A student of William A. Dunning at Columbia, a colleague of Frederick Jackson Turner at Wisconsin, Phillips later claimed to have been the frontier historian's "constant disciple."[110] Phillips depicted slavery as a positive system of adjustment to civilization for Africans; complementing this belief are his assertions that slavery arose from the South's characteristic environmental conditions.[111] For Phillips, the black presence in the South was the key to the region's history. At the base of the Old South stood the Negro; the South was (and continued to be) a different place than the North, and the differences were far deeper than merely economic. On the eve of the Civil War, Phillips maintained, American Negro slavery was no longer generally profitable, but maintained nevertheless by benign slaveholders; he thus raised two major points of contention for the writing on slavery that followed.

Unlike the Hopkins *Studies, American Negro Slavery* places much weight on the testimony of plantation records. Phillips downplays the legal evidence of slave codes and court decisions, relied upon so heavily in the *Studies:* "the government of slaves was for the ninety and nine by men, and only for the hundredth by laws."[112] And the accounts of travelers in the antebellum South he sets down as impressionistic and unreliable. What the records told him was that slavery was at heart a genial, inoffensive system. Cruel beatings and overwork were calumnies, or isolated instances, Phillips held. Instead, the institution was necessary and paternal: "the plantations were the best schools . . . for the training of that sort of inert and backward people which the bulk of the American negroes represented."[113] This emphasis on white owners and overseers' records is instructive. Phillips selected materials that allowed some narratives and choked off the possibility of others.

It is not new to suggest that Phillips painted a picture of African American character and culture that strikes any contemporary reader as racist. More than once, Phillips unfavorably contrasts freedom with conditions under slavery; in terms of food, housing, and health, the old days were for blacks truly the good old days, he argues; the slave cabins, for instance, "denote" a "sounder construction and greater comfort than most of the negroes in freedom have since been able to command." Indeed, Phillips more than suggests that for the slaves, material comfort was sufficient. The exercise of religion displayed not a desire for deliverance, but was comic, an indication of blacks' "proneness toward superstition" or taste for things "exhilarating." And on the subject of family, "the birth-rate [took] care of itself. The pickaninnies were winsome, and their parents, free of expense and anxiety for their sustenance, could hardly have more of them than they wanted."[114]

Phillips's litany of racist stereotypes is wide ranging, if familiar. But again, his portrait of plantation slavery is an oblique portrait of white southerners, and an argument about their character and identity. For Phillips, African Americans were essentially *tabulae rasae,* "with an implicit reservation as to limits," of course. "While produced only in America," argued Phillips, "the plantation slave was a product of old-world forces." Characterizing African Americans as products raises, of course, the question of the producer. Phillips quotes approvingly the old saying that "a negro was what a white man made him."[115] If blacks were, as Phillips argues, happy, healthy, fecund, well provided for, and well ordered, what can we help but conclude about the whites who made them that way? Other contemporary studies confirmed Phillips's characterization of the benevolence of white rule. "She loved her 'lil chillin,'" wrote one historian of the "Black Mammy," "and they loved her, and why should they not love one another when their lives were . . . so closely combined."[116]

The profession's reception of *American Negro Slavery* was laudatory. For example, Theodore D. Jervey, writing in the *American Historical Review*, called Phillips's book "a substantial addition to the general store of knowledge" and praised the author's objectivity, noting that he permitted "the facts to speak for themselves."[117] And Tipton R. Snavely of the University of Virginia, in a glowing review, characterized *American Negro Slavery* as "impartial" and "a valuable contribution to American economic history."[118] Others, however, did not share these views. W. E. B. Du Bois called the work "incomplete" and "unfortunately biased," objecting that "the Negro as a responsible human being has no place in the book."[119] But Phillips's narrative of a benevolent white South ordering and regulating a childlike race was deeply culturally resonant. It remained the dominant interpretation of slavery until the civil rights movement, and displayed a tenacious half-life even longer in textbooks, popular fiction, and well-visited historical sites. "The negro," wrote one scholar, "took his captivity lightly. . . . His laugh is hearty, extending over his whole face, and is so surely contagious that it would crack the skin of a hypochondriac who dared to venture within its bounds."[120] Mastered by the kind of benevolent slaveholder Phillips and other white scholars depicted, who would not smile?

A White South in a White Nation

By the beginning of the twentieth century, postwar reconciliation narratives had reached for white Americans a satisfying degree of closure. The racialized domestic narratives of Thomas Dixon and Thomas Nelson Page mirrored what was happening on a larger political, social, and cultural scale; they embodied as well as shaped what was happening across American society. The story of America as a nation of white regions had become canonical and respected. Few white Americans seemed prepared to argue with the judgments of mainstream academic discourses about the South and the nation. Few argued with assertions that the South had supplied the nation with its earliest political leadership and had shaped the new nation in important ways. North Carolina's J. G. de R. Hamilton summed up this orthodox view in no uncertain terms:

> First, that in the person of Thomas Jefferson, the South gave to the nation its foremost political theorist and political leader. Second, that in Jackson, Clay and Calhoun, the South produced three of the four remaining great national leaders, and so far as birth and blood are concerned, produced another, Abraham Lincoln. Third, that in the period from the adoption of the Constitution until 1860 a large number of public men of unusual ability appeared in the South, whose influence was so great that for practically all that time the South was dominant in Congress, in the White House, and in the Supreme Court.[121]

The end of the nineteenth century was a particularly fortuitous time for this reconceptualization of the South's place in the nation, for the American nation as well as the South was undergoing wide-scale reevaluation and redefinition. From the middle of the nineteenth century through the turn of the twentieth, industrialization, urbanization, and the development of national markets and the modern corporation challenged older definitions of American and Americanness dependent upon the republican ideology of independent production, a relatively inactive national government, and "island communities."[122] By century's end, America was an industrial colossus, possessed of an increasingly racially diverse and conscious urban proletariat, an overseas empire, and the desire for a useable past. Like European nations touched by Darwinist rhetoric of competition, challenge, and struggle, Americans went searching, half-anxiously, for evidence that the nation was rooted in a vital tradition. And like their European colleagues, American scholars of history and literature compiled massive multivolume histories and collections of primary sources as the straw to make the bricks to build satisfying, triumphalist national narratives.

By the twentieth century, white southerners had been left to order the region's affairs largely as they saw fit. Appeals to southern tradition and southern history became inextricably linked to a definition of southern-ness in which black southerners were not southerners in any real sense at all. In historians' and literary scholars' narratives of a white South, African Americans played vital but painfully circumscribed roles: as contented slaves in stories of the antebellum past, or clowns, criminals, or impediments to regional progress in assessments of the contemporary South. As one account of turn-of-the-century Virginia wrote: "The negro as a freedman has made some progress, but as yet the greater number of criminals is of this race. . . . On the whole, the negroes are indispensable for field hands." A photograph in the same book shows "A type of the illiterate negro, now fast disappear-ing," leaving somewhat ambiguous whether the illiteracy or the "negro" were disappearing.[123]

Was this, then, a grand southern conspiracy—a fast move in which the South foisted its definition of Union off on a preoccupied North in order to further its project of white supremacy and consolidation (or reconsolida-tion) of class privilege? Not that crude, perhaps, but certainly that effective, especially because most white Americans basically agreed with the white South's project of racial "ordering." As the work of Frederick Jackson Turner makes especially clear, people who thought about politics wished to find a way to avoid the sectional bitterness that culminated in the South's thwarted attempt to leave the Union.

The context of the 1890s is crucial, as the battles over the tariff and the gold standard took on an unmistakable sectional cast, even appearing for a while that the South and West might rally behind William Jennings Bryan against the rapacious East. Dominant Democratic interests in the South had every interest in presenting the appearance of a solid South to the rest of the nation. Southern Democrats had their own battles to fight in the 1890s, as the Republican Party appeared poised to once again become a threat, allied with disgruntled Democratic Populists on Fusion tickets. Nearly everyone except black southerners had something to gain from this arrangement. The "Redeemers" consolidated their power in the South free of federal interference, the people interested in applied political science got a template for later dreams of regional planning and coordination, and others outside the South got a happy partner within a stable Union.

In the meantime, white southerners like Thomas Nelson Page by turn cooed soothing reassurances and handed down stern words to white America, words so revealing and influential that they are worth quoting at length. Page maintained that from time to time "the race question was in process in settlement," though he never mentioned how this was being done or who was doing it, except to note that whenever a final solution seemed to be at hand, it was "dashed to the ground" (viii). "Next to Representative Government, this is to-day the most tremendous question which faces directly one-third of the people of the United States, and only less immediately all of them. . . . It affects all those conditions which make life endurable and, perhaps, even possible in a dozen states of the Union" (ix). The question is so vexing, so time-consuming, to the people of the South that it "excludes due consideration of every other question whatsoever." During Reconstruction, "national passion was allowed to usurp the province of deliberation, and the Negro was taught two fundamental errors: first, the Southern white was inherently his enemy, and, secondly, that his race could be legislated into equality with the white" (ix). But northern whites can be taught, Page continues. Northerners do not believe southern testimony on the race question until they come to the region themselves. "Evidence upon a most vital matter has been accepted rather with reference to the sectional status of the witness rather than to his opportunity for exact knowledge" (x). "A Southerner may be a high-minded and philanthropic gentleman; [his] lifetime of knowledge of the Negro's character . . . counts for nothing with a large class who fancy themselves the only friends of the Negro" (x–xi). Page, however, did ultimately have hope that the white South's stories of African Americans were growing increasingly persuasive and accepted: "Men of all sections are awakening to the need for a proper solution" (xi).[124]

White southern writers were not all of one mind on the subject they were creating. John Spencer Bassett, political progressive, founder of the *South Atlantic Quarterly,* and Trinity College (now Duke University) academic, was typical of the generation of southerners so comfortable with his professional identity and Americanness that he moved happily to a position at Massachusetts' Smith College after his remark placing Booker T.

Washington second only to Robert E. Lee among southern men of greatness excited considerable wrath. Other writers displayed a similar critical temper. In his considerations of the Old South (especially his critical biography of William Gilmore Simms), William P. Trent could be as harsh as anyone in arguing that the region was an intellectually sterile slaveocracy. Where Trent and more seemingly unreconstructed writers such as Thomas Nelson Page and United Daughters of the Confederacy activist Mildred Lewis Rutherford meet is that at bottom no one by 1900 truly wanted a seceded South, but instead a South within a new nation the terms of which white southerners would help to define. They insisted as well that the story of the white South was a story of a common people with common experiences, values, and interests. And they largely got it. By the 1920s and 1930s conservatives such as the Nashville Agrarians would not like the terms of the bargain that allowed the South rhetorically to rejoin the American mainstream. But the assertion that the South was fundamentally American (if economically somewhat backward) mostly held until the civil rights movement, when black Americans and their allies demonstrated the ways in which that narrative and its consequences were incompatible with the stories about melting pots and freedom and leadership of the free world that Americans liked to tell. Until then, however, turn-of-the-century southern and American narratives meshed comfortably, for binding them were assumptions not only about blackness but about whiteness as well. Their assumptions about whiteness were no more based upon innate characteristics than were their assumptions about blackness, of course, but were the products of an imaginative process that proceeded along with and helped create the space for a white South within a white nation.

The canonization of southern letters and emerging historical definitions of a distinct but fundamentally American South played a central role in the cultural formation of narratives of a white South in a white nation. "The South is making marvelous strides," wrote one scholar in 1909, "and its activities are being directed by its own people who understand its own conditions."[125] The results were enormous. As Joel Williamson argues: "One could lynch just as effectively by genteel means as crudely by rope and faggot. Negroes could be lynched by account books. And they could be lynched by written history."[126] Amused by the reception of Margaret Mitchell's *Gone With the Wind*, Douglas Southall Freeman, the biographer of Lee and Washington,

 "The South Is a Single, Homogeneous People"

recalled that the novel awakened a wave of sympathy in the southern cause from northerners and westerners, who turned to him for further suggestions for the story of the Civil War from the South's point of view. In 1939, the year the movie was released, Freeman obliged with *The South to Posterity: An Introduction to the Writing of Confederate History,* an extended examination of the southern historical literature on the Civil War. "I never quite swallowed," he wrote, "the story of the Connecticut lady of abolitionist stock who was alleged to have exclaimed, 'Those damn Yankees!' as she read Miss Mitchell's description of the march to the sea; but I began to wonder if the children of the Confederates who lost the war in the field were, in the realm of letters, winning the peace." Considering the bulk of southern writing on the Civil War, Freeman concluded that "Confederate history was most persuasive where authors had the least intention of making it so. Those authors who sought to overwhelm by mustered argument and paraded declamation succeeded only in destroying interest; those made friends who told simply or quaintly, with humor or with color, of what they had seen and experienced."[127] This success in defining a racialized regional "we" within a white nation allowed the white South to claim a fundamental community with the broader white nation while retaining its right to judge and order its own affairs, proceeding as they did from organic imperatives.

Just how well the white South succeeded in its task of explaining its history on its own terms was well illustrated on June 2, 1931, when the state of Mississippi unveiled two statues in the National Statuary Hall of the United States Capitol in Washington, D.C. Since 1864 each state had been invited to contribute two statues "of deceased persons who have been citizens thereof, and illustrious for their historic renown or for distinguished civic or military services such as each State may deem to be worthy of this national commemoration." In 1931 the National Statuary Hall held statues of men such as Henry Clay, John Winthrop, Daniel Webster, and Andrew Jackson.[128]

The men the state of Mississippi chose as "worthy of . . . national commemoration" were Jefferson Davis and James Z. George. These statues and the placing of them are a striking example of the white South's power in shaping unmistakable visual reminders of the asserted values of white Mississippians. With the United States Marine Band providing music, including "America" and the "Star-Spangled Banner," Jefferson Finis Davis was honored in the Capitol Building of the nation against whose authority he rebelled. At the time of the unveiling, Davis was not a U.S. citizen, an eventuality that the authors of the 1864 statute creating Statuary Hall had almost certainly not anticipated. Davis, characterized by one speaker as "the soldier, the patriot, the statesman," was "the Cicero of the Senate."[129] Davis, said another speaker, was "the idol of his people."

The "mighty figure" of Davis, said U.S. Senator Pat Harrison, "was crowned with coronets and chained in irons; he pardoned thousands, but was denied one himself . . . he created a nation and died a disfranchised citizen."[130] But sectional feelings, argued Harrison, no longer prevented Davis's enshrinement: "the scars of strife and the wounds of conflict" had healed, and Mississippi presented Davis to the nation "without apology." By 1931 Davis was not the only former Confederate honored in Statuary Hall; Davis joined his former vice president Alexander Stephens and military leaders Robert E. Lee, Joe Wheeler, and Kirby Smith. So when Davis's statue was unveiled, and the United States Marine Band played "Dixie," it no longer seemed daring or awkward for the nation to honor the man who, more than any other figure, represented unrepentant rebellion against its authority. White America's acceptance of Jefferson Davis as a national icon was, and continues to be, apparent to anyone who visits the U.S. Capitol.

Mississippi's other honored dignitary, James Zacharias George, is less familiar than Davis, although his enshrinement was equally significant for what it said about white Mississippians' sense of history, power, and display. George was a key figure in the overthrow of Reconstruction in the state in 1875 and chief architect of the state's disfranchising 1890 constitution, a model followed by practically all the southern states in the 1890s and 1900s. George was praised for his work in "reestablishing free government among his people":

> Under his direction it was to be demonstrated, as has so often been demonstrated in history among those of his race and of his people's race, that under proper leadership, intelligence will triumph over ignorance in government . . . and that it is possible to establish and maintain, with approximate certainty, justice and righteousness in government.[131]

In 1931, then, Mississippi honored in the U.S. Capitol the man most associated with secession and the man most responsible for the overthrow of

Reconstruction and the generations-long disfranchisement of black Mississippians. Members and officers of the United States Senate listened to George, the "Great Commoner," praised as a man who, "in the name of the people of Mississippi," "brought hope and peace to the people of Mississippi of both races."[132] It is difficult to imagine how the nation could have come any farther in agreeing with white Mississippians that their heroes were American heroes and that the vision of the white South they presented—orderly and masterful—was true and right.

Following the Civil War, white southerners' studies of the region's literature and history steadily advanced a new vision not only of the South but of the American polity as well. The post–Civil War moment invited a rethinking of the nature of the Union, and of the composition and purpose of the American people. Contemporaries in all regions of the country realized that they were living in an era of profound transformation of American life and institutions. "It is hardly an exaggeration," wrote Frederick Jackson Turner, "to say that we are witnessing the birth of a new nation in America."[133]

Before the Civil War, Americans commonly argued that they were a special, indeed a chosen people, especially when compared with Europeans. But the terms of Union and the character of American nationalism were by no means clear-cut. Americans of the Revolutionary War generation contested the meaning of liberty and union, a process that continued until the Civil War. During the war Lincoln drew on romantic-inspired nationalism to argue that a teleology informed the American experience, something more transcendent and unbreakable than a strictly construed constitutional pact between semisovereign states.[134] Once secession and disunion were dead, the postwar generation explored the changed context of American nationalism, as well as the expanded state Americans were creating and attempting to manage.[135]

Dominant voices in the white South in the 1880s and 1890s imagined the American nation not as dualistic, uneasily balanced sections quarreling over the Great West, as Frederick Jackson Turner had it, but were beginning to think of the nation in terms of a depoliticized aggregate of diverse regions, each with its own organic history and traditions. Historian Michael O'Brien correctly sees nineteenth-century "sectionalism" as a political doctrine. Imbued with romantic nationalist notions of a land and people, sectionalism "helped to fashion a conception of southern identity, which many thought should be embodied in political independence." As the Civil War demonstrated, the sense of southern identity founded upon sectionalism thus defined was insufficient to guarantee political independence for the South. Sectionalism was judged by the post-Reconstruction generation a chief precipitant of the Civil War, and cast into disrepute as a foundational argument for southern distinctiveness and regional semiautonomy, especially on the all-important question of race policy. Consequently, continues O'Brien, the next generation "developed the transmuted romantic doctrine of regionalism," an (apparently) "depoliticized version of the theory of cultural distinctiveness, whereby portions of the Union retain their special character."[136]

Yet regionalism too was a potentially unstable foundation upon which to construct narratives of a post–Civil War South; after the Civil War, any conception of "the South" was dependent upon some imagined southernness beyond the state, or at least assumed a definition of the South not based solely on political definition. The crucible of war had shown just how fracturable antebellum assertions of southern nationness were. Any claim for southern identity tied not to a polity but to an organic southernness, then, risked running afoul of its own logical imperative toward devolution and localism. Literary scholar William P. Trent noted the tenacity of state and local loyalties:

> The South Carolinian . . . is not merely glad to hail from his native state, he is not merely anxious to return thither to die, he is miserable whenever and as long as he is not living there. Nay, he actually wishes to be rooted to a particular parish or town. The *genius loci* is the god he worships, and he stands for everything that is not cosmopolitan.[137]

The former Confederate States (a "South" defined in political terms) was a diverse region, even by American standards. Far more complicated than the Cotton South and two races of mainstream American narratives of the South, the region covered by the former Confederacy held climate zones from mountain to subtropical; many "races" and every conceivable combination thereof.[138] But in the postwar era, an imagined South emerged that proved longer-lived and more resilient than the Confederate nation. "Owing to peculiar conditions, the South" shared, wrote one group of scholars, "an interrelated and separate history, special problems and distinct life."[139] This assertion of southern identity emerged from and aided late-nineteenth-century racialist and American nationalist imperatives.

What the dominant voices of the white South were at pains to deny was not the word "section" so much as "sectionalism," by which they meant rhetoric or actions liable to excite a belief that the South was not a happy member of the Union. Southerners who preached national reconciliation and maintained that the South had adopted commercial values had their eyes on northern support and northern dollars.[140] The rhetoric of Henry Grady or Henry Watterson was, of course, meant for national as well as southern consumption. Watterson asked a Grand Army of the Republic reunion in 1895:

> What is left for you and me to cavil about, far less to fight about? . . . The institution of African slavery, with its irreconcilable conditions, got between the North and the South, and—. But I am not here to recite the history of the United States. You know what happened as well as I do, and we all know that there does not remain a shred of those old issues to divide us. . . . Slavery is gone. Secession is dead. The Union, with its system of Statehood still intact, survives; and with it a power and glory among men passing the dreams of the fathers of the republic.[141]

By the turn of the twentieth century, many Americans were beginning to imagine their nation not as two sections arrayed against each other, nor, as in much postwar fiction, as a pair of reconciled lovers, but rather as a variety of regions—New England, the South, the West, and the Southwest, among them.[142] Theoretically, at least, all regions were politically equal, and each had its own culturally specific, yet nonthreatening, claims to distinctiveness.[143]

The studies of southern history and letters that emerged at the turn of the century depended upon implicit definitions of the South in which the region was distinct yet fundamentally American. With the divisive questions of secession and slavery resolved, so it seemed, white southerners and other white Americans pointed proudly to signs that the South was thoroughly American in institutions and temperament. White northern and southern agreement about the wisdom of the color line especially worked to bring all white Americans together, despite the quite recent Civil War. Indeed, evolving definitions of the Civil War did not complicate, but rather made easier, the task of reconciliation. The war was increasingly imagined, as it is represented today on television and in the movies as an epic, tragic quarrel among (white) brothers, rather than as a problematic and contested struggle over freedom, equality, and citizenship. The Civil War, like the American nation itself, was represented as a white man's affair.[144]

The example of Woodrow Wilson was often used by northerners and southerners alike as evidence that white southern Americans need not be internally conflicted or feel any irreconcilable duality as southerner and American. In 1902 Wilson was appointed president of Princeton University, and the *Baltimore American* declared: "To Virginia and to the South, the appointment of Dr. Wilson . . . demonstrates the obliteration of sectionalism and the mark which men of Southern birth are making in the North."[145] When Wilson assumed the presidency, a chorus of voices read his victory as "a kind of vindication for the South," in George Tindall's phrase, and an end to sectional bitterness. The scholar Edwin Mims argued that Wilson's southern origins were significant: "he seemed to be bringing his native section back into the house of the fathers." But at the same time, according to Mims, Wilson "was, if man ever was, a representative American, saturated with its history, animated by its ideals."[146] With Wilson's inauguration, most observers agreed, the nation had reached the end of the "road to reunion."[147] The South, then, seemed to have taken up the post-Reconstruction challenge issued by voices such as Louisville's *Southern Bivouac* to imagine and craft a South "not as something separate from the national but as an inseparable and integral part of it."[148]

An agreement upon white superiority and racial segregation facilitated this sense of white integration. White Americans shared quasi-Darwinian convictions about racial hierarchies and white men's burdens.[149] White southern studies of the South's history and literature allowed a national audience to place potentially un-American-looking disfranchisement and the violence of the lynching decades within culturally resonant tropes of order, management, and racialism. In catechism-like fashion Julian A. C. Chandler asked in 1909: "What then constitutes the chief things for us to consider in the Southern civilization of to-day? First, the determination of the Southern whites to rule in the lands which they themselves have developed—white supremacy but with civil rights to all."[150] In an era of scientific racialism and widespread anxieties over the effects of unregulated immigration, such frank statements of white determination were not out of place. In fact, the southern narratives and the southern disenfranchising project were politically acceptable to the North precisely because broader cultural narratives of whiteness and the disordered/disorderly Other had enabled them to imagine a white North and a white South engaged in a common task. White southerners realized this fact. Said a senator from Virginia: "The instinct of race integrity is the most glorious, as it is the most predominate characteristic of the Anglo-Saxon race, and the sections have it in common."[151]

By the 1890s, veterans of the Blue and the Gray shook hands at numerous and celebrated Civil War reunions, rituals reaching their culmination perhaps in the fiftieth anniversary of the Battle of Gettysburg in 1913. At July 4 celebrations at Gettysburg that summer, President Wilson displayed a common white southern understanding of the war, especially one intended for a national audience: "How complete the union has become and how dear to all of us, how unquestioned, how benign and majestic." The "quarrel," said Wilson, is "forgotten."[152] Such an understanding of the war was based upon an assumption that all white men were now brothers, and that black interpretations of the war did not particularly matter. But while whiteness was the *sine qua non* of the new American nation, whiteness did not seem able by itself to carry the national project. The white republic was held together by the darker Other, whether in the pages of plantation fiction or in Gilded Age campaigns against the Plains Indians.

By the end of the nineteenth century white northerners and southerners were able to take up arms against the Spanish in a brief and satisfying war, and afterward against darker foes, as Filipino guerillas showed themselves unappreciative of the fruits of American empire.[153] Offering the South's assistance to other Americans with their eyes on imperial prizes, Ben Tillman explained: "We of the South have borne this white man's burden of a colored race in our midst."[154] With their shared commitments to whiteness and order, the North and South were by century's end again on the same side. At the turn of the century, wrote Woodrow Wilson,

> The old landmarks of politics … seemed … submerged. The southern States
> were readjusting their elective suffrage so as to exclude the illiterate negroes

and so in part undo the mischief of Reconstruction; and yet the rest of the country withheld its hand from interference. Sections began to draw together with a new understanding of one another.[155]

White Americans, especially such pure Anglo-Saxons as southerners claimed to be, merited an honored position in an America that to northern urban whites was beginning to look less like the face in the mirror.

For all of white America's rhetoric about its supremacy and fitness, many narratives of white southern identity display uneasiness over just whether whiteness was predetermined to eclipse the dark. For every white southerner who argued that the Negro problem would disappear because blacks themselves would disappear through disease, vice, and an inability to rein their passions and civilize themselves, other alarmed voices looked into the coming century and saw not a brilliant whiteness but the dawn of dusk. Thomas Nelson Page, in *The Negro: The Southerner's Problem* (1904), attempted on the one hand, as the title suggests, to persuade white northerners that the white South should be allowed to manage blacks without interference or even much careful attention. On the other, Page, like Vardaman, Thomas Dixon, and other prophets of the apocalypse, stressed that black America was an Enemy Within, beginning to exact the revenge of the cradle. "Where ten millions of one race," wrote Page, "which increases at a rate that doubles its numbers every forty years, confront within the borders of one country another race, the most opposite to it on earth, there must exist a question grave enough in the present and likely to become stupendous in the future."[156] The fecundity of black Americans—nationally, not just regionally, argued Page—endangered the promise of American life. Such rhetoric need not be psychologized to discern what the white South really thought. Instead, it is instructive to think of how far broader American narratives would eventually come in agreeing with the South that the best stories about America and the South were those that emphasized their lily-whiteness: not only America's complexion, of course, but its exceptionalism and freedom from sin.

This work by white southerners in helping to create pan-white American narratives posited the existence of an essential white soul as biologically deterministic as were the inferior souls of black folk. In the name of keeping order along that color line, white Americans were invited to join hands with

   "The South Is a Single, Homogeneous People"

as much gusto as the aged boys in blue and gray displayed at the numerous veterans' reunions of the turn of the century. Only this time the fact of Union victory was muted, as at the Gettysburg anniversary, where Confederates made it to the top of Seminary Ridge this time, joining hands across the stone wall with their now-comrades. Southerners took the wall this time by persuading Yankees to invite them over to their side. To these narrators and most other Americans, "black" meant "southern black" in the unquestioning way that "southern" meant "white." The narrators of the 1890 to 1920 period were southerners with a broad national vision; they persuaded America that the problem of the twentieth century was the problem of the color line.

CONCLUSION

"MISSISSIPPI'S GIANT HOUSE PARTY": WHITENESS AND COMMUNITY AT THE NESHOBA COUNTY FAIR

"In Neshoba County, Mississippi, the basement of the past is not very deep."
—Florence Mars, *Witness in Philadelphia*

"This is not a place to come to burn the American flag."
—Fairgoer to author, July 2000

"The Neshoba County Fair is not for everybody."
—Fairgoer to author, July 2001

For more than one hundred years, Mississippians have braved their long hot summer to head to the eastern part of the state for the Neshoba County Fair. For one week in late July, thousands of men and women from Philadelphia (the county seat), the rest of the state, and even farther afield descend upon the fairgrounds to create a Mississippi town of respectable size.[1] Joined by well more than fifty thousand additional visitors, including the occasional reporter from a Washington or Boston newspaper, they gather to enjoy food, drink, horse racing, gospel singing, and political oratory—in short, as *National Geographic* accurately if perhaps accidentally characterized it, to "join in tribal rites of fellowship . . . where . . . a whole way of life finds affirmation." This annual ritual is an assertion that one can go home again. "It's a place," as one admirer explained, "where there is comfort in knowing that tomorrow will be little changed from today."[2]

The fair's most striking feature is the cabins that fan out from centrally located Founder's Square. More than six hundred in all, these magnificent specimens of vernacular architecture are lovingly decorated and named— "The Fox Den," "Green Acres," and "Ye Old King's Kastle" among them; purists argue whether such conveniences as screened windows and air conditioning compromise their aesthetic integrity. In contrast to the SUVs and minivans parked outside them, these two- and three-story structures are self-consciously Spartan, in keeping with the fair's early history as a camp meeting: "iron bedsteads and homemade wood bunks stand in rows dormitory-style, their covers wilting in 99-degree heat." Coveted, but in limited supply, the cabins are practically a medium of exchange. As one owner noted, "It's a common thing in Neshoba County to have a divorce where they would decide the child custody, alimony, cash settlement and who gets the house, but the only thing they can't resolve is who is going to get the fair cabin."[3] Jealously passed from generation to generation, the cabins and the relaxed living they encourage—strangers may find themselves invited inside for supper, or at least a drink—are seen by longtime fairgoers as a key to the fair's meaning. They are correct, for each summer the cabins, all owned by white families, become the heart of a Disneyesque "Southland," a racially segregated imagining of a Mississippi town. In a county almost one-third black, the fair remains, in the eyes of many Neshoba County residents, largely for whites only. "It's for them, not for us," a black Philadelphian told me matter-of-factly.

The fair exemplifies the most critical development in race and public culture in Mississippi over the last generation: a move from explicit public commemoration of whiteness such as that forged at the turn of the twentieth century and reinvigorated in the 1950s and 1960s to an implicit rhetoric signaled obliquely in cultural practices and artifacts. This rhetoric of white identity is now, in some ways, even more tenacious in the state's public culture than it was in the 1950s and 1960s because it wields a largely unspoken power. At the fair, whiteness and racially exclusive definitions of community are embodied in the very walls of the cabins and encoded in the seemingly benign cultural practices of singing, visiting, and celebrating family life.

In the last two decades, white Mississippians have been confronted with potent reminders of their state's defiant years: the release of the movie *Mississippi Burning,* the grudging opening of the State Sovereignty Commission's files, and the conviction of Byron de la Beckwith for the murder of Medgar Evers. But fairgoers, for all their obeisance to tradition and the past, display a curious, even conscious, will to ignorance of the county's and state's history of violent resistance to racial change. The fair represents a paradox most white Mississippians have yet to grasp: their cherished celebrations of family and community are not separable from the state's racialist past. Those narratives, so central to white Mississippians' understandings of who they are, are built upon a deeply racialized foundation, a foundation laid at the turn of the twentieth century and still productive of narratives of family, region, and race.[4]

The domestic traditions of the fair, epitomized by self-consciously old-fashioned southern dinners for friends and family, are at the heart of this construction of "whiteness," an identity defining the descendents of most European immigrants as members of one "race." All cabin owners and practically all guests at the Neshoba County Fair are white, a fact literally unremarkable to white fairgoers. Around the fair's quasi-sacramental dinner tables, whiteness is invisible and unspoken. Politicians no longer occupy center stage at the fair with speeches celebrating white womanhood and the purity of whites-only institutions, but racial difference is no less central to the fair's meaning. Sites like the fair, with their self-consciously commemorative domesticity, give insight into what still underpins definitions of a racially exclusive community in Mississippi. Access to the cabins, celebrations of family, and dinner tables is so zealously treasured because "social equality"—admittance to white domestic space on terms of equality—remains one of the most stubborn taboos in the Deep South. These domestic spaces are central to the fair's definition of community and identity. The traditions that the fair celebrates were built in part upon the state's commitment to black oppression, but at the fair today, there is no overt discussion of this history of white privilege. Instead, nostalgia replaces memory in support of the implicit, near-universal practice of a racially exclusive white identity.[5]

At its origin in the late 1880s, the fair resembled other southern livestock and agricultural exhibitions. In 1889, farmers from Neshoba County's

Coldwater community held a picnic near the Coldwater School to encourage the development of a livestock and produce fair in Neshoba County. They had earlier attended social and agricultural functions held under the auspices of the agrarian Patrons' Union of Lake, Mississippi, in adjacent Scott County.

In the beginning, farmers and their families came in ox-drawn wagons to the fairgrounds, some eight miles southwest of Philadelphia, and camped at night in the open air. Soon, they formed the Neshoba County Stock and Agricultural Fair Association, a private corporation, and on August 28, 1891, elected their first board of directors. Construction of the cabins began in 1893, after the association formally acquired property in February of that year. Incorporated under state law in 1933, the Neshoba County Fair, unlike other state and county fairs, was and remains a private corporation owned by local stockholders. The Fair Association still owns all 150 acres on which the cabins stand; any transfer or sale of cabins, which in prime locations can command prices from $60,000 to $100,000, must be approved by the board of directors. Black Philadelphians believe that price is not the only factor accounting for the continued all-white ownership of the cabins.[6]

A nonprofit organization, the fair supports itself largely through revenue from admissions and the concession stands. Even the concession business is closely linked to family and tradition at the fair. The right to sell bottled water, fried pickles, and cotton candy is coveted; spots along the midway open infrequently, and seem to go to those with long-standing connections to the fair. But getting in the gate is trouble enough for some Neshoba Countians. In 2001, daily admission was $10.00 per person, a considerable expense to low-income families.

The fair began at a volatile moment in Mississippi. The 1890s witnessed disfranchisement of a majority of the state's voters, and the triumph of Jim Crow and a conservative Democratic Party. Until the end of the nineteenth century, Neshoba County was sparsely populated. Most residents were white settlers of modest means who had moved into its red clay hills to coax out a cotton crop each summer.[7] There were a few black citizens and a small Choctaw population, which gave the county a noticeable tri-racial tenor. Life for Neshoba Countians changed when the railroad came through in 1905, producing a moderate spike in the county's population.[8]

In a time of rapid social change, the fair became an attempt to affirm the equality and dignity of white Neshoba Countians who felt threatened by their black neighbors' attempts to claim some measure of equality. Assertions of *Herrenvölk* community soon became central to the fair's image and the rhetoric used to describe it. "No normal person," newspaperman Clayton Rand bragged in 1940, "could resist the gregarious contagion of this congenial event where merchants and farmers, visiting celebrities and natives met and mingled on terms of democratic equality." Egalitarian mores apparently did prevail at the early fair. For years, the fair had a common privy—a deluxe twenty-holer, as one self-described old-timer recalled. "This fair," she remembered, "has always had about the same atmosphere, one of family feelings." Traditionally, one of the fair's highlights has been the day of the governor's speech, when fairgoers turn out in fashion: "Dress at the Fair was formal. Women wore hats and gloves and their best dresses." When they tired of political oratory, the crowd could turn to horse races, a beauty contest, exhibits of livestock and produce, amateur theatricals and school declamations, and tent shows. "The first tent show," remembered one Philadelphia resident, "featured a petrified man with one arm."[9]

Today, the language of family and equality is largely unchanged: "what the fair is famed most for is a dish of good old-fashioned southern hospitality."[10] The fair's admirers work hard to cultivate an "old-timey" image of family and community untouched by events of the past decades. As in the beginning, assertions of an undifferentiated, democratic (white) community prevail today: "no where on God's green earth," wrote the *Daily Mississippian,* "will you find doctors, lawyers, accountants, store owners, farmers, teachers, and politicians living just a cut above poverty. The average cabin is a two story, wooden framed, hell-to-clean shack." A *National Geographic* reporter rhapsodized: "Kids run safe and free at the fair, what with traffic mostly pedestrian, crime unknown, every door open, and every grown-up a friend." "Everybody is *so* laid back and friendly," wrote Jill Conner Browne, "that you'd really have to go out of your way to piss somebody off."[11]

It is tempting to dismiss such language as memory dulled by nostalgic longing for a small-town past that never was. After all, such fair regulars as Governor James K. Vardaman in the early 1900s and Senator Theodore Bilbo in the 1930s and 1940s preached that white families and white communities were under constant danger from sexually predatory black men or a meddlesome federal government. But nostalgia should be distinguished from memory when considering the fair, for nostalgia is in fact a way of forgetting rather than remembering. Fairgoers wish to have the old and allegedly simpler days, but the county's troubled past, especially the summer of 1964, when three young civil rights field workers were abducted and brutally murdered, is the unavoidable skeleton at the fried chicken and butterbean feast. "People would rather forget those days [of 1964]," a reporter noticed. But for Neshoba County's African American residents, precisely when in time one places the good old days is problematic, with memories still inconveniently fresh of Jim Crow laws and folkways, and federal agents digging the bodies of civil rights workers out of an earthen dam.[12]

The fair in its early decades should be placed within the context of similar Progressive Era efforts at encouraging scientific farming and home economics throughout the South; it was "a short course in better farming and better living." But the Neshoba County Fair has survived and prospered in ways that other county fairs did not. The explanation is surely the way the townlike cabin setting enabled a potent sense of place and community for the fairgoers. Neshoba County newspaperman Clayton Rand rightly observed that "unlike other county fairs, this fair preceded the season of harvest, so the agricultural exhibits were secondary" to politics and socializing.[13]

Founded just before the adoption of Mississippi's disfranchising 1890 constitution, the fair worked to check populist discontent with the state's status quo. Speakers ranging from gubernatorial candidates to prominent farmers to schoolboy orators made no mention of the economic differences that divided white Mississippians, except to assert that they themselves came from the ranks of the common man (more recently, "working families") and understood his needs. Instead, fair orators told the attendees that theirs was a high and noble culture, and their women the flower of the Southland. Mississippi's leaders identified threats from outside the white community, claiming to stand as their champions against predatory interests and violent threats, ranging from Wall Street plutocrats to railroad barons to vicious and "uppity" blacks run amok.

The fair was so politically potent because Mississippi holds its primary elections in August. In the days of one-party politics, victory in the primary was, as everyone puts it, tantamount to election. A speaking appearance at the fair was quickly deemed indispensable for would-be state officeholders. The WPA Guide to Mississippi declared that "it has become the political ring into which State politicians toss their hats during election years. . . . The impression a candidate makes here at the fair often remains in the minds of the public on election day."[14]

The first candidate for statewide political office to appear at the fair was the "White Chief," James K. Vardaman, and almost every governor since Anselm McLaurin (1896–1900) has spoken there. The fair became well known for the speakers' blistering invective, whether directed by Vardaman and Pat Harrison against each other in their 1918 bid for the Democratic nomination for the U.S. Senate, for example, or by Vardaman, Theodore Bilbo (1916–1920, 1928–1932), and Ross Barnett (1960–1964) against black Mississippians and outside agitators down through the 1960s. And make no mistake, political rhetoric in Neshoba County was often heatedly partisan. Pat Harrison, for instance, attacked incumbent Senator James K. Vardaman as a tool of the Kaiser, one of the "little group of willful men," as Wilson put it, who opposed American entry into World War I. Did, then, the fair support the disfranchisers' arguments that white southerners could differ politically if blacks were removed from the political scene? In fact, African Americans were "removed" from neither politics nor the fair. In the 1950s and 1960s, especially, Mississippi politicians, with precious few exceptions, seemed to speak of little else other than massive resistance to "racial amalgamation." Black Mississippians were always present at the fair: in rhetoric, in the fairgoers' imagination, and literally in servile domestic roles. Black Mississippians, then, were always a palpable force, hidden in plain sight; the fair's "present absence," as literary critics might put it.

At the Neshoba County Fair in the 1890s and later, patrons and speakers asserted a stable, consensual tradition of white southern identity, the same narratives white Mississippians heard from their schools, pulpits, and political forums. "Nothing in Neshoba County's history," argued one admirer of the fair, "has done so much to . . . bring Neshoba County family and friends together."[15] Office seekers such as James Vardaman and Theodore Bilbo delighted generations of fairgoers with their broad theatricality. In the closed society of the Neshoba County Fair, political disagreement seemed more a family quarrel than a clash of irreconcilable principles.

"Under Vardaman's poetic influence," Clayton Rand recalled, "Fair patrons became sweaty and popeyed." In a typical performance, Vardaman recited "Tennyson's 'Locksley Hall,' Leigh Hunt's 'Abou ben Adhem,' Edwin Markham's 'The Man with the Hoe,' and Bob Ingersoll's 'Peroration' to his speech to the Union Veterans in 1876." In one speech Theodore Bilbo compared himself to St. Paul, John Bunyan, and Jefferson Davis, all men who, like himself, Bilbo reminded his audience, were jailed for their beliefs. One Mississippian expressed the opinion of thousands of state residents as he spit his tobacco juice on the ground and conclusively declared: "They ain't no use talkin,' some folks is called to preach and some folks is called to be governor."[16] Years afterward, the spirit of "The Man," Bilbo, lingered at the fair. "The only ambition I ever had was to vote for Sen. Bilbo," a Neshoba county officeholder reflected in 1983.[17] The fair advanced, both explicitly, with the segregationist rhetoric of political aspirants, and implicitly with the prescribed place of black Mississippians in the festivities, a construction of white southern identity whose foundation was the acceptance of the Jim Crow settlement as orthodoxy.

These days no serious aspirant for Mississippi political office speaks so explicitly the language of Vardaman or Bilbo. But the story of the Neshoba County Fair since the 1960s reveals the powerful influence that the rhetoric of whiteness wields in shaping contemporary Mississippi culture. At the fair now the language of whiteness is rarely heard above a whisper. But the fair itself, an institution forged in the very crucible of assertions of white community and identity, remains as popular as ever. White fairgoers insist that the fair does not and never has had anything to do with whiteness or the politics of race. But consider this unself-conscious assertion by the *Jackson (Miss.) Daily News* in 1974: "It's an insider's world. . . . It's Mississippi tradition, roots and culture. . . . It's where the next generation of Mississippians is being groomed to carry on. . . . It's their Mississippi, like it always has been."[18] Many black Mississippians suspect that as Lincoln said of slavery and the Civil War, race has something to do with the fair. Indeed, in Neshoba County, the love of whiteness—veiled as it is in the language of family, community, "the old days," and a conveniently undefined "we" and "our"—is not dead, but now instead the love that dares not speak its name.

The career of Governor Ross Barnett is characteristic of the fair's pattern of memory and forgetting. In his retirement, Barnett hardly underwent the same conversion—real or apparent—that his one-time ally George Wallace experienced. Barnett did, however, work to cultivate a benign image, and used his appearances at the fair to remake himself, a task that included such blatant non sequiturs as Barnett's riding in Jackson, Mississippi's annual Medgar Evers Homecoming Parade, a tribute to the slain civil rights leader. "I remember when Ross first understood that he couldn't say 'nigger' anymore," recalled one acquaintance. "When he told his jokes that year [at the fair], he changed it to 'colored boy.' It was quite a step." A Mississippi reporter took issue with a *Boston Globe* impression that Mississippians came to laugh at the antics of the segregationist governor–turned Chautauqua-like entertainer, with his much-beloved rendering of the vaguely irredentist "Are You From Dixie?" "Not so," wrote the Mississippi newspaperman. "The large crowd, even former political foes, laughed with, and not at Barnett. Barnett is now something of a folk hero." "I adore, I love my Mississippians," Barnett told a cheering crowd in 1976, echoing his language of 1962, when he told a crowd in Jackson's Veterans' Memorial Stadium that he loved the state and its customs, one of which forbade the admission of African Americans such as James Meredith to Ole Miss. To many Mississippians, the fair is just not the same since Barnett's passing: "It was death to speak after Ross Barnett because so many people came to hear him," recalled one man in 1994. "He told these stories and Kennedy jokes." Not all Mississippians miss Barnett, however. "All bad things must also come to an end," observed Mississippi NAACP field director Robert Walker in 1984, the year failing health forced the eighty-six-year-old Barnett to miss the fair. For Walker, the fair conjured up not images of family, community, and good old-time values, but something less palatable; to him, the fair was "the mecca for white politicians who have not had fairness and true representation of black citizens on their minds."[19]

Despite the claims of its defenders, the fair's rhetoric in the 1970s and 1980s continued to display some of the harsh edge of previous years. Of course, the fair has always been home to some harmless eccentrics, such as presidential candidate Buck Ladner, who in 1979 advocated a punitive military strike against "the Arabs" and the conversion of Washington, D.C., to a national museum; the executive branch was to be moved to the desert Southwest and the legislative branch to a site on the Louisiana-Arkansas line. But well into the 1980s, orators at the fair reminisced about their friendships with arch-segregationists such as Theodore Bilbo. In 1974, Ross Barnett attacked "desegregation, busing and income and inheritance taxes," and paying poetic tribute to the fair, added: "you listened to my virtues way back in '59." At it again in 1978, Barnett continued to lambaste school busing: "The bureaucrats are talking about racial balance," he thundered. "Who cares about racial balance?" Warming to his task, Barnett quickly lapsed into old-fashioned rhetoric, identifying the racial taboos that busing was designed to break. The bureaucrats intended that black and white children were to eat, sit, study, and even dance together. The solution, in Barnett's estimation, was simple: "We need some men in Congress who'll stand up and fight like James K. Vardaman and Theodore Bilbo." Black Mississippians such as Henry Kirksey, a Jackson businessman and several-time candidate for state and national office, had a good idea that cries for "neighborhood schools" signaled a not-too-subtle call for a return to segregated schools. But despite his rather sinister image outside—and to many within—the Magnolia State, the fair's directors never expressed qualms over Barnett's appearances: "Our problem with Ross Barnett is that they just love him so much, we have a hard time getting him off the stage." Other Mississippians agreed. A member of the North Jackson Exchange Club declared in 1979: "No man can make you prouder to be a Mississippian than Ross Barnett!"[20]

The fair attracts tens of thousands of visitors each summer, perhaps justifying its Web site's claim to be "*the* political forum for the state of Mississippi."[21] Black Mississippians argue that the fair's subtext has remained unchanged, hardly a dead issue when such figures as Jack Kemp, Michael Dukakis, John Glenn, and Ronald Reagan, who launched his 1980 post-convention presidential campaign at the fair, have found the large, politically conscious audiences too tempting to pass up. Today, the politicians continue to come, shaking hands, kissing babies, and cooing that Mississippi's fundamental values are sound. Former Senate majority and minority leader Trent Lott is a fair favorite. In the late 1990s he and fellow Republican heavyweights John Ashcroft, Jim Jeffords, and Larry Craig, the "Singing Senators," entertained the crowds with polished versions of old favorites. Back in Washington and out of this seemingly nonpartisan pose, Ashcroft, Lott, and Craig consistently struck some of the Senate's most conservative notes. Although Ashcroft's rejection by Missouri voters and Jeffords's break with the Republican Party broke up the Singing Senators, Lott remained a favorite at the fair. Some say that the fair no longer has the political immediacy that it once did, but the old excitement is still discernable, especially in election years.

In 2002, for instance, relatively slow population growth cost Mississippi a seat in the House of Representatives, and after a contentious redistricting battle, sitting U.S. Representative Chip Pickering (Republican, Third District) faced sitting U.S. Representative Ronnie Shows (Democrat, Fourth District) for the newly drawn Third District seat. On August 1, Pickering debated Shows beneath the tin-roofed pavilion in Founders' Square. While for one hundred years candidates had lambasted each other in fair speeches, such debates were rare in fair history. The weather was sweltering; the pavilion overflowed with a highly partisan Republican crowd. Shows was no liberal, boasting a long record of antiabortion votes in the Mississippi and U.S. House of Representatives. Still, Shows's attempts to excite the crowd to populist anger over Brookhavenite Bernie Ebbers's WorldCom financial follies proved unsuccessful.

The thirty-eight-year-old Pickering bragged about the number of sons he had fathered (five), pledged his support for President George W. Bush, and tarred Shows's party with the epithet "liberal." The Founders' Square crowd howled its approval at Pickering's jabs at Hillary Clinton and Bennie Thompson, the Democrat representing Mississippi's Second District. Making sure that no one missed the point, Pickering's supporters distributed church-house fans with Shows's photo on one side and Hillary Clinton's on the reverse; other fans featured Shows on one side and Thompson (an African American) on the other. Clinton and Thompson seemed particularly egregious to the fair crowd not simply because they were Democrats—Mississippi did have another Democratic U.S. representative, as well as a Democratic governor. Instead, Thompson's and Clinton's assertions that there are such things as women's issues or black issues contradict most fairgoers' assertions about the fundamental stability and rightness of the status quo, especially their idea that people who bring up race or gender are troublemakers who are simply "playing politics." Before the friendly crowd, Pickering also spent a good deal of his allotted time lamenting his father Charles Pickering's failure to win confirmation as a federal judge, a failure he attributed to his father's Southern Baptist religious faith, and not, for instance, civil rights groups' worries about Pickering's publication and voting record across four decades.[22]

Although some elements of the Mississippi stump tradition remain unchanged, in other ways the fair is a site where inversions of the state's traditional mores are sanctioned and even encouraged. Alcohol has always flowed freely at the fair, at least in some cabins. "It's a dry state," reported the *Memphis Press-Scimitar* in 1947, "but there's plenty of good drinking whisky around." That tradition had not changed by 1986, when a University of Southern Mississippi student declared, "It's illegal to drink. And we have drunk over 100 cases of beer in a weekend." A recent observer agreed that heavy drinking and the fair go together: "Eating is the primary fair entertainment for those who don't favor alcohol poisoning."[23] And since 1922, the fair's harness races represent the only legal horse racing in the state.

But in other matters old-time Mississippi mores are still tenaciously observed. Lott and Ashcroft might find Neshoba hospitality appealing, but others closer to home are less sanguine. "I've never been," said a thirty-four-year-old native of Philadelphia in 1991. "My father told me, 'The Neshoba County Fair is no place for black folks.'" Yet the fair has never been lily white. Black Mississippians have long had a place there, as jockeys, custodians, or characters in the segregationists' cautionary tales, but apparently African Americans are welcome even today only so long as they know their place. An incident in 1991 underscored the often unspoken ways in which atavistic racial etiquette still informs the Neshoba County Fair. Several black drivers withdrew from competition to protest the treatment of a black jockey after a disputed race was awarded to the only white jockey entered. Despite the jockey's complaints of physical abuse and racial slurs, the head of the fair's all-white, twenty-two-member board of directors doubted that any racism was involved. Making quite clear the role in which blacks were welcomed at the fair, the director remarked, "We've used black drivers since back in the '30s. I don't know of any problems."[24]

Not knowing of any problems with the state's past is a common theme at the fair. One wonders just what gubernatorial candidate Kirk Fordice had in mind during his successful 1991 campaign when he promised to deliver "an 'old-style stump speech' to the Neshoba audience." Some Mississippians heard in his fair rhetoric echoes of massive resistance and challenge to outsiders. After his election, Fordice continued to visit the fair, shouting to his audience in 1995: "I don't believe we need to run this state for 'Mississippi Burning,' referring to the movie about the Neshoba County murders. 'Never apologize! Never look back! Forward together.'" A decade earlier, former Governor John Bell Williams spoke confidently of Ronald Reagan's sympathy with the old time states' rights agenda: "I'm happy to say we have a president now who talks our language and we don't have to apologize." Andrew Young, at that time U.S. ambassador to the United Nations, on the other hand, found Reagan's willingness to speak states' rights language to the fair audience ill advised, given the county's history. The presence of Confederate flags and the singing and playing of "Dixie" continue to dismay many African Americans. "Many blacks," one man argued, "believe in an unwritten law of the fair: You can go out there. You can stand around at the pavilion on Founder's Square, go see the exhibits or go to the rides. But, no blacks in the cabins unless they are working for somebody."[25]

Robert Craycroft, the author of an architectural study of the Neshoba County Fair, called it "an intermittent yet continuing community, temporary yet permanent."[26] Craycroft observed that the fair's significance lies in its "annual reaffirmation of the institutions of family and community." Some years ago Cleanth Brooks wrote that "though we tend to praise the fact of community as a good thing (as in general we tend to praise unity or freedom as 'good' things) its goodness is not a priori or absolute . . . the South, as an authentic community, has held to some values that surely were, and are, questionable.[27] No one can expect to see the fair fade away any time soon, like other Jim Crow relics such as "White" and "Colored" signs, the poll tax, or Ross Barnett. For one thing, the fair is big business, bringing thousands of dollars of tax money to the county's coffers and big profits to the local Wal-Mart and other merchants: "The fair time compares favorably to Thanksgiving, Christmas and Fourth of July weekend."[28] Candidates for state and national office still flock to the fairgrounds to stump for votes. But in a county still working to overcome the notoriety it earned in 1964 as Americans looked in horror upon the murders of James Chaney, Andrew Goodman, and Michael Schwerner, the fair's supporters would be well served to consider how the fair perpetuates a racially divisive vision of community in the name of family and nostalgia. Instead, nostalgia might be shaped into memory and healing to make the fair indeed a "Giant House Party for all Mississippians," as the promotional literature proclaims.

Such claims are easier made than accomplished, however. For historians, social scientists, and policy makers in the South to treat white southerners' narratives of memory and identity lightly is to make a mistake. For one thing, it is naive to assume that white southerners will willingly accept a characterization of their past and present that points to deep flaws in their conceptualization of family and community. Insisting to people that the stories that they tell about themselves are racist or otherwise harmful is to invite disbelief or ridicule. The disappearance of overt narratives of whiteness and identity from southern public forums like textbooks, the political stump, and churches have not removed the need for the ordering and definition they performed. People visit relatives at the Neshoba County Fair, or embrace markers of southernness such as fried catfish, *Southern Living* magazine, or NASCAR, all without feeling a conscious thrill of racial hegemony. What, their defenders argue, do these customs and pastimes have to do with forgotten politicians and a legally discredited system of Jim Crow? These things are merely family, they say. Or tradition. Or fun. It is not pleasant to consider that explicit racism of the old style and a vaguer, still-present language of family and nostalgia not only serve the same ends, but also tell stories that are essentially parallel.

White southerners rightly insist that it is no longer 1965, and that the region has made real progress in dismantling the legal and other structural mechanisms that gave teeth to Jim Crow. But such an assertion, while correct, is not complete. To point to differences between the 1960s and the present may in fact serve as an argument, tacit or otherwise, that nothing profitable remains to be said about race, whether past or present.

Generations-old habits of thinking, speaking, and feeling cannot be changed overnight, and it is not cynicism to admit that fact. What, then, is to be done? First, it seems necessary to recognize, for whites, just how abruptly change seemed to come to the region, especially when coupled with the increasingly obstreperous and violent white resistance that accompanied the seeds of change. The late 1960s and early 1970s were thus difficult, uneasy years for the South, especially the Deep South. Black southerners were frustrated and impatient after years of Jim Crow and white foot dragging in the implementation of school integration and other social change. White southerners, especially those who grew up in the defiant years of the 1950s and 1960s, watched as the segregation that they had been taught was God-ordained and the only bulwark against chaos, crumbled beneath a grass-roots assault and the insistence of the federal government.[29]

When it comes to the stories that white southerners tell about themselves, their history, and their culture—what I have called in this book narratives of pan-white identity—white southerners who lived through the 1960s and 1970s have not sufficiently recognized the dissonance created by the social change of those years. More specifically, history has rarely seemed to give the South the time it has needed to absorb social change and to incorporate those changes into the stories it tells about itself and its values. Narratives of white community and black disorder had been deliberately ramped up just as the transition to a new legal and social order was underway. Those narratives had to disappear from public life, most whites accepted, some gladly, others grudgingly. Thus many southerners, black and white, chose in the 1970s for a variety of reasons, some self-serving, some pragmatic, to focus on negotiating the present rather than revisiting the past, and it seems unfair or at least unproductive to criticize them for those decisions.

But such an abrupt and basically unaddressed shift in formative, foundational narratives was bound to exact a price. Narratives of a basically homogeneous white community facing a common threat from black disorder shaped the region's culture in fundamental ways from the early nineteenth century through the civil rights movement of the 1950s and 1960s. Through the 1960s, of course, post-Reconstruction iterations of whiteness, blackness, order, and danger were reenergized in the South, particularly in places such as Mississippi, as the white establishment faced a civil rights movement predicated upon a wholesale rejection of narratives of benevolent white male authority.

During this period of challenge to white male authority, the gendered as well as racialized elements of the narratives of a white South showed themselves clearly. In *Black Monday,* his attack on the *Brown* decision, Yale-educated circuit court Judge Thomas Brady argued: "No true, loyal, Southern man will agree to [public school integration] or permit it. It shall not be!" Such resistance might bring economic or other hardships, but "This will be the acid test which the white men of the South will have to meet."[30] Along with this assertion that the affairs of the South were best ordered and maintained by the benevolent authority of white men, Brady's attack on *Brown* contains other central elements of turn-of-the-century white South narratives of white community and black threats to it. First, Brady asserts that the common threat posed by *Brown*—by disorderly blacks and their champions, that is— creates a community of interest stretching across the South, and indeed to all "seventeen States involved in the 'Black Monday' decision." Next, Brady repeats the claim, familiar since the antebellum period, that white southerners knew and understood black southerners, while other Americans did not. Brady writes: "If you had a negro mammy take care of you . . . if you played with negro boys . . . if you have worked with and among them, laughed at their ribald humor; if you can find it in your heart to overlook their obscenity and depravity . . . then you are beginning to understand the negro." Brady, then, repeats a familiar, sentimentalized image of the black southerner as good-natured clown.[31]

As his characterization of "the southern negro" continues, however, it becomes clear that what he is really offering is praise for the orderly, masterful, white southern man as clear and strong as that found in the plantation fiction of Thomas Nelson Page. First, Brady points to the "loyalty and devotion" that black southerners show to whites, a not-so-implicit rebuke to the Supreme Court and the social scientists on whom the *Brown* decision drew. Next, Brady contrasts the black man's irresponsibility to his home and family to the care and responsibility shown by white southern men to black families as well as their own:

> If you have had a negro man and his wife and children live and work with you on your place . . . if you have fed and clothed all of them and protected them from anyone *who would harm them* [emphasis in original] . . . if you bought the school books for their children . . . if you have bailed the husband out of jail on Monday morning . . . if you have taken him to the doctor and had his wounds treated, paid his bill and fine without expecting to be or having been reimbursed . . . if you have given him, in addition to his salary, extra money at Christmas time and at other times in order that he might buy some presents for the three or four illegitimate children which he acknowledges as his own, THEN you are beginning to know the negro and understand his problems.

Finally, much as Thomas Dixon and other turn-of-the-twentieth-century writers did, Brady explains what is truly at stake in maintaining white male control of the South: "The loveliest and purest of God's creatures, the nearest thing to an angelic being that treads this terrestrial ball is a well-bred, cultured Southern white woman or her blue-eyed, golden-haired little girl."[32]

In the 1960s, increasing pressure from a grass-roots civil rights movement, federal civil rights legislation, and the coming of school desegregation brought these narratives of white manhood, black disorder, and sexual danger to a shrill crescendo. In the late 1960s, when Brady's fellow white Mississippians began to realize that the *Brown* decision was finally going to be enforced, groups such as "Parents for Segregation" and "Americans for the Preservation of the White Race" began to unpack and explain in clearly gendered terms the threat that school desegregation posed. Despising the Mississippi state government's "knuckling under to Federal pressure," one group asked in revealingly gendered language, "don't you wish they would stand up and act like MEN instead of Federal pimps?"[33]

Mississippi's move to reestablish a compulsory school attendance law (it had been abolished in 1956) prompted one group to state flatly that the purpose of such a law was "to take white children from their parents and force them into association with negroes. . . . Integrated schools lead to interracial marriages."[34] The organization Americans for the Preservation of the White Race carried the narrative to its logical conclusion. Claiming that communists were behind the NAACP and the school integration movement, the APWR presented its cautionary tale in an easy-to-understand comic strip format, with distinct "stages" along the road to miscegenation: "Classes in High School Together" (showing not a schoolroom scene but a black boy and white girl in an embrace), "Calling on your Daughter," "Marrying your daughter" (perhaps accidentally, "daughter" is no longer capitalized), and finally, a befuddled-looking white man slapping his forehead in amazement upon meeting "Your grandchildren—one white—one black."[35]

Southern public culture no longer carries such overtly racialized messages of white womanhood and black defilement. At the Neshoba County Fair, for instance, the few candidates who do use the word "white" are marginal. In 2002 Jim Giles, an independent candidate for Mississippi's Third District seat, was not allowed by the Neshoba County Fair Association to participate in the debate. The association, citing its status as a private organization, refused to invite Giles to speak. Giles, a quasi-populist, fond of defending the Confederate flag and attacking the American invasion of Iraq, opined that the association was "scared of my white country rebels." Giles's Web site argues that "It's okay to put your own people first. Jews and Negroes do." Giles had no chance of winning Mississippi's Third District seat, and no one would suggest that Mississippi is any the poorer for failing to listen to his divisive rhetoric.

But the clear rejection of Giles by a great majority of white Mississippians leads too easily to the conclusion that racial exclusivity is confined to marginal characters, or is a relic of the 1960s, the 1950s, or earlier. On December 1, 2003, Mississippi State University hired Sylvester Crooms as the head coach of its football team. Crooms thus became the first African American head football coach in the history of the Southeastern Conference. The *Jackson Clarion-Ledger* celebrated with an editorial cartoon. The cartoon contained split panels, labeled 1953 and 2003. The first showed two young white men holding a newspaper telling of Mississippi State's hiring a football coach. "I hope he's white," says one boy to the other. The second panel shows presumably the same pair, but older, fatter, and presumably wiser. The same newspaper headline now elicits a far-different reaction. "I hope he's a winner," says one man to the other.[36] The cartoon is at once self-congratulatory and makes the not-so-subtle point that one has to return to the 1950s to find such racism in the state of Mississippi.

Panels labeled "1983" and "2003" would have made a rather different point. To admit that white Mississippi State fans might have objected to hiring a black coach any later than 1953—say in the 1960s, 1970s, and 1980s, when Mississippi State did hire head football coaches—would be to contradict the position taken since the early 1970s by semiofficial state organs like the *Jackson Clarion-Ledger.* Most white Mississippians are now willing to admit that while the state's past may have had its regrettable moments, all has been basically well in terms of race since 1970 or thereabouts. This narrative of a changed Mississippi seems as important to the state's culture today as the narratives of a white South that I have explored in this book were to the state and the region at the turn of the twentieth century. The Compromise of the 1970s, we might call it, like the Compromise of the 1890s, has allowed white Mississippians to save face and to retain power.

The white narrative of a changed South, one in which white supremacist attitudes and racism have simply melted away, manifests itself in most of the South's official rhetoric, and also in most of its everyday public language. Central to these stories of the region's past and present is the definition of racism as state-sanctioned, direct race-based oppression, such as Jim Crow laws or quasi-official lynching. Now that these unpleasantries are gone, racism is gone. For the most part, white southerners accept the Civil Rights Act, the Voting Rights Act, and the integration of the public schools, but this acceptance comes with a moratorium on public discussion of race. At the Neshoba County Fair and elsewhere in the state, the past for many white Mississippians is country best undiscovered. Anyone who argues otherwise is thus guilty of practicing racially divisive politics. The state's dead should bury their dead, so the argument goes. "Never look back!" as Governor Kirk Fordice told the Neshoba County Fair crowd in 1995.

This is not to say that nothing in the state has changed. By almost every quantifiable measure, the South is a better place for African Americans to live and work now than it was a generation or two ago. Many black Americans realize this fact, and are returning to the region, either to raise their families or to come to terms with their past. But the change for the better seems to have come at a price, especially in Mississippi: massive white population shift from the capital city of Jackson to its suburbs, a continued racial polarization of the state's political parties and occasionally its political campaigns, and an insistence by many white Mississippians that no substantive work on matters of race remains to be undertaken. Other Mississippians, white and black, realize that silence on race is not a useful strategy. Observing the 2003 state elections, Jackson State University political scientist Leslie McLemore argued: "Race is not going to be the overt factor, but is going to be an unspoken major factor in November. . . . That story has to be told, has to be analyzed." Mississippi State University's Marty Wiseman agreed: "We've got to talk about race."[37] There is in fact a good deal of public and private talk about race in the state, but not in ways that have resolved deeply rooted problems.

As Mount Olive native Ralph Eubanks wrote, "Though Mississippi is not the same place it used to be, the forces of its darker era can still rise up and make themselves known . . . coded speech . . . is still at work in Mississippi and plays a role in daily life." As an example of this coded speech, Eubanks cites the December 2002 political embarrassment of Trent Lott for statements Lott made at Senator Strom Thurmond's hundredth birthday party. Lott said: "I want to say this about my state: When Strom Thurmond ran for president, we voted for him. We're proud of it. And if the rest of the country had followed our lead, we would not have had all these problems over all these years, either."[38] Though Eubanks is no doubt correct that in Mississippi and the South generally, "forces of its darker era can still rise up," Lott's comments seem too sincere and too ingenuous to be coded speech. Lott knows very well what Mississippi was like as he grew up in the 1940s and 1950s, and as he attended the University of Mississippi during the James Meredith integration crisis. In praising Thurmond, Lott was hardly making a coded appeal for racist support of the Republican Party. Indeed, Senator Lott could point to a good record of constituent support for Mississippians of all races, not the least of which was his tenacious pursuit of big-dollar defense contracts for the state, especially his old congressional district.[39]

Instead, Lott's remarks are better understood as an example of the tenacious persistence of the old ways of talking about community, not only in Mississippi, but throughout much of the rest of the South. The following distinction may be subtle, but it seems vital: Mississippians, especially white Mississippians born in the 1940s and 1950s, have for the most part successfully accepted the fact that black Mississippians share with them the workplace, public schools, and places of public accommodation. But for many white Mississippians, their fundamental conceptions of community, of who "we" are, continue to be shaped by the racially polarizing narratives of the late–Jim Crow years. Trent Lott was, of course, too young in 1948 to have voted for Strom Thurmond. For him to say that "we" voted for Thurmond, then, makes sense only if at some level his conception of "we" means the broad community of white Mississippians, and not the disfranchised black Mississippians of that era. No black Mississippi politician, and there are now many, would ever say that "we" voted for Strom Thurmond. Finally, it is worth noting that after a brief period as the subject of foot-in-mouth editorial cartoons and as the butt of late-night television talk show hosts' jokes, Lott's political position in Mississippi quickly seemed as strong as ever. Ask almost any customer, wrote the *Jackson Clarion-Ledger* in 2003 after a visit to a restaurant in Lott's old congressional district, "and they'll tell you U.S. Sen. Trent Lott is no less than a hero."[40]

Is there truly no way to conceive of identity and community at the Neshoba County Fair, in Mississippi or in the South generally, other than in racialized terms? The highly influential work of Benedict Anderson suggests how people come to see themselves as part of a larger "imagined community."[41] But definitions of community can easily turn exclusionary, especially in cultures such as Mississippi's, with its history of legal and folkish segregation. Paradoxically, the less internally coherent the definition of community, the greater the need for sharp lines at some imagined edges. Certainly the history of the rhetoric of community in the South suggests that its uses have, on the whole, been questionable, to borrow from Cleanth Brooks. The difficulty comes in finding an equally satisfying way to conceptualize and discuss the aggregations in which human beings willingly or unwillingly find themselves. Probably the chief obstacle in addressing the divisive effects of white southerners' narratives of family, community, and identity is their refusal to see them for what they are—deeply racialized constructs with enormous power to shape the culture of which they are a part. The need for identity will not, of course, end. And conceptions of identity cannot change overnight. What faces the South is a daunting task. It flies in the face of much of southern history, not to say the larger history of nationalism and its Pandora's box of ills of the twentieth century. But this is perhaps a start. It is at least time for white southerners to cease insisting that their narratives of family, community, and belonging at places like the Neshoba County Fair—deeply rooted in New South visions of whiteness and blackness, gender and mastery, region and community, order and disorder—have nothing to do with race. They always have, and so long as the categories of whiteness and blackness continue to matter in America and the South, they always will.

In this new century, there are voices proclaiming, just as they did one hundred years ago and more, that a coalition of Yankees and racial equalizers intends menace toward the South. Organizations like the League of the South (called the Southern League until attorneys for the so-named baseball league noticed) talk of cultural and eventual political secession. Of course, few white southerners notice or take seriously the talk of groups such as the League of the South. But what *is* striking about groups like the League of the South is their rhetoric, which in its essentials is little different from that of a century ago: "Community is natural society—an organic matrix of values, memories, and blood ties . . . we must build a new community and institutions of our own. . . . For education we will homeschool today, but envision a Southern university tomorrow."[42]

White southerners at the turn of the twentieth century had, and intended to retain, political, cultural, and social power in their most fundamental forms. Land ownership, political participation, control of public space—all would be enforced, whether by law, custom, or eruptions of violence, as white realms. Definitions of the threatened domestic, crafted by New Southerners, and reshaped by later generations, continue to enable systems of racial control and prevent the formation of a broader community in the Deep South, although many white southerners display a tenacious refusal when it comes to seeing what is before their eyes. Perhaps this failure to see the shaping narratives of community, race, and power for what they are is understandable. Acknowledging them might exact a high price. Works of reconstruction can be messy. Marx observed that we make history from materials handed us from the past. But nowhere does he promise that ridding ourselves of the old ghosts will be easy.

NOTES

Introduction

Epigraph: Sallie Colvin, speaking to a Louisiana county fair, 1907; quoted in Ted Ownby, *Subduing Satan: Religion, Recreation and Manhood in the Rural South, 1865–1920* (Chapel Hill: University of North Carolina Press, 1990), 167.

1. Two excellent recent histories of southern uses of the past and southern identity generally are James C. Cobb, *Away Down South: A History of Southern Identity* (New York: Oxford University Press, 2005) and W. Fitzhugh Brundage, *The Southern Past: A Clash of Race and Memory* (Cambridge, Mass.: Harvard University Press, 2005). In studying the turn-of-the-century South, I have been influenced by the definition of culture provided by Clifford Geertz, who writes: "The concept of culture I espouse . . . is essentially a semiotic one. Believing, with Max Weber, that man is an animal suspended in webs of significance he himself has spun, I take culture to be those webs, and the analysis of it to be therefore not an experimental science in search of law but an interpretive one in search of meaning." Geertz, "Thick Description: Toward an Interpretive Theory of Culture," in *The Interpretation of Cultures: Selected Essays* (1973; reprint, New York: Basic Books, 2000), 5.

2. Basil Lanneau Gildersleeve, "The Creed of the Old South," in Maurice Garland Fulton, *Southern Life in Southern Literature: Selections of Representative Prose and Poetry* (Boston: Ginn and Co., 1917), 377–88; quote at 387. On the other hand, literary critic William P. Trent argued: "A 'Solid South' would seem to presuppose a homogeneous Southern people . . . but to draw this inference would be to make a mistake." Even so, Trent speaks throughout his essay of "the Southern people," "Southern civilization," and "Southern brethren." Further, Trent repeats the familiar argument that the civilization of the South was Cavalier, while that of the North was Puritan, and admits that "the institution of slavery gave a more or less uniform patriarchal tone to society in every Southern state." William P. Trent, "The Diversity Among Southerners," in Fulton, *Southern Life in Southern Literature*, 389–98; quote at 389. Black southerners do not figure as southerners in either scholar's account of the South. In thinking of the blood ties that constituted the South, Gildersleeve referred of course only to the acknowledged, legitimate blood ties.

3. In the past two decades historians have written extensively on whiteness as a racial category in the United States. This book draws on that scholarship, while recognizing that "whiteness studies" is a fluid, evolving field of inquiry. Below I indicate works I have found particularly helpful. On whiteness in a broad Western context, see Richard Dyer, *White* (London: Routledge, 1997). For excellent general works on whiteness in America, see the anthology *Critical White Studies: Looking Beyond the Mirror,* ed. Richard Delgado and Jean Stefancic (Philadelphia: Temple University Press, 1997); and Valerie Babb, *Whiteness Visible: The Meaning of Whiteness in American Literature and Culture* (New York: New York University Press, 1998). The best study of whiteness in the American South is Grace Elizabeth Hale, *Making Whiteness: The Culture of Segregation in the South, 1890–1940* (New York: Pantheon, 1998). Pioneering works on American whiteness, dealing

principally with the nineteenth century, are those of David R. Roediger, Noel Ignatiev, and Alexander Saxton. See Roediger, *The Wages of Whiteness: Race and the Making of the American Working Class* (London: Verso, 1991), and *Toward the Abolition of Whiteness: Essays on Race, Politics and Working Class History* (London: Verso, 1994); Ignatiev, *How the Irish Became White* (New York: Routledge, 1995); and Saxton, *The Rise and Fall of the White Republic: Class Politics and Mass Culture in Nineteenth-Century America* (London: Verso, 1990). For a useful attempt to define more rigorously whiteness studies, see Birgit Brander Rasmussen, Eric Klinenberg, Irene J. Nexica, and Matt Wray, ed., *The Making and Unmaking of Whiteness* (Durham, N.C.: Duke University Press, 2001). For an attempt to complicate explorations of whiteness, see Matt Wray and Annalee Newitz, ed., *White Trash: Race and Class in America* (New York: Routledge, 1997). Some historians have proved skeptical of this scholarship, criticizing it as ahistorical or insufficiently rigorously defined. See Eric Arnesen, "Whiteness and the Historians' Imagination," *International Labor and Working Class History* 60 (Fall 2001): 2–32. On public skepticism of whiteness studies, see Darryl Fears, "Hue and Cry on 'Whiteness Studies,'" *Washington Post* 20 June 2003; thanks to Marc Kilmer for bringing this story to my attention. I share most scholars' conviction that the idea of race has a complex history that overshadows any asserted biological or genetic foundations of the concept. Barbara J. Fields writes: "Race is a product of history, not of nature." Fields stresses the economic roots of racialist thought in America. See Fields, "Ideology and Race in American History," in J. Morgan Kousser and James M. McPherson, ed., *Region, Race, and Reconstruction: Essays in Honor of C. Vann Woodward* (New York: Oxford University Press, 1982), 143–77; quote at 152. For works that stress the intellectual and cultural history of race, see George M. Frederickson, *The Black Image in the White Mind: The Debate on Afro-American Character and Destiny, 1817–1914* (Hanover, N.H.: Wesleyan University Press, 1987), orig. ed. 1971; and Winthrop Jordan, *White Over Black: American Attitudes Toward the Negro, 1550–1812* (Chapel Hill: University of North Carolina Press, 1968). Frederickson rightly cautions that "strictly 'idealist' or strictly 'materialist'" explanations fail to account for the "complex interplay between culture and society" that produces racialist thought. See Frederickson, *Black Image,* xiii. See also Thomas C. Holt, *The Problem of Race in the Twenty-First Century* (Cambridge, Mass.: Harvard University Press, 2000).

4. Hilary A. Herbert, ed., *Why the Solid South?* (New York: Negro Universities Press, 1969), 438; orig. ed. 1890.

5. As I argue in chapters 1 and 2, a central trope of narratives of white southern identity was that of the white household under assault by blacks, a charge that lent authority to white oppression of blacks. "One of the key ways of constructing moral power," writes Linda Williams, "is the icon of the good home." See Williams, *Playing the Race Card: Melodramas of Black and White from Uncle Tom to O. J. Simpson* (Princeton, N.J.: Princeton University Press, 2001), 7.

6. "War and emancipation shook the antebellum household to its foundations," argues Laura Edwards, "destabilizing the configuration of private and public power it supported." See Edwards, *Gendered Strife and Confusion: The Political Culture of Reconstruction* (Urbana and Chicago: University of Illinois Press, 1997), 7. On the broader public context of contemporary southern family and household, see Peter W. Bardaglio, *Reconstructing the Household: Families, Sex, and the Law in the Nineteenth-Century South* (Chapel Hill: University of North Carolina Press, 1995). On black and white understandings of the household in the Mississippi Delta during the Civil War and Reconstruction, see Nancy D. Bercaw, *Gendered Freedoms: Race, Rights and the Politics of Household in the Delta, 1861–1875* (Gainesville: University Press of Florida, 2003).

7. Frances Willard quoted in Michael A. McGerr, *A Fierce Discontent: The Rise and Fall of the Progressive Movement in America, 1870–1920* (New York: Free Press, 2003), 53. McGerr characterizes such a rhetorical move as "[s]wathing aggressive intentions in the reassuring warmth of home and hearth." McGerr, *Fierce Discontent,* 54. On southern progressivism, see Dewey W. Grantham, *Southern Progressivism: The Reconciliation of Progress and Tradition* (Knoxville: University of Tennessee Press, 1983); William A. Link, *The Paradox of Southern Progressivism, 1880–1930* (Chapel Hill: University of North Carolina Press, 1992); Marjorie Spruill Wheeler, *New Women of the New South: The Leaders of the Woman Suffrage Movement in the Southern States* (New York: Oxford University Press, 1993).

8. See Link, *Paradox of Southern Progressivism,* 58–91.

9. On the power of narrative and metaphor to forge a community's sense of identity, see the pioneering work of Benedict Anderson, *Imagined Communities: Reflections on the Origin and Spread of Nationalism,* 2nd ed. (New York: Verso, 1991); Ernest Gellner, *Nations and Nationalism* (Ithaca, N.Y.: Cornell University Press, 1983); Eric Hobsbawn and Terence Ranger, ed., *The Invention of Tradition* (Cambridge, U.K.: Cambridge University Press, 1983). On broader American ideas of a collective identity, see Michael Kammen, *Mystic Chords of Memory: The Transformation of Tradition in American Culture* (New York: Vintage: 1991). For a collection of essays emphasizing the contingency and historical context of assertions of one category of identity, see Werner Sollors, *The Invention of Ethnicity* (New York: Oxford University Press, 1989).

10. My understanding of narrative is informed by Peter Brooks, *Reading for the Plot: Design and Intention in Narrative* (Cambridge, Mass.: Harvard University Press, 1984). Brooks writes: "We live immersed in narrative, recounting and reassessing the meaning of our past actions, anticipating the outcome of our future projects, situating ourselves at the intersection of several stories not yet completed" (3). In the last two decades scholars in the social sciences and humanities have produced fruitful examinations of the narratives and rhetoric of their disciplines. See, for instance, John S. Nelson, Allan Megill, and Donald McCloskey, *The Rhetoric of the Human Sciences: Language and Argument in Scholarship and Public Affairs* (Madison: University of Wisconsin Press, 1991); Donald N. McCloskey, *If You're So Smart: The Narrative of Economic Expertise* (Chicago: University of Chicago Press, 1992).

11. Richard Gray, "Inventing Communities, Imagining Places," in Suzanne W. Jones and Sharon Monteith, ed., *South to a New Place: Region, Literature, Culture* (Baton Rouge: Louisiana State University Press, 2002), xix.

12. See Douwe Draaisma, *Metaphors of Memory: A History of Ideas about the Mind,* trans. Paul Vincent (Cambridge, U.K.: Cambridge University Press, 2000), 10. He continues: "Precisely what the relationship is between two contexts, how metaphors are related to reality or whether all metaphors can be exchanged for literal descriptions, even whether literal descriptions exist at all—there is a fundamental lack of consensus on all these matters" (10).

13. See, for example, Zoltan Kovecses, *Metaphor: A Practical Introduction* (New York: Oxford University Press, 2002); Sheldon Sacks, ed., *On Metaphor* (Chicago: University of Chicago Press, 1979).

14. For a historian's examination of the stakes involved in interpreting a familiar icon, see Holly Beachley Brear, "We Run the Alamo, and You Don't: Alamo Battles of Ethnicity and Gender," in W. Fitzhugh Brundage, ed., *Where These Memories Grow: History, Memory and Southern Identity* (Chapel Hill: University of North Carolina Press, 2000), 299–317.

For a collection of essays, articles, and court decisions on recent Confederate flag controversies in the South, including the 2001 Mississippi state flag referendum, see the archive maintained by the University of Mississippi School of Law, available at http://library.law.olemiss.edu/library/news/flag.shtml (accessed 11 May 2003).

15. For instance, Joel Williamson points out that the figure of the "'nigger beast'" assaulting white women was a fixture of turn-of-the-century rhetoric, a "scene that came all too easily to Southern white minds." See Williamson, *The Crucible of Race: Black-White Relations in the American South Since Emancipation* (New York: Oxford University Press, 1984), 116. For an older examination of white southern iconography and myth, see W. J. Cash, *The Mind of the South* (New York: Knopf, 1941).See Anne Firor Scott, *The Southern Lady: From Pedestal to Politics, 1830–1930* (Chicago: University of Chicago Press, 1970). See Jane Turner Censer, *The Reconstruction of White Southern Womanhood, 1865–1895* (Baton Rouge: Louisiana State University Press, 2003).

16. For an excellent study of the broader history of white southern narratives, see Scott Romine, *The Narrative Forms of Southern Community* (Baton Rouge: Louisiana State University Press, 1999). Romine's is a study of narratives strictly construed: fiction and memoir from A. B. Longstreet through William Faulkner and beyond. On representations of the South in American culture since the 1930s, see Tara McPherson, *Reconstructing Dixie: Race, Gender, and Nostalgia in the Imagined South* (Durham, N.C.: Duke University Press, 2003). For an examination of a later genre of white southern narrative of identity, see Fred Hobson, *But Now I See: The White Southern Racial Conversion Narrative* (Baton Rouge: Louisiana State University Press, 1999). See also Hobson's study of southern self-examination, *Tell About the South: The Southern Rage to Explain* (Baton Rouge: Louisiana State University Press, 1983). Hobson terms southern apologists "the Southern school of remembrance" (5).

17. Fred Hobson refers to white southerners who criticized the region's racism and other flaws as the "school of shame and guilt." See his discussion of Louisiana's George Washington Cable in Hobson, *Tell About the South,* 106–26.

18. Richard Gray, "Foreword: Inventing Communities, Imagining Places: Some Thoughts on Southern Self-Fashioning," in Jones and Monteith, *South to a New Place,* xiii–xxiii; quote at xvii.

19. Classic studies of the making of Lost Cause and New South ideology are Gaines M. Foster, *Ghosts of the Confederacy: Defeat, the Lost Cause, and the Emergence of the New South, 1865–1913* (New York: Oxford University Press, 1987); Charles Reagan Wilson, *Baptized in Blood: The Religion of the Lost Cause* (Athens: University of Georgia Press, 1980); Paul M. Gaston, *The New South Creed: A Study in Southern Mythmaking* (New York: Knopf, 1970).

20. See David Goldfield, *Still Fighting the Civil War: The American South and Southern History* (Baton Rouge: Louisiana State University Press, 2002), 33. Goldfield adds: "What distinguished white southerners from other Americans is that they set about to create a heritage, not to re-create a history" (33).

21. Stephanie McCurry, *Masters of Small Worlds: Yeoman Households, Gender Relations and the Political Culture of Antebellum South Carolina* (New York: Oxford University Press, 1995), 92–93, 240, and elsewhere. The Genoveses' work on slaveholders and the patriarchal ideal includes Eugene D. Genovese, *Roll, Jordan, Roll: The World the Slaves Made* (New York: Random House, 1972), and Elizabeth Fox-Genovese, *Within the Plantation Household: Black and White Women of the Old South* (Chapel Hill: University of

North Carolina Press, 1988). See also William K. Scarborough, *Masters of the Big House: Elite Slaveholders of the Mid-Nineteenth-Century South* (Baton Rouge: Louisiana State University Press, 2003). For a reminder that white male mastery over household and dependents was neither universally recognized nor absolute, see Laura F. Edwards, "Law, Domestic Violence, and the Limits of Patriarchal Authority in the Antebellum South," in Nancy Bercaw, ed., *Gender and the Southern Body Politic* (Jackson: University Press of Mississippi, 2000), 63–86.

22. Some southern historians have called for a moratorium on the question of the persistence of southern identity. See, for example, Ted Ownby, "'Does the South Still Exist?': A Historian's Critique of the Question," *Crossroads: A Journal of Southern Culture* 5 (Spring 1998): 3–12. Within the academy, a contrary position is presented in the work of John Shelton Reed. See, for instance, Reed, *The Enduring South: Subcultural Persistence in Mass Society* (Chapel Hill: University of North Carolina Press, 1974).

23. See Edward L. Ayers, "What We Talk about When We Talk about the South," in Ayers, Patricia Nelson Limerick, Stephen Nissenbaum, and Peter S. Onuf, ed., *All Over the Map: Rethinking American Regions* (Baltimore: Johns Hopkins University Press, 1996), 62–82.

24. The "separate spheres" concept is prescriptive, and fails to indicate that American men and women did not lead nearly so neatly gendered an existence. I employ it here for two reasons. It was language that late-nineteenth-century Americans used. Second, that it was prescriptive rather than descriptive makes it more rather than less useful for my purpose, which is to explore the forces in southern society doing the prescribing and setting the boundaries. Barbara Welter, "The Cult of True Womanhood: 1820–1860," *American Quarterly* 18 (Summer 1966): 151–74; Nancy F. Cott, *The Bonds of Womanhood: "Woman's Sphere" in New England, 1780–1835* (New Haven, Conn.: Yale University Press, 1977); Linda Kerber and others, "Beyond Roles, Beyond Spheres: Thinking about Gender in the Early Republic," *William and Mary Quarterly* 3, no. 46 (July 1989): 565–85; Linda Kerber, "Separate Spheres, Female Worlds, Woman's Place: The Rhetoric of Women's History," *Journal of American History* 75 (June 1988): 9–39. For a further critique, see Cathy N. Davidson and Jessamyn Hatcher, ed., *No More Separate Spheres!* (Durham, N.C.: Duke University Press, 2002).

25. From the 1890s until the 1960s, mainstream historiography concurred with white southerners, characterizing Reconstruction-era southern state governments as corrupt failures. A widely read work of popular history is Claude Bowers, *The Tragic Era: The Revolution After Lincoln* (New York: Blue Ribbon Books, 1929).

26. V. O. Key, *Southern Politics in State and Nation* (1949; reprint, Knoxville: University of Tennessee Press, 1984), 233.

27. Joseph B. Parker, ed., *Politics in Mississippi,* 2nd ed. (Salem, Wisc.: Sheffield, 2001), 4.

28. Jane Tompkins, "'Indians': Textualism, Morality, and the Problem of History," *Critical Inquiry* 13 (Autumn 1986): 101–19; quote at 115.

29. For a recent narrative survey, see Leon F. Litwack, *Trouble in Mind: Black Southerners in the Age of Jim Crow* (New York: Knopf, 1998).

30. The best recent survey of what Howard Rabinowitz called the "First New South" is Edward L. Ayers, *The Promise of the New South: Life After Reconstruction* (Oxford, U.K.: Oxford University Press, 1992); on the volatility of the New South, see especially 3–33. See Rabinowitz, *The First New South, 1865–1920* (Arlington Heights, Ill.: Harlan Davidson, 1992). The classic account remains C. Vann Woodward, *Origins of the New South, 1877–1913*

(Baton Rouge: Louisiana State University Press, 1951). Also see the relevant chapters in Dewey W. Grantham, *The South in Modern America: A Region at Odds* (New York: Harper Collins, 1994).

31. For a narrative survey of these years that emphasizes class, ethnic, racial, and gender tensions, see Nell Irvin Painter, *Standing at Armageddon: The United States, 1877–1919* (New York: Norton, 1987). See also McGerr, *Fierce Discontent;* Gail Bederman, *Manliness and Civilization: A Cultural History of Gender and Race in the United States, 1880–1917* (Chicago: University of Chicago Press, 1995); and Alan Trachtenberg, *The Incorporation of America: Culture and Society in the Gilded Age* (New York: Hill and Wang, 1982).

32. Charles W. Kent, *The Revival of Interest in Southern Letters* (Richmond, Va.: B. F. Johnson, 1901), 8, 4. On the intellectual history of the South, see the work of Michael O'Brien, especially *The Idea of the American South, 1920–1941* (Baltimore: Johns Hopkins University Press, 1979), and *Rethinking the American South: Essays in Intellectual History* (Baltimore: Johns Hopkins University Press, 1988).

33. Ayers, *Promise of the New South,* 411.

34. Holland Thompson, *The New South* (New Haven, Conn.: Yale University Press, 1919), 5.

35. George Frederickson observes that the South "push[ed] the principle of differentiation by race to its logical outcome—a kind of *Herrenvolk* society in which people of color . . . are treated as permanent aliens or outsiders." Frederickson, *White Supremacy: A Comparative Study in American and South African History* (New York: Oxford University Press, 1981), xi–xii. W. J. Cash famously argued that the defense of slavery created a "proto-Dorian bond of white men" in the South. Cash, *Mind of the South,* 111. Unlike Cash, I examine here the assertion and operation of such a bond at this historical moment without assuming that it operated seamlessly or consistently. On asserted white manhood in an earlier period and in a broader context, see Dana D. Nelson, *National Manhood: Capitalist Citizenship and the Imagined Fraternity of White Men* (Durham, N.C.: Duke University Press, 1998).

36. Quoted in McGerr, *Fierce Discontent,* 187.

37. Barbara Fields writes: "White supremacy is a slogan, not a belief. And it is a slogan that cannot have meant the same to all white people. Those who invoke it as a way of minimizing the importance of class diversity overlook this simple but basic point." See Fields, "Ideology and Race in American History," 156. Like Fields, I recognize that class diversity marked the New South. But I argue here that assertions of white supremacy and white community served to complicate and obscure class differences among white southerners.

38. Thompson, *The New South,* 140. See William A. Link, ed., *The Rebuilding of Old Commonwealths and Other Documents of Social Reform in the Progressive Era South* (Boston and New York: Bedford, 1996), 36. For a study of southern community that employs the metaphor of family, see Jacquelyn Dowd Hall, James Leloudis, and others, *Like a Family: The Making of a Southern Cotton Mill World* (New York: Norton, 1987). "Again and again in our interviews," write the authors, "people chose a family metaphor to describe mill village life" (xvii). William A. Link writes that at the end of the nineteenth century most white southerners worried that "disorder and conflict among whites comprised the most dangerous threat of the racial powder keg." See Link, *Paradox of Southern Progressivism,* 58. Though muted in dominant public discourse, the rhetoric of pan-white southernness can still be easily found, especially on the Internet. The Council of Conservative Citizens explained that

black activists, northern liberals, and other forces have long targeted "the values of the traditional white South." Web site available at http://www.cofcc.org/ourwar2.htm (accessed 10 February 2003).

39. Kantrowitz, *Ben Tillman and the Reconstruction of White Supremacy* (Chapel Hill: University of North Carolina Press, 2000), 3, 2. Kantrowitz writes that in Ben Tillman's South, "The meanings of 'manhood' and 'womanhood' were open to question and contest, as were the meanings of 'black' and 'white'" (4).

40. For a sophisticated examination of the political and social effects of the rhetoric of white supremacy, see Glenda E. Gilmore, *Gender and Jim Crow: Women and the Politics of White Supremacy in North Carolina, 1896–1920* (Chapel Hill: University of North Carolina Press, 1996).

41. In examining the work of another group of culturally dominant texts, Scott Romine writes that they demonstrate "how a hegemonic social order in a given place and time attempted to resolve its internal conflicts and legitimate its hegemony," a description that aptly fits the process I see here. See Romine, *Narrative Forms of Southern Community,* 4.

42. On turn-of-the-century white impressions of blacks, see Frederickson, *Black Image,* 256–82.

43. Dunbar Rowland, *Mississippi: Comprising Sketches of Counties, Towns, Events, Institutions, and Persons, Arranged in Cyclopedic Form* (Spartanburg, S.C.: Reprint Company, 1976), 1:853; orig. ed. 1907. On railroads in the New South, see Ayers, *Promise of the New South,* 9–13. Scholars are now producing a rich body of literature on memory and identity in the late-nineteenth and twentieth-century South. For a representative example, see Brundage, ed., *Where These Memories Grow.* See also Jacquelyn Dowd Hall, "'You Must Remember This': Autobiography as Social Critique," *Journal of American History* 85 (September 1998): 439–65.

44. W. Fitzhugh Brundage, "White Women and the Politics of Historical Memory in the New South, 1880–1920," in Jane Dailey, Glenda E. Gilmore, and Bryant Simon, ed., *Jumpin' Jim Crow: Southern Politics from Civil War to Civil Rights* (Princeton, N.J.: Princeton University Press, 2000), 115–39; quote at 126. For an excellent study of white southern women's efforts to shape public memory of the Confederate experience, see Karen L. Cox, *Dixie's Daughters: The United Daughters of the Confederacy and the Preservation of Confederate Culture* (Gainesville: University Press of Florida, 2003).

45. Mayes quoted in Thomas N. Boschert, "A Family Affair: Mississippi Politics, 1882–1932," (PhD diss., University of Mississippi, 1995), 19.

46. See Woodward, *Thinking Back: The Perils of Writing History* (Baton Rouge: Louisiana State University Press, 1986), 15. Link, ed., *Rebuilding of Old Commonwealths,* 29.

47. See Grace Elizabeth Hale, *Making Whiteness: The Culture of Segregation in the South, 1890–1940* (New York: Random House, 1998), xi; Williamson, *Crucible of Race.* For Williamson's categories of racial conservative, moderate, and radical, see *Crucible of Race,* 5–7.

48. See especially Hale, *Making Whiteness,* 121–97. I do, however, recognize in chapter 2 the powerful effect of popular fiction, itself a form of popular consumption.

49. Stephen Greenblatt, "Culture," in Frank Lentricchia and Thomas McLaughlin, ed., *Critical Terms for Literary Study* (Chicago: University of Chicago Press, 1990), 230.

50. James C. Cobb, *The Most Southern Place on Earth: The Mississippi Delta and the Roots of Regional Identity* (New York: Oxford University Press, 1992), vi.

Chapter 1

Epigraphs: Quoted in David M. Oshinsky, *"Worse Than Slavery": Parchman Farm and the Ordeal of Jim Crow Justice* (New York: The Free Press, 1996), 90; Barnett quote available at http://www.usnews.com/usnews/issue/980330/30miss.htm (accessed 20 January 2001); James W. Silver, *Mississippi: The Closed Society* (New York: Harcourt, Brace, 1964), 34.

1. *New York Times,* 2 January 1963, 9. The Rebels finished the regular season with a 9-0 record, and defeated Arkansas 17-13 in the 1963 Sugar Bowl. The team was ranked third in the nation in the final Associated Press poll. During the integration crisis, *Time* recognized the university's "perennially powerful football team," and characterized Ole Miss as a "cheerfully unintellectual institution." *Time* 5 October 1962, 16.

2. See Charles W. Eagles, *The Price of Defiance: James Meredith and the Integration of Ole Miss* (Chapel Hill: University of North Carolina Press, 2009), 336–37.

3. Wright Thompson, "Ghosts of Mississippi," *ESPN Outside the Lines;* available at http://sports.espn.go.com/espn/eticket/story?page=mississippi62 (accessed 19 March 2009).

4. Eagles, *The Price of Defiance,* 333–34; Silver, *Mississippi,* 118–19; Russell H. Barrett, *Integration at Ole Miss* (Chicago: Quadrangle, 1965), 121–22; Erle Johnston, *Mississippi's Defiant Years, 1953–1973* (Forest, Miss.: Lake Harbor, 1990), 153–58; Derek C. Catsam, "The Jackass Brays: Massive White Resistance to the Integration of Ole Miss" (master's thesis, University of North Carolina at Charlotte, 1996), 21–30. As Catsam notes, in different sources the lyrics to this tune vary slightly. This song suggests that supporters of Ole Miss were aware of the racial implications of the university's Confederate symbols. During the governor's race in 1964, a campaign poster for Paul B. Johnson Jr., Ross Barnett's lieutenant governor, "showed Ole Miss's Colonel Rebel kicking John Kennedy and carried the caption 'Forget, Hell! I'm standing with Paul Johnson.'" See W. Ralph Eubanks, *Ever is a Long Time: A Journey Into Mississippi's Dark Past: A Memoir* (New York: Basic Books, 2003), 63. For an account of Ole Miss concentrating on the Meredith years and after, see Nadine Cohodas, *The Band Played Dixie: Race and the Liberal Conscience at Ole Miss* (New York: Free Press, 1997). See also Frank Lambert, *The Battle of Ole Miss: Civil Rights v. States' Rights* (New York: Oxford University Press, 2010).

5. Erle Johnston, *I Rolled with Ross: A Political Portrait* (Baton Rouge, La.: Moran, 1980), 2. The story is more complicated than Johnston suggests. Before the Meredith crisis, Barnett was not a consistently popular governor, and in fact was booed at an earlier appearance at an Ole Miss football game. See Cohodas, *Band Played Dixie,* 83. In 1963 Johnston became head of Mississippi's State Sovereignty Commission, an executive-branch agency charged with shielding the state from desegregation efforts. See Yasuhiro Katagiri, *The Mississippi State Sovereignty Commission: Civil Rights and States' Rights* (Jackson: University Press of Mississippi, 2001), 119.

6. Johnston, *I Rolled with Ross,* 3–4. After the integration of Ole Miss, the following bumper stickers appeared in the state: "Made in Occupied Mississippi," "Mississippi: Kennedy's Hungary," and "The Castro Brothers 'Have Moved into the White House.'" Barrett, *Integration at Ole Miss;* see the illustrations following 128. See also William Doyle,

An American Insurrection: The Battle of Oxford, Mississippi, 1962 (New York: Doubleday, 2001) and Charles W. Eagles, "'The Fight for Men's Minds': The Aftermath of the Ole Miss Riot of 1962," *Journal of Mississippi History* 71 (Spring 2009): 1–53.

7. C. Vann Woodward, "The Search for Southern Identity," in *The Burden of Southern History* (Baton Rouge: Louisiana State University Press, 1968), 11–12. The essay was originally published in *Virginia Quarterly Review* 34 (1958): 258–67.

8. Quoted in Barrett, *Integration at Ole Miss,* 122.

9. See Doyle, *American Insurrection,* 109–12; 316.

10. Barnett died in 1987, but contemporary Mississippians are regularly reminded of the former governor: five miles northeast of Jackson lies the fifty-two-square-mile Ross Barnett Reservoir. Created in 1965, the year after Barnett left office, the reservoir is used for flood control and water supply, but chiefly for boating, fishing, and other recreational use. "If you drove in [to Jackson], then it's likely you saw at least one highway sign, probably many more, pointing to it. . . . Named for a former governor who supported segregation in fist-pounding speeches, The Rez, as we Jacksonians like to call it, now provides tons of fun for everyone." *Jackson Clarion-Ledger,* "Discover Greater Jackson." Available online at http://www.clarionledger.com/discover2001/q28.html (accessed 12 October 2003).

11. *Jackson Clarion-Ledger,* 12 October 2003.

12. *Jackson Clarion-Ledger,* 5 October 2003. On the renaming of New Orleans public schools named for slaveholders, including George Washington, see *New Orleans Times-Picayune,* 5 April 1988; on the commemoration of Arthur Ashe on Richmond's Monument Boulevard and larger issues of public commemoration, see Kirk Savage, "The Life of Memorials," *Harvard Design Magazine* 9 (Fall 1999), 1–5; available online at http://www.gsd. harvard.edu/research/publications/hdm/back/9savage.pdf (accessed 3 October 2003). There is a large literature considering the influence of "southern" institutions and culture on the larger American nation. A good recent example is Peter Applebone, *Dixie Rising: How the South is Shaping American Values, Politics, and Culture* (New York: Harcourt Brace, 1996). An equally old and vast literature contends that the distinctiveness of the South is disappearing or has disappeared (with different writers, of course, hold varying opinions whether this is a good or bad thing). See John Egerton, *The Americanization of Dixie: The Southernization of America* (New York: Harper's Magazine Press, 1974). A provocative popular study of southern identity and the commemoration of the South's past is Tony Horwitz, *Confederates in the Attic: Dispatches from the Unfinished Civil War* (New York: Pantheon, 1998).

13. James K. Vardaman, [speech delivered to the Mississippi House of Representatives on 14 March 1904], Letterbook, Administration of James K. Vardaman, Governor's Office, Mississippi Department of Archives and History (hereafter MDAH), Jackson, Mississippi.

14. Quoted in Thomas D. Clark, *The Southern Country Editor* (Indianapolis: Bobbs-Merrill Company, 1948), 228.

15. Dewey W. Grantham, *The Life and Death of the Solid South: A Political History* (Lexington: University Press of Kentucky, 1988), 32.

16. Bureau of Governmental Research, *Inaugural Addresses of the Governors of Mississippi, 1890–1980* (Oxford: University of Mississippi), 29, 20, 21, 22, 23. On post-Reconstruction celebrations of national unity, see David W. Blight, *Race and Reunion: The Civil War in American Memory* (Cambridge, Mass.: Harvard University Press, 2001), and

Nina Silber, *The Romance of Reunion: Northerners and the South, 1865–1900* (Chapel Hill: University of North Carolina Press, 1993), especially 159–96.

17. See, for instance, John B. Boles, *The South Through Time: A History of an American Region* (Englewood Cliffs, N.J.: Prentice Hall, 1995), 401–7. There is a large literature considering just what a southern demagogue is, just who ought to be considered one, and whether the term is in fact useful. Some standard biographies are Raymond Arsenault, *The Wild Ass of the Ozarks: Jeff Davis and the Social Bases of Southern Politics* (Knoxville: University of Tennessee Press, 1988); William F. Holmes, *The White Chief: James Kimble Vardaman* (Baton Rouge: Louisiana State University Press, 1970); Francis Butler Simkins, *Pitchfork Ben Tillman: South Carolinian* (Baton Rouge: Louisiana State University Press, 1944); and C. Vann Woodward, *Tom Watson: Agrarian Rebel* (New York: Macmillan, 1938). See Robert Dean Pope, "Of the Man at the Center: Biographies of Southern Politicians from the Age of Segregation," in *Region, Race, and Reconstruction: Essays in Honor of C. Vann Woodward,* J. Morgan Kousser and James M. McPherson, ed. (Oxford, U.K.: Oxford University Press, 1982), 89–112. See also Allan Michie and Frank Rhylic, *Dixie Demagogues* (New York: Vanguard Press, 1939); Wilma Dykeman, "The Southern Demagogue," *Virginia Quarterly Review* 33 (Autumn 1957): 558–69; Allan Louis Larson, "Southern Demagogues: A Study in Charismatic Leadership" (PhD diss., Northwestern University, 1964); "The Demagogue," in *The Oratory of Southern Demagogues,* ed. Cal M. Logue and Howard Dorgan (Baton Rouge: Louisiana State University Press, 1981), 1–11. The most sophisticated recent study of a turn-of-the-century southern politician is Stephen Kantrowitz, *Ben Tillman and the Reconstruction of White Supremacy* (Chapel Hill: University of North Carolina Press, 2000).

18. The best biography of Vardaman is Holmes, *White Chief.* See also Holmes, "James Kimble Vardaman," in *The Encyclopedia of Southern History,* ed. David C. Roller and Robert W. Twyman (Baton Rouge: Louisiana State University Press, 1979), 1270. Uncritical and much less satisfactory is George C. Coleman, *James Kimble Vardaman: Southern Commoner* (Jackson, Miss.: Hederman Brothers, 1981). An admiring contemporary study is Archibald S. Coody, *Biographical Sketches of James Kimble Vardaman* (Jackson, Miss.: A. S. Coody, 1922).

19. A long-influential account of Mississippi politics in the Vardaman era is Albert D. Kirwan, *The Revolt of the Rednecks: Mississippi Politics, 1876–1925* (Lexington: University of Kentucky Press, 1951); see also Charles Granville Hamilton, *Progressive Mississippi* (Aberdeen, Miss.: n.p., 1978). Two good, more recent studies are Boschert, "A Family Affair," and Stephen Cresswell, *Multiparty Politics in Mississippi, 1877–1902* (Jackson: University Press of Mississippi, 1995). See also Cresswell, *Rednecks, Redeemers, and Race: Mississippi After Reconstruction, 1877–1917* (Jackson: University Press of Mississippi, 2006), especially 190–212.

20. See William M. Strickland, "James Kimble Vardaman: Manipulation Through Myths in Mississippi," in *The Oratory of Southern Demagogues,* ed. Cal M. Logue and Howard Dorgan (Baton Rouge: Louisiana State University Press, 1981), 66–82. A newspaper opposed to Vardaman maintained that he was "only playing on the passions and prejudices of the populace in order to obtain office." *Jackson Clarion-Ledger,* 13 August 1903.

21. William Alexander Percy, *Lanterns on the Levee: Recollections of a Planter's Son* (1941; reprint, Baton Rouge: Louisiana State University Press, 1973); quoted in Holmes, *White Chief,* v.

22. John Ray Skates, *Mississippi: A Bicentennial History* (New York: W. W. Norton, 1979), 129, 131.

23. Vardaman's rhetoric was popular in the North as well as the South. "'He was applauded frequently,' came one report from Crookston, Minnesota, 'and many persons crowded forward to shake his hand after the meeting. Most of these were women.'" Williamson, *Crucible of Race,* 379. For an attempt at a measured assessment of Vardaman, see Nannie Pitts McLemore, "James K. Vardaman: A Mississippi Progressive," *Journal of Mississippi History* 24 (February 1967): 1–11. But for a reminder of how Vardaman's reform agenda was shaped by his attitudes toward black Mississippians, see Oshinsky, *"Worse Than Slavery,"* 85–106.

24. Thomas C. Holt, "Marking: Race, Race-Making, and the Writing of History," *American Historical Review* 100 (February 1995): 3.

25. See Cresswell, *Multiparty Politics in Mississippi,* especially 126–55; Boschert, "A Family Affair," 61–79; Kirwan, *Revolt of the Rednecks,* 40–49.

26. Bradley G. Bond, *Political Culture in the Nineteenth-Century South: Mississippi, 1830–1900.* (Baton Rouge: Louisiana State University Press, 1995), 285; Creswell, *Multi-Party Politics in Mississippi,* 198.

27. Traditionally, historians stress regional or class divisions among Mississippi whites of the period, with many historians viewing the rise to power of men like Vardaman as a "redneck revolt." See Kirwan, *Revolt of the Rednecks;* Grantham, *Life and Death of the Solid South,* 32; Skates, *Mississippi,* 127–28; Cobb, *Most Southern Place on Earth,* 176. Cobb argues that "many Delta aristocrats readily professed a greater degree of respect and compassion for blacks than for whites on the lower rungs of the socioeconomic ladder" (177). For such impressions, Cobb and others draw upon William Alexander Percy's autobiography, *Lanterns on the Levee,* an influential if unrepresentative account. In terms of education, cosmopolitanism, and elite sensibilities, Percy had few peers in the Delta or elsewhere in the state. Further, while I do not mean to take easy potshots at Percy for his paternalistic views, it is difficult to imagine that many black Mississippians felt that he or other Delta planters treated them with much respect or compassion.

28. Boschert, "A Family Affair," 17. Boschert adds that electoral reforms such as the 1902 primary law "tightened restrictions on primary voting" and concludes that "its primary purpose was to preserve the traditional patterns of white rule" (173).

29. Quoted in Boschert, "A Family Affair," 125.

30. Bradley G. Bond, *Mississippi: A Documentary History* (Jackson: University Press of Mississippi, 2003), 153.

31. See Grantham, *Southern Progressivism.* See also Grantham's "Review Essay: The Contours of Southern Progressivism," in *American Historical Review* 86 (December 1981): 1039–59. For two works that explore the complex interplay of race and reform in the South, see Jack Temple Kirby, *Darkness at the Dawning: Race and Reform in the Progressive South* (Philadelphia: Lippincott, 1972); and Bruce Clayton, *The Savage Ideal: Intolerance and Intellectual Leadership in the South, 1890–1914* (Baltimore: Johns Hopkins University Press, 1972).

32. *Brookhaven Semi-Weekly Leader,* 27 July 1907.

33. *Jackson Clarion-Ledger,* 3 September 1903.

34. Williams, *Playing the Race Card,* xiv.

35. Vardaman was not alone, of course, in understanding that public perceptions of race relations and southern history were most effectively inscribed in the language of fiction. Consider the tremendous influence of his contemporary, Thomas W. Dixon, and for a less obvious example, Thomas Nelson Page, the subjects of chapter 2 here. As Martha Vicinus sees it, melodrama "refers pejoratively to an excess of emotion, disproportionate to the object, excessively simplified characters who appeal to each other and the audience by means of exaggerated expressions of right and wrong, and many remarkable and improbable coincidences, spectacular effects, and plot complications." Martha Vicinus, "'Helpless and Unfriended': Nineteenth-Century Melodrama," *New Literary History* 8, no. 1 (Autumn 1981): 127. On the work of domestic fiction in the post–Civil War United States, see Silber, *Romance of Reunion.*

36. Nancy Armstrong, *Desire and Domestic Fiction: A Political History of the Novel* (New York: Oxford University Press, 1987), 21. Although Armstrong writes of British fiction, her insights are valid for the United States for an age when British cultural productions exercised such a strong hold upon American markets and tastes.

37. Jane Tompkins, *Sensational Designs: The Cultural Work of American Fiction, 1790–1860* (New York: Oxford University Press, 1985), xvii.

38. See J. Morgan Kousser, *The Shaping of Southern Politics: Suffrage Restriction and the Establishment of the One-Party South, 1880–1910* (New Haven, Conn.: Yale University Press, 1974); Michael Perman, *Struggle for Mastery: Disfranchisement in the South, 1888–1908* (Chapel Hill: University of North Carolina Press, 2001).

39. I have drawn this term from Judith R. Walkowitz, *City of Dreadful Delight: Narratives of Sexual Danger in Late-Victorian London* (Chicago: University of Chicago Press, 1992), see especially 5–13.

40. Quoted in Williamson, *Crucible of Race,* 379.

41. See Pete Daniel, "Cotton Culture," in *Encyclopedia of Southern Culture,* ed. William R. Ferris and Charles Reagan Wilson (Chapel Hill: University of North Carolina Press, 1989), 34; see also Pete Daniel, *Breaking the Land: The Transformation of Cotton, Rice, and Tobacco Cultures since 1880* (Urbana: University of Illinois Press, 1985).

42. A McComb newspaper observed in 1905: "A very large crowd of negroes were here on circus day, but money among them must have been scarce, for not more than half the crowd entered the show." *McComb City Enterprise,* 30 November 1905.

43. On southern revivalism, see Ownby, *Subduing Satan,* 144–64. On shopping and consumerism in turn-of-the-century Mississippi, see Ted Ownby, *American Dreams in Mississippi: Consumers, Poverty, and Culture, 1830–1998* (Chapel Hill: University of North Carolina Press, 1999), 82–97.

44. Nannie Pitts McLemore, "The Progressive Era," in *A History of Mississippi,* ed. Richard A. McLemore (Jackson: University Press of Mississippi, 1973), 2:43.

45. The direct primary, adopted in 1903, replaced the state's much-criticized convention system.

46. George C. Osborn, "Mississippi's Closest Senatorial Contest: John Sharp Williams and James K. Vardaman, 1907," *Journal of Mississippi History* 12 (1950): 203.

47. For a common national reaction to Vardaman, see *New York Times,* 8 February 1907; 3 August 1907.

48. Quoted in Dunbar Rowland, *Mississippi; Comprising Sketches of Counties, Towns, Events, Institutions, and Persons, Arranged in Cyclopedic Form* (Atlanta: Southern Historical Publishing Association, 1907), 2:852.

49. *Meridian Weekly Star,* 19 June 1902, quoted in Orleane Pope Bolian, "The Meaning of James K. Vardaman" (master's thesis, Tulane University, 1933), 11.

50. *New Orleans Times-Democrat,* 17 October 1902, quoted in Bolian, "Meaning of James K. Vardaman," 18.

51. *Memphis Scimitar,* 17 October 1902, quoted in Bolian, "Meaning of James K. Vardaman," 18.

52. Bolian, "Meaning of James K. Vardaman," 18.

53. *The Greenwood Commonwealth,* 24 October 1902, quoted in Bolian, "Meaning of James K. Vardaman," 18–19.

54. *Greenwood Commonwealth,* 31 October 1902, quoted in Bolian, "Meaning of James K. Vardaman," 19.

55. James W. Loewen and Charles Sallis, ed., *Mississippi: Conflict and Change* (New York: Pantheon, 1974), 193.

56. James W. Garner, "A Mississippian on Vardaman," *Outlook* 75 (12 September 1903): 139.

57. Boschert, "A Family Affair," 177.

58. Rowland, *Mississippi; Comprising Sketches,* 2:854.

59. Percy, *Lanterns on the Levee,* see especially the chapter "Bottom Rail on Top" (140–55), where Percy writes of Vardaman: "A likable man, as a poolroom wit is likable, but surely not one to set in the councils of the nation. . . . He was not a moral idiot of genius like Huey Long; he was merely an exhibitionist playing with fire" (144).

60. Garner, "Mississippian on Vardaman," 139.

61. Quoted in Boschert, "A Family Affair," 192.

62. *New York Times,* 3 August 1907.

63. James E. Watson, *As I Knew Them* (New York: Bobbs-Merrill, 1936), 284.

64. Willie Morris, *North Toward Home* (Boston: Houghton Mifflin, 1967), 8.

65. See, however, Boschert, "A Family Affair," especially 175–293.

66. Woodward, *Origins of the New South,* 272. On the naming of a Highway 49 bridge over the Yazoo River for Williams, see *Mississippi Code of 1972, As Amended,* SEC. 65-3-71.8. "John Sharp Williams Memorial Bridge" designated; available at: http://www.mscode. com/free/statutes/65/003/0071.8.htm (accessed 1 November 2003). On Williams's portrait (along with those of former Mississippi senators Jefferson Davis, L. Q. C. Lamar, and Pat Harrison) in Cochran's office, see Barbara Lago, "Path to Power," *UM Lawyer* (Fall/Winter 2002–3); available at: http://www.olemiss.edu/depts/law_school/UM%20 LAWYER/UMlaw/pathtopower.html (accessed 1 November 2003). See Williamson, *Crucible of Race,* 364.

67. John Sharp Williams, "Issues of the War Discussed," *Confederate Veteran* 12 (November 1904); available online at: http://members.cox.net/confed/1904/article14.html (accessed 1 November 2003).

68. See John C. Willis, *Forgotten Time: The Yazoo-Mississippi Delta After the Civil War* (Charlottesville: University Press of Virginia, 2000). Also, Robert L. Brandfon, *Cotton Kingdom of the New South: A History of the Yazoo Mississippi Delta from Reconstruction to the Twentieth Century* (Cambridge, Mass.: Harvard University Press, 1967).

69. Quoted in Cobb, *Most Southern Place on Earth,* 5.

70. George C. Osborn, *John Sharp Williams: Planter-Statesman of the Deep South* (Baton Rouge: Louisiana State University Press, 1943). The only other full-length study is Harris Dickson, *An Old-Fashioned Senator: A Story-Biography of John Sharp Williams* (New York: Frederick A. Stokes Company, 1925).

71. Quoted in Rayford W. Logan, *The Betrayal of the Negro: From Rutherford B. Hayes to Woodrow Wilson* (1954; reprint, New York: Collier Books, 1965), 99.

72. The U.S. Supreme Court case *Williams v. Mississippi,* 170 US 213 1898, arose from a challenge by a black Mississippian to his conviction for murder by an all-white jury. The Supreme Court held unanimously that the suffrage restrictions of the 1890 Mississippi constitution were constitutional. See J. Morgan Kousser, "Williams v. Mississippi," in *Encyclopedia of Southern History,* 1345–46.

73. Neil R. McMillen, *Dark Journey: Black Mississippians in the Age of Jim Crow* (Urbana: University of Illinois Press, 1989), xv.

74. *McComb City Enterprise,* 18 January 1906.

75. Quoted in Nan Elizabeth Woodruff, *American Congo: The African American Freedom Struggle in the Delta* (Cambridge, Mass.: Harvard University Press, 2003), 151.

76. *Yazoo Herald,* quoted in *Greenwood Commonwealth,* 12 April 1907.

77. Williams to J. F. Gray, 10 January 1907, George C. Osborn Collection, Accretion, MDAH.

78. Williams to E. A. Ringold, 26 April 1912, George C. Osborn Collection, Accretion, MDAH.

79. *Yazoo Herald,* quoted in *Greenwood Commonwealth,* 12 April 1907.

80. See Woodward, *Origins of the New South,* 321–49; Kousser, *Shaping of Southern Politics,* 139–45; and James P. Coleman, "The Mississippi Constitution of 1890 and the Final Decade of the Nineteenth Century," in *A History of Mississippi,* ed. Richard A. McLemore (Jackson: University and College Press of Mississippi, 1973), 2:3–28.

81. John Sharp Williams to R. L. East, 11 January 1907, George C. Osborn Collection, Accretion, MDAH.

82. See Frederick Palmer, "Williams-Vardaman Campaign," *Collier's* 39 (27 July 1907): 11–12.

83. Laura Nan Fairley and James T. Dawson, *Paths to the Past: An Overview History of Lauderdale County, Mississippi* (Meridian, Miss.: Lauderdale County Department of Archives and History, 1988), 91–105.

84. Rowland, *Mississippi; Comprising Sketches,* 2:221.

85. William D. Jelks to James K. Vardaman, 21 December 1906, Governor's Office, Administration of James K. Vardaman, Correspondence, MDAH.

86. Jelks shared Vardaman's conviction that education spoiled black southerners, maintaining that "for the most part, the negro teacher . . . has either taught the beauty of idleness and the decency of theft, or has, at least, made no impression to the contrary on the plastic mind of the child." Quoted in I. A. Newby, *Jim Crow's Defense: Anti-Negro Thought in America, 1900–1930* (Baton Rouge: Louisiana State University Press, 1965), 178. See also William Dorsey Jelks, "The Acuteness of the Negro Question," *North American Review* 174 (15 February 1907): 391–94.

87. Quoted in McMillen, *Dark Journey*, 226.

88. Ibid., 232.

89. Ibid., 1.

90. Garrard Harris, *Harper's Weekly* (11 February 1905), quoted in Bolian, "Meaning of James K. Vardaman," 44.

91. Harris, quoted in Bolian, "Meaning of James K. Vardaman," 44.

92. James K. Vardaman, "Biennial Message of Gov. Jas. K. Vardaman to the Legislature of Mississippi," Governor's Office, Administration of James K. Vardaman, Correspondence, 3 January 1906, 24, MDAH.

93. Ibid., 24.

94. *Jackson Clarion-Ledger,* 7 October 1906.

95. For general accounts of the debate, see *Meridian Weekly Star,* 4 July 1907; 5 July 1907.

96. *Meridian Weekly Star,* 5 July 1907.

97. Williams to Vardaman, 16 February 1907, Williams Papers, Official Archives, RG #59, Container #1, Box 1, MDAH.

98. Vardaman to Williams, 1 March 1907, Williams Papers.

99. Osborn, "Mississippi's Closest Senatorial Contest," 199.

100. Holmes, *White Chief,* 186; Woodward, *Origins of the New South,* 375; Osborn, "Mississippi's Closest Senatorial Contest," 213.

101. *Jackson Clarion-Ledger,* 27 November 1906.

102. *Meridian Weekly Star,* 5 July 1907.

103. "Hon. John Sharp Williams Replies to Gov. Vardaman," *Jackson Clarion-Ledger,* 12 February 1907.

104. "Great Speech of John Sharp Williams," *Jackson Clarion-Ledger,* 27 November 1906.

105. John Sharp Williams, "'Tariff Barons' and 'Tariff Beggars.' Trusts. The Mississippi constitution and supremacy of the white man's code of ethics; his family life and civilization" [speech delivered to the Mississippi House of Representatives, 24 February 1902], MDAH.

106. John Sharp Williams, "Address to Company 'A,' Confederate Veterans," 31 May 1904, MDAH, 10, 11.

107. *Jackson Clarion-Ledger,* 27 November 1906.

108. "Hon. John Sharp Williams Replies to Gov. Vardaman," *Jackson Clarion-Ledger,* 12 February 1907.

109. *Meridian Weekly Star,* 5 July 1907.

110. On Vardaman's distaste for imperialism, see Kirwan, *Revolt of the Rednecks,* 178–85; Holmes, *White Chief,* 184–89.

111. Dudley Weldon Woodard and Charles Banks, *Negro Progress in a Mississippi Town, Being a Study of Conditions in Jackson, Mississippi* (Cheyney, Pa.: Committee of Twelve for the Advancement of the Interests of the Negro Race, 1909), 7.

112. Vicinus, "Nineteenth-Century Domestic Melodrama," 128. See also Peter Brooks, *The Melodramatic Imagination* (New Haven, Conn.: Yale University Press, 1976).

113. *Jackson Clarion-Ledger,* 21 July 1907; quoted in Holmes, *White Chief,* 188.

114. On the mammy figure in the postbellum period, see Grace Elizabeth Hale, *Making Whiteness: The Culture of Segregation in the South, 1890–1940* (New York: Pantheon, 1998), 85–119; for an examination of America's best-known mammy figure, see M. M. Manring, *Slave in a Box: The Strange Career of Aunt Jemimah* (Charlottesville: University Press of Virginia, 1998).

115. See, for instance, Gilbert M. Hoffman, *Dummy Lines Through the Longleaf: A History of the Sawmills and Logging Railroads of Southwest Mississippi* (Oxford: Center for the Study of Southern Culture, University of Mississippi, 1992); Ayers, *Promise of the New South: Life After Reconstruction,* 123–31.

116. B. W. Whittington to James K. Vardaman, n.d. [1907?], Governor's Office, Administration of James K. Vardaman, Correspondence, MDAH.

117. *Jackson Clarion-Ledger,* 27 November 1906.

118. *Meridian Weekly Star,* 4 July 1907.

119. Quoted in Osborn, *John Sharp Williams,* 214.

120. Ibid., 215.

121. Rowland, *Mississippi; Comprising Sketches,* 1:308–9.

122. On the visit to Brookhaven, see *Brookhaven Semi-Weekly Leader,* 27 July 1907.

123. Quoted in *Brookhaven Semi-Weekly Leader,* 17 July 1907.

124. See *Brookhaven Semi-Weekly Leader,* 18 May 1910; *Lincoln County Times,* 19 May 1910. See Julius E. Thompson, *The Black Press in Mississippi, 1865–1985: A Directory* (West Cornwall, Conn.: Locust Hill Press, 1988), 60, 88.

125. Osborn, "Mississippi's Closest Senatorial Contest," 209.

126. Williams to Hunter S. Williams, 10 June 1907, quoted in Osborn, *John Sharp Williams,* 209.

127. Logan wrote unambiguously that "The last decade of the nineteenth century and the opening of the twentieth century marked the nadir of the Negro's status in American society." See Logan, *Betrayal of the Negro,* 62.

128. Ralph Ellison writes that "Southern whites cannot walk, talk, sing, conceive of laws or justice, think of sex, love, the family or freedom without responding to the presence of

Negroes." Ellison, *Shadow and Act* (London: Secker and Warburg, 1964; reprint, New York: Vintage, 1972), 116.

129. Quoted in Nannie Pitts McLemore, "The Progressive Era," in Richard Aubrey McLemore, ed., *A History of Mississippi* (Jackson: University and College Press of Mississippi, 1973) 2:44.

130. Quoted in McMillen, *Dark Journey*, 240.

131. Bertram Wyatt-Brown, *The House of Percy: Honor, Melancholy, and Imagination in a Southern Family* (New York: Oxford University Press, 1994), 187; see also 178–91.

132. Nannie Pitts McLemore, "The Progressive Era," in Richard Aubrey McLemore, ed., *A History of Mississippi* 2:49–54; Percy, *Lanterns on the Levee*, 143–53. Percy added: "The herd is on the march, and when it stampedes, there's blood galore and beauty is china under its hoofs" (153).

133. Percy, *Lanterns on the Levee*, 143–51; quote at 149. William Alexander Percy laid the blame for much of the region's ills at the feet of the "poor whites," a group that in Percy's vague description sounds like a majority of the South's white population. Of them he writes: "I can forgive them as the Lord God forgives, but admire them, trust them, love them—never." Percy, *Lanterns on the Levee*, 20.

134. Hamilton, *Progressive Mississippi*, 103.

135. Holmes, *White Chief*, 187.

136. "Longino's Negro Record," *Vardaman's Weekly*, 17 July 1919.

137. "Hanging Negroes for Rape," *Vardaman's Weekly*, 19 June 1919.

138. Quoted in Dunbar Rowland, *History Of Mississippi: The Heart Of The South* (Chicago: S. J. Clarke, 1925), 2:652.

Chapter 2

Epigraphs: Thomas W. Dixon Jr., *The Clansman: An Historical Romance of the Ku Klux Klan* (1905; reprint, with an introduction by Thomas D. Clark, Lexington: University Press of Kentucky, 1970), 150–51; Thomas Nelson Page, *The Old Dominion; Her Making and Her Manners* (New York: Scribner's, 1908), 272–73.

1. The literature on Page and Dixon is large, and in recent years has become increasingly sophisticated. Two excellent studies of race and American literature are Sandra Gunning, *Race, Rape, and Lynching: The Red Record of American Literature, 1890–1912* (New York: Oxford University Press, 1996), and Mason Stokes, *The Color of Sex: Whiteness, Heterosexuality, and the Fictions of White Supremacy* (Durham, N.C.: Duke University Press, 2001). There are also many fine essays in Anne Goodwyn Jones and Susan V. Donaldson, ed., *Haunted Bodies: Gender and Southern Texts* (Charlottesville: University Press of Virginia, 1997).

2. In addition to the implied, often oblique whiteness inscribed in westerns such as Owen Wister's *The Virginian*, much popular turn-of-the-century fiction very explicitly engaged racialist, eugenicist ideas. Along with Jack London's well-known *Call of the Wild* (1903), see his Klondike tales, *The Son of the Wolf* (Boston: Houghton Mifflin, 1900), and *South Sea Tales* (New York: Macmillan, 1911). On American imperialism and the making of white

identity, see Matthew Frye Jacobson, *Whiteness of a Different Color: European Immigrants and the Alchemy of Race* (Cambridge, Mass.: Harvard University Press, 1998), 203–22. On idealized white manhood in the Progressive Era, see John F. Kasson, *Houdini, Tarzan, and the Perfect Man: The White Male Body and the Challenge of Modernity in American* (New York: Hill and Wang, 2001), especially 3–19.

3. Alexander Saxton, *The Rise and Fall of the White Republic: Class Politics and Mass Culture in Nineteenth-Century America* (New York: Verso, 2003; orig. ed. 1990), 377. See also Matthew Basso, Laura McCall, and Dee Garceau, ed., *Across the Great Divide: Cultures of Manhood in the American West* (New York: Routledge, 2001), especially 109–68.

4. Glenda Elizabeth Gilmore, *Gender and Jim Crow: Women and the Politics of White Supremacy in North Carolina, 1896–1920* (Chapel Hill: University of North Carolina Press, 1996), 137–38.

5. Sandra Gunning argues that the "black male body, hypersexualized and criminal-ized, has always functioned as a crucial and heavily determined metaphor in an evolv-ing national discourse on the nature of a multiethnic, multiracial American society." See Gunning, *Race, Rape, and Lynching,* 3.

6. Caroline Gebhard, "Reconstructing Southern Manhood: Race, Sentimentality, and Camp in the Plantation Myth," in Jones and Donaldson, ed., *Haunted Bodies,* 132–55; quote at 133.

7. Eric J. Sundquist, *To Wake the Nations: Race in the Making of American Literature* (Cambridge, Mass.: Harvard University Press, 1993), 426.

8. Quoted in Jacobson, *Whiteness of a Different Color,* 207.

9. Stokes, *Color of Sex,* 134.

10. First published in *Century* ["Meh Lady: A Story of the War," *Century* 32 (October 1886): 187–96, "Marse Chan," *Century* 27 (April 1884): 932–42] and later in 1887 as *In Ole Virginia* (New York: Scribner's, 1887). On Page, see Hobson, *Tell About the South,* 133–57. See also Matthew R. Martin, "The Two-Faced New South: The Plantation Tales of Thomas Nelson Page and Charles W. Chesnutt," *Southern Literary Journal* 30 (Spring 1998): 17–36; Lucinda H. MacKethan, "Thomas Nelson Page: The Plantation as Arcady," *Virginia Quarterly Review* 54 (1978): 314–32; Joseph B. Keener, *Shakespeare and Masculinity in Southern Fiction: Faulkner, Simms, Page, and Dixon* (New York: Palgrave McMillan, 2008), 43–72.

11. Theodore L. Gross, *Thomas Nelson Page* (New York: Twayne Publishers, 1967), 7.

12. Grace King, *Memories of a Southern Woman of Letters* (New York: MacMillan, 1932), 377; quoted in Michael Flusche, "Thomas Nelson Page: The Quandary of a Literary Gentle-man," *Virginia Magazine of History and Biography* 84 (1976): 464.

13. Gross, *Thomas Nelson Page,* 8.

14. Flusche, "Thomas Nelson Page," 471.

15. Nina Silber, *The Romance of Reunion: Northerners and the South, 1865–1900* (Chapel Hill: University of North Carolina Press, 1993).

16. Quoted in Edmund Wilson, *Patriotic Gore: Studies in the Literature of the American Civil War* (New York: Oxford University Press, 1962), 606.

17. Quoted in Flusche, "Thomas Nelson Page," 465.

18. Flusche, "Thomas Nelson Page," 465. Fred Hobson argues too that Page "had a political intent." Hobson, *Tell About the South,* 137.

19. Wilson, *Patriotic Gore,* 613.

20. Armistead Gordon recalls one of Page's southern and western reading tours in "Thomas Nelson Page: An Appreciation," *Scribner's Magazine* (January 1923): 79–80. After hearing Page read "Marse Chan," a southern listener wrote: "To us of younger years that sad romance / Seems like some legend of the days of old. / As when King Arthur and his knights drew lance / Ere yet the flame of chivalry grew cold." Quoted in Gordon, "Thomas Nelson Page," 80.

21. Edwin Mims, "Thomas Nelson Page," in *Southern Writers, Biographical and Critical Studies* (Nashville: Church, 1903), 2:137. Mims spent much of his career at Vanderbilt University, though generally at odds with the University's Fugitives and Agrarians. For a biographical sketch of the progressive Mims, see Randall G. Patterson, "Edwin Mims," in *Southern Writers: A Biographical Dictionary,* ed. Robert Bain, Joseph M. Flora, and Louis D. Rubin Jr. (Baton Rouge: Louisiana State University Press, 1979), 310–12.

22. Hobson, *Tell About the South,* 134; Page, *Red Rock: A Chronicle of Reconstruction* (New York: Scribner's, 1898), vi–viii.

23. Gross, *Thomas Nelson Page,* 14. There is no satisfactory biography of Page. Harriet Holman, "The Literary Career of Thomas Nelson Page, 1884–1910" (PhD diss., Duke University, 1947), is useful. Page's brother is the author Rosewell Page, who penned *Thomas Nelson Page: A Memoir of a Virginia Gentleman* (New York: Scribner's, 1923).

24. A biographical sketch written shortly after Page's death saw "Uncle Gabe's White Folks" as semiautobiographical, calling it "a tender story in the negro vernacular, depicting the affectionate relations between the races as he had known them on the old plantation." Gordon, "Thomas Nelson Page," 79.

25. Albion Tourgée, "The South a Field for Fiction," *Forum* 6 (1888–89): 406–8. Tourgèe authored a semiautobiographical novel detailing the thankless task of reconciling white southerners to Reconstruction experiments in democracy. See Tourgée, *A Fool's Errand* (New York: Fords, Howard and Hulbert, 1879).

26. Page, *The Novels, Stories, Sketches, and Poems of Thomas Nelson Page,* Plantation Edition (New York: Scribner's, 1906–18), 10:293.

27. As a spoof of such efforts as Page's, Mark Twain wrote a similar foreword to his *Adventures of Huckleberry Finn.* "In this book a number of dialects are used, to wit: the Missouri negro dialect; the extremest form of the backwoods Southwestern dialect; the ordinary 'Pike County' dialect; and four modified varieties of this last. The shadings have not been done in a haphazard fashion, or by guesswork; but painstakingly, and with the trustworthy guidance and support of personal familiarity with these several forms of speech. I make this explanation for the reason that without it many readers would suppose that all these characters were trying to talk alike and not succeeding."

28. Toni Morrison, *Playing in the Dark: Whiteness and the Literary Imagination* (Cambridge, Mass.: Harvard University Press, 1992), 68.

29. All parenthetical citations to "Marse Chan" are to Page, "Marse Chan," in *In Ole Virginia, Or, Marse Chan and Other Stories,* Southern Classic Series, ed. M. E. Bradford (Nashville: J. S. Sanders, 1991). The narrator maintains that the landscape was "most significant of the character of the race" that once inhabited it (1).

30. Wilson, introduction to *In Ole Virginia,* xv.

31. Gebhard, "Reconstructing Southern Manhood," in Jones and Davidson, ed., *Haunted Bodies,* 142.

32. Here is the same political constellation (that of moderate Whig versus secessionist Democrat) that we will find in Thomas Dixon's fiction, examined later in the chapter. Fred Hobson notes Page's use of Whigs as heroes and Democrats as villains; see Hobson, *Tell About the South,* 137.

33. By the late 1880s one of the things that *was* gone with the wind was the memory that the South had ever had a Whig Party. In the era of the Democratic Solid South, few white politicians pointed out that the "White Man's Party," as the southern "Democracy" proudly called itself, faced stiff Whig opposition from the 1830s through the 1850s. Especially after the Populist challenge of the 1890s, Democrats preferred to invoke the specter of what might happen should the white vote be split, rather than remember a time when it was—regularly and competitively in many southern states. See Michael F. Holt's authoritative study *The Rise and Fall of the American Whig Party: Jacksonian Politics and the Onset of the Civil War* (New York: Oxford University Press, 1999).

34. Noah's son Ham (*Genesis* 9) was a stock figure in antebellum defenses of slavery. Having looked on his father's drunken nakedness, so the story was interpreted, Ham and his descendents were doomed to serve as hewers of wood and drawers of water for their brothers and their progeny. But in Page's use of Ham, the biblical story intersects with a postbellum commonplace: that slavery was in fact a burden to the slave owners, rather than the slaves, and that holding slaves was philanthropy toward a benighted race.

35. The work of social and cultural historians on the Civil War and Reconstruction era is now rich. On gender in the period, see, for instance, LeeAnn Whites, *The Civil War as a Crisis in Gender: Augusta, Georgia, 1860–1890* (Athens: University of Georgia Press, 1995), George Rable, *Civil Wars: Women and the Crisis of Southern Nationalism* (Urbana: University of Illinois Press, 1989), Victoria E. Bynum, *Unruly Women: The Politics of Social and Sexual Control in the Old South* (Chapel Hill: University of North Carolina Press, 1992), Edwards, *Gendered Strife and Confusion,* and Silber, *Romance of Reunion.*

36. Gebhard, "Reconstructing Southern Manhood," in Jones and Davidson, ed., *Haunted Bodies,* 135, 139, 142, 133.

37. Thomas Nelson Page, "Recollections and Reflections," typescript, n.d., *Thomas Nelson Page Papers,* Special Collections, Duke University Library, Durham, North Carolina. I am grateful to Professor Fred A. Bailey of Abilene Christian University for supplying me with a copy of this document. Page included the same account of the genesis of "Marse Chan" in the preface to the Plantation Edition of his works (New York: Scribner's, 1892): 1:xii. See also Edwin Mims, "Thomas Nelson Page," in *Southern Writers* (Nashville: Church, 1903), 2:134–35.

38. One thinks, for instance, of Nathaniel Hawthorne's *Scarlet Letter,* Emily Brontë's *Wuthering Heights,* Mary Shelley's *Frankenstein,* or Henry James's *The Turn of the Screw,* all of which use frame stories and found documents to account for the romantic or the improbable in their narratives.

39. His tale told, Sam humbly receives money from the white listener, a continuation of Page's darkface performance in the text.

40. Wilson, *Patriotic Gore,* 615.

41. Gunning, *Race, Rape, and Lynching,* 22. See also Thomas W. Dixon Jr., *The Leopard's Spots; A Romance of the White Man's Burden, 1865–1900* (New York: Doubleday, Page, 1903).

42. Older studies of Dixon include Raymond A. Cook, *Fire from the Flint: The Amazing Careers of Thomas Dixon* (Winston-Salem, N.C.: John F. Blair, 1968), and Cook, *Thomas Dixon* (New York: Twayne, 1974). See Joel Williamson's subtle reading of Dixon and *The Leopard's Spots* in *Crucible of Race,* 140–76; Judith Jackson Fossett, "(K)night Riders in (K)night Gowns: The Ku Klux Klan and Constructions of Masculinity," in *Race Consciousness: African-American Studies for the New Century,* ed. Judith Jackson Fossett and Jeffrey A. Tucker (New York: New York University Press, 1997), 35–49; Glenda Elizabeth Gilmore, "'One of the Meanest Books': Thomas Dixon Jr., and *The Leopard's Spots," North Carolina Literary Review* 2, no. 1 (Spring 1994): 87–101; Keener, *Shakespeare and Masculinity in Southern Fiction,* 73–107; Michele K. Gillespie and Randal L. Hall, ed., *Thomas Dixon Jr., and the Birth of Modern America* (Baton Rouge: Louisiana State University Press, 2006).

43. See, for instance, Williamson, *Crucible of Race,* 140–41.

44. On the Klan's use of *Birth of a Nation,* see David M. Chalmers, *Hooded Americanism: The History of the Ku Klux Klan* (Durham, N.C.: Duke University Press, 1987), 23–27, 29–30, 32, 420, 430. Interestingly, Dixon despised the revived "Renegade Klan," as he called it: "Its persecution of the negro race under the conditions of modern life is utterly uncalled for, stupid and inhuman." In the wake of Klan violence in Louisiana in 1924, Dixon argued: "There can be but one end to a secret order of disguised men. It will grow eventually into a reign of terror which only martial law will be able to put down." Quoted in Chalmers, *Hooded Americanism,* 93. Note that Dixon was considered by some of his contemporaries an authority on the Klan and issues of law and order.

45. Thomas D. Clark, introduction to *The Clansman,* v.

46. Dixon, *The Clansman,* 149.

47. James Kinney, "The Rhetoric of Racism: Thomas Dixon and the 'Damned Black Beast,'" *American Literary Realism, 1870–1910* 15 (Autumn 1982): 145–54. I depart from Kinney's reading of Dixon as a man out of sympathy with the progressive reforms of his era. Segregation clearly partook of Progressive-era ideals of management, order, and eugenics. That blacks were objects to be ordered (problems, as Du Bois remarked) does not make segregation any less modern in temper.

48. He wrote a trilogy on socialism—*The One Woman* (1903), *Comrades* (1909), and *The Root of All Evil* (1911). Dixon opposed the ruinous imposition of social equality, contending that socialism threatened home, family, and society.

49. Williamson, *Crucible of Race,* 158. Williamson writes: "As an event in the life of Thomas Dixon, *The Leopard's Spots* was an attempt by him to achieve a psychic cure. . . . Central to this psycho-play was the setting of himself aright in relation to his mother" (164–65).

50. Dixon, "An Author's Answer to His Critics," *New York Times* (9 August 1902). He continued: "There is not a bitter or malignant line in it. It may shock the prejudices of those who worshipped the negro as canonized in 'Uncle Tom.' Is it not time they heard the whole truth?"

51. Quoted in Sam G. Dickson's celebratory introduction to a recent edition of the reconstruction trilogy. See Dickson, introduction to *The Reconstruction Trilogy: The Clansman,*

The Leopard's Spots, The Traitor by Thomas Dixon (Newport Beach, Calif.: Noontide Press, 1994), xiv.

52. Diane Roberts, *The Myth of Aunt Jemima: Representations of Race and Region* (London: Routledge, 1994), 156. Although I ultimately find his use of psycho-sexual motivations important but not sufficient as an analysis of rape narratives, Joel Williamson has perceptively noted the importance of the pollution taboo in white southern culture: "In the South, the absoluteness of the role race plays directly into the absoluteness of the sex role and roles of good and bad. . . . [A] 'good woman' (white) cannot be a little bit bad, or a little bit masculine, any more than she can be a little bit black." See Williamson, *Crucible of Race,* 497.

53. Simmons (1854–1940) was for thirty years (1901–31) a Democratic senator from North Carolina. He entered politics in the 1880s, was elected to the U.S. House of Representatives in 1886, and lost his seat two years later to a black Republican. Chairman of the state party, he engineered the "white supremacy campaign of 1898" and Aycock's election two years later, the same election in which voters passed a disfranchising amendment to the state constitution. See Richard L. Watson Jr., "Furnifold McLendel Simmons," in *Encyclopedia of Southern History,* 1105–6; quote at 1105. Daniels (1862–1948) was for years the editor of the regionally influential *Raleigh News and Observer.* An ardent Democrat, he supported the candidacy of Woodrow Wilson in 1912, and served as secretary of the navy. See Melvin Urofsky, "Josephus Daniels," in *Encyclopedia of Southern History,* 328.

54. See Jim Cullen, "'I's a Man Now': Gender and African American Men," in Darlene Clark Hine and Earnestine Jenkins, ed., *A Question of Manhood: A Reader in U.S. Black Men's History and Masculinity* (Bloomington: Indiana University Press, 1999), 489–501.

55. Joel Chandler Harris, *Life of Henry W. Grady* (New York: Cassell Publishing Co., 1890), 15–16.

56. Grantham, *South in Modern America,* 23–59. The classic study is Gaston, *New South Creed.*

57. See David T. Courtwright, "Alcohol and Alcoholism," in Ferris and Wilson, ed., *Encyclopedia of Southern Culture,* 1347. See Williamson, *Crucible of Race,* 282. Earlier, C. Vann Woodward noted that the correlation between race and prohibition could be overstated. See Woodward, *Origins of the New South,* 390. There is no doubt, though, of the rhetorical connection between race and prohibition efforts.

58. See David Cecelski and Timothy Tyson, ed., *Democracy Betrayed: The Wilmington Race Riot of 1898 and Its Legacy* (Chapel Hill: University of North Carolina Press, 1998). Not until the pioneering work of C. Vann Woodward was southern Populism seriously studied. See Woodward, *Tom Watson, Agrarian Rebel* (1938; reprint, London: Oxford University Press, 1988).

59. Andrea Meryl Kirshenbaum, "'The Vampire that Hovers Over North Carolina': Gender, White Supremacy, and the Wilmington Race Riot of 1898," *Southern Cultures* 4 (1998): 6–30.

60. Armstrong, *Desire and Domestic Fiction,* 20.

61. Quoted in Wayne Burns, *Charles Reade: A Study in Victorian Authorship* (New York: Bookman Associates, 1961), 284.

62. See Bederman, *Manliness and Civilization.* Bederman rightly cautions against viewing turn-of-the-century manhood as experiencing a period of crisis: "Middle-class men were

unusually obsessed with manhood at the turn of the century . . . [but] there is no evidence that most turn-of-the-century men ever lost confidence in the belief that people with male bodies possessed both a man's identity and a man's right to wield power" (11).

63. Page, "The Gray Jacket of 'No. 4,'" in *The Burial of the Guns and Other Stories* (New York: Scribner's, 1894); available online at http://www.pinkmonkey.com/dl/library1/digi111.pdf (accessed 18 November 2003).

64. On southern congressmen's efforts to derail antilynching legislation, see George B. Tindall, *The Emergence of the New South, 1913–1945* (Baton Rouge: Louisiana State University Press, 1967), 550–55.

65. Page, "The Negro Question," in *The Old South: Essays Social and Political* (New York: Scribner's, 1905), 284–85. See also Frederickson, *Black Image.*

66. Page, *Red Rock,* 357.

67. Williamson, *Crucible of Race,* 140–76; quote at 141.

68. Hobson, *Tell About the South,*134.

69. Sarah Watts, *Rough Rider in the White House: Theodore Roosevelt and the Politics of Desire* (Chicago: University of Chicago Press, 2003), 21.

70. Richard Wright, *White Man, Listen!* (New York: Doubleday, 1957), 109.

Chapter 3

Epigraphs: Thomas Nelson Page, "The Want of a History of the Southern People," in *The Old South: Essays Social and Political in The Novels, Stories, Sketches and Poems of Thomas Nelson Page* [also called "The Plantation Edition"] (New York: Scribner's, 1904), 12:346. Cleanth Brooks, "Thematic Problems in Southern Literature," in Louis D. Rubin and C. Hugh Holman, ed., *Southern Literary Study: Problems and Possibilities* (Chapel Hill: University of North Carolina Press, 1975), 209.

1. Julian A. C. Chandler, "Introductory Outline to the History of the States," in Chandler, ed., *The South in the Building of the Nation* (Richmond, Va.: Southern Historical Publication Society, 1909), 1:xxi. Educated at William and Mary and Johns Hopkins, Chandler taught history and political science at Richmond College.

2. R. L. Dabney, *A Defense of Virginia and the South* (1867; reprint Harrisonburg, Va.: Sprinkle, 1977), 5. Dabney's characterization of Virginia is also, of course, gendered and anthropomorphized, a common way of metaphorizing the South.

3. Executive Committee of the Southern Historical Society, *Southern Historical Society Tracts* 1 (January 1876): 41; reprint Millwood, N.Y.: Kraus Reprint Co., 1977.

4. The best study of the American historical profession is Peter Novick, *That Noble Dream: The 'Objectivity Question' and the American Historical Profession* (Cambridge, U.K.: Cambridge University Press, 1988); on the 1880s and 1890s, see especially 72–85. On early attempts by white southerners to shape historical understandings of secession and Civil War, see Blight, *Race and Reunion,* 78–79, 273–74, 291–92. See also Bethany Leigh Johnson, "Regionalism, Race, and the Meaning of the Southern Past: Professional History in the American South, 1896–1961" (PhD diss., Rice University, 2001). For a comparative study of French, German, and American southern acceptance of defeat, see Wolfgang

Schivelbusch, *The Culture of Defeat: On National Trauma, Mourning, and Recovery* (New York: Metropolitan Books, 2003).

5. Douglas Southall Freeman calls Stephens's *Constitutional View* "one of the most unusual books ever written in the United States by a man of high intelligence." The work is a 1,200 page series of dialogues between Stephens and three fictitious characters: a radical Republican from Massachusetts, a conservative Republican from Connecticut, and a northern Democrat from Pennsylvania. See Freeman, *The South to Posterity: An Introduction to the Writing of Confederate History* (1939; reprint, New York: Scribner's, 1983), 32–33.

6. Dabney, *A Defense of Virginia and the South;* Albert Taylor Bledsoe, *Is Davis a Traitor, or, Was Secession a Constitutional Right Previous to the War of 1861?* (Baltimore: Innes, 1866); Joseph E. Johnston, *Narrative of Military Operations Directed, During the Late War Between the States* (New York: Appleton, 1874); Alexander Stephens, *A Constitutional View of the Late War Between the States; Its Causes, Character, Conduct and Results. Presented in a Series of Colloquies at Liberty Hall* (Philadelphia: National Publishing Co., 1868); Jefferson Davis, *The Rise and Fall of the Confederate Government* (New York: Appleton, 1881).

7. Editors [J. A. C. Chandler, Franklin L. Riley, James Curtis Ballagh, John Bell Henneman, Edwin Mims, Thomas E. Watson, Samuel Chiles Mitchell, and Walter Lynwood Fleming], "Editors' Introduction," in Chandler, ed., *The South in the Building of the Nation,* 1:xv. The twelve-volume project is subtitled: "A History of the Southern States Designed to Record the South's Part in the Making of the American Nation; to Portray the Character and Genius, to Chronicle the Achievements and Progress and to Illustrate the Life and Traditions of the Southern People."

8. Don H. Doyle, *Nations Divided: America, Italy, and the Southern Question* (Athens: University of Georgia Press, 2002), 40.

9. Doyle, *Nations Divided,* 37. In the quoted passage, Doyle refers to Italian nationalism, but the description seems apt for the white American South as well.

10. Kent, *Revival of Interest in Southern Letters,* 5, 8.

11. Chandler, "Introductory Outline to the History of the States," in Chandler, ed., *The South in the Building of the Nation,* 1:xxi–xxii. For a common formulation showing both the lingering bogey of New England's cultural hegemony and an assertion of a nation of regions, see Kent, *Revival of Interest in Southern Letters:* "I venture the assertion that our southern youth to-day are as familiar with the writers of the New England school as are the boys of Boston or of Concord, but the New England boys—alas! It is true of our Southern youth as well—are lamentably ignorant of the literature of the South. Our American boys, without in any wise undervaluing these Puritan productions, should recognize that the knee-buckled knickerbockers, the quiet Quakers, the wide-awake Westerners and the self-conceited Southerners have not failed to contribute their share to the sum total of this American literature" (7).

12. Among them are Louise Manly, *Southern Literature, from 1579–1895* (Richmond, Va.: B. F. Johnson Publishing Co., 1895); W. M. Baskervill and others, *Southern Writers,* 2 vols. (Nashville: Church, 1897 and 1902); Charles W. Kent, *The Revival of Interest in Southern Letters* (Richmond, Va.: B. F. Johnson Publishing Co., 1900); F. V. N. Painter, *Poets of the South* (New York: American Book Co., 1903); William Lander Weber, *Selections from the Southern Poets* (New York: Macmillan, 1903); Carl Holliday, *A History of Southern Literature* (New York: Neale Publishing Co., 1906); Charles W. Hubner, *Representative Southern Poets* (New York: Neale Publishing Co., 1906); Kate Orgain, *Southern Authors in Poetry and Prose*

(New York: Neale Publishing Co., 1908); Leonidas Warren Payne Jr., ed., *Southern Literary Readings* (Chicago: Rand McNally, 1913); and Edwin A. Alderman, Joel Chandler Harris, and Charles W. Kent, ed., *The Library of Southern Literature* (New Orleans: Martin & Hoyt, 1907–23).

13. Turner, "Dim Pages in Literary History," in Rubin and Holman, ed., *Southern Literary Study*, 45.

14. "There is at present a new interest in literature in the South. The people read more; and in recent years an encouraging number of Southern writers have achieved national distinction." F. V. N. Painter, *Poets of the South* (1903; reprint Freeport, N. Y.: Books for Libraries Press, 1968), 3.

15. On the interplay of ideas of regionalist and nationalist canons, see the entry on John Bell Henneman, a professor of English at Vanderbilt and Sewanee, and editor of the *Sewanee Review,* in Robert Bain, Joseph M. Flora, and Louis D. Rubin, ed., *Southern Writers: A Biographical Dictionary* (Baton Rouge: Louisiana State University Press, 1979), 220–21. "Henneman believed that romantic southern local color was more indicative of a national literary heritage and point of view than the realism of Howells and James, but in 'The Modern Spirit in Literature,' *Sewanee Review* (August 1894) he had maintained that all regional and national literatures would shortly lose identities in world literature." He and others, including Baskervill, were heavily influenced by a series of lectures given by the southern poet Sidney Lanier at Johns Hopkins University in 1880.

16. A similar modernist/traditionalist battle was being waged on the other side of the Atlantic, of course. For nineteenth- and twentieth-century examples of English language and literature examination papers from British universities, see Stephen Potter, *The Muse in Chains: A Study in Education* (London: Jonathan Cape, 1937), 267–80.

17. David R. Shumway, *Creating American Civilization: A Genealogy of American Literature as an Academic Discipline* (Minneapolis: University of Minnesota Press, 1994), 6. See also Kermit Vanderbilt, *American Literature and the Academy: The Roots, Growth, and Maturity of a Profession* (Philadelphia: University of Pennsylvania Press, 1986); Gerald Graff, *Professing Literature: An Institutional History* (Chicago: University of Chicago Press, 1987); Lawrence W. Levine, *The Opening of the American Mind: Canons, Culture, and History* (Boston: Beacon, 1996), especially 54–90; On similar developments in history, see Novick, *That Noble Dream;* and John Higham, *History: The Development of Historical Studies in the United States* (Princeton, N.J.: Princeton University Press, 1965).

18. On efforts to make an American English, see Kenneth Cmiel, *Democratic Eloquence: The Fight over Popular Speech in Nineteenth-Century America* (New York: William Morrow, 1990); on composition courses, see 240–42; 260.

19. Scholars of southern history and literature were not the only ones creating narratives of the South in these years. Other academic/professional, institutionally sanctioned discourses, particularly in sociology, anthropology, and the heavily racialized sciences, were also developing "histories" of the South, with particular attention to the corollary "Negro Question." For the situation in the South, see Kirby, *Darkness at the Dawning.*

20. "There have been collections of the war poetry of the South . . . but the following pages are given over entirely to selections from the writings of those who have made contributions to American verse." Joel Chandler Harris, introduction to *Songs of the South,* ed. Jennie Thornley Clarke (1896; reprint, Garden City, N.Y., and New York: Doubleday, Page, 1913), v.

21. Harris, *Songs of the South,* v–vi.

22. For a useful collection of primary sources, see John E. Bassett, ed., *Defining Southern Literature: Perspectives and Assessments, 1831–1952* (Madison, N.J.: Fairleigh Dickinson University Press, 1997). See also M. Thomas Inge, "The Study of Southern Literature," in *The History of Southern Literature,* ed. Louis D. Rubin Jr. and others (Baton Rouge: Louisiana State University Press, 1983), 589–99.

23. See, for instance, L. W. Payne Jr., "Program of the Group-Study Course in Southern Literature" (Gonzales, Tex.: Inquirer Print, [1914?]). Payne's was a project conducted under the auspices of the Extension Department of the University of Texas. Like most of other efforts at shaping southern literature I explore here, Payne's bibliography lists the writings of all the scholars I mention in this chapter, as well as many others. Members of the reading group are advised to build their own personal libraries of southern literature (1). They take up such topics as "The First Distinct American Note in Our Literature" (7), "My favorite mocking-bird poem" (10), and "Contrast Northern and Southern War-songs for vituperation and harsh lyrics" (14).

24. Advertisement printed on the inside front cover of Kent, *Revival of Interest in Southern Letters.*

25. Montrose J. Moses, *The Literature of the South* (New York: T. Y. Crowell, 1910), ix.

26. Kent and others, ed., *Library of Southern Literature* 1:xvi, 1:xx. The anthology was published by a southern house (Martin & Hoyt) and "published under the approval and patronage of distinguished citizens of the South," among them Charles B. Aycock, ex-governor, North Carolina; Henry Cohen, rabbi, Texas; Stephen D. Lee, general commanding United Confederate Veterans, Mississippi; and Hoke Smith, governor of Georgia, figures not well known for their scholarly achievement. The set was available both in plain brown cloth library binding and a red leather-bound Edition De Luxe, the front covers of the latter adorned with southern state seals.

27. Gaines M. Foster, "Mirage in the Sahara of the Bozart: The Library of Southern Literature," *Mississippi Quarterly* 28 (Winter 1974–75): 3–19.

28. O'Brien, ed., *All Clever Men, Who Make Their Way: Critical Discourse in the Old South* (Fayetteville: University of Arkansas Press, 1982), 8. O'Brien continues: "the *Library of Southern Literature* still has value as a starting point for inquiry into lesser or unjustly obscure writers."

29. Alderman and others, ed., *Library of Southern Literature,* 15:457.

30. "Only ten selections discussed slavery, none of which adopted the radical pro-slavery attitude." "Only five selections mentioned [Reconstruction]." Foster, "Mirage in the Sahara of the Bozart," 11.

31. On Rutherford, see Fred A. Bailey, "Mildred Lewis Rutherford and the Patrician Cult of the Old South," *Georgia Historical Quarterly* 78 (Fall 1994): 509–35; Grace Elizabeth Hale, "'Some Women Have Never Been Reconstructed': Mildred Lewis Rutherford, Lucy M. Stanton, and the Racial Politics of White Southern Womanhood 1900–1930," in *Georgia in Black and White: Explorations in the Race Relations of a Southern State, 1865–1950,* ed. John C. Inscoe (Athens: University of Georgia Press, 1994): 173–201; Virginia Pettigrew Clare, *Thunder and Stars: The Life of Mildred Rutherford* (Oglethorpe, Ga.: Oglethorpe University Press, 1941); and Sarah H. Case, "The Historical Ideology of Mildred Lewis

Rutherford: A Confederate Historians' New South Creed," *Journal of Southern History* 68 (August 2002): 599–628. On similar efforts to memorialize the Lost Cause, see Fred A. Bailey, "Free Speech and the Lost Cause in the Old Dominion," *Virginia Magazine of History and Biography* 103 (April 1995): 237–66. For a representation of Rutherford's considerable writings, see Rutherford, *Truths of History: A Historical Perspective of the Civil War from the Southern Viewpoint* (1914; reprint Atlanta: Southern Lion Books, 1998).

32. Mildred Lewis Rutherford, *The South in History and Literature. A Handbook of Southern Authors, from the Settlement of Jamestown, 1607, to Living Writers* (Atlanta: Franklin-Turner, 1906).

33. On the redefinition of Faulkner as a great writer in the 1940s and 1950s, see Lawrence H. Schwartz, *Creating Faulkner's Reputation: The Politics of Modern Literary Criticism* (Knoxville: University of Tennessee Press, 1988).

34. The note was common. See Painter, *Poets of the South,* 11. "The South has not been as unfruitful in literature as is often supposed." But inverting a usual formulation in which slavery is usually been taken to have sapped the energies of southern writers, he continues: "the leading writers of the South . . . have been exempt, in large measure, from the narrowing influence of one-sided theological or philosophical tenets. They have not aspired to the role of social reformers; and in their loyalty to art, they have abstained from fanatical energy and extravagance."

35. Rutherford's fears echo chapter 2's discussion of Thomas Dixon's novel *The Leopard's Spots,* in which I refer to this contagion theme as it appears in the novel. Many white southerners believed that blacks were disease-ridden and increasingly dangerous to be around. Steeped in this cultural figure, Rutherford turns it on a character, the old-time black mammy, usually not represented this way. For a broader discussion of fin de siècle venereal disease and contagion fears and representations, see Elaine Showalter, *Sexual Anarchy* (New York: Penguin, 1990).

36. Maurice Garland Fulton, a professor of English at North Carolina's Davidson College, for instance, rejected the strategy of indiscriminate compilation in his anthology: "I have omitted the historians, the biographers, and the political writers so frequently used to swell the bulk of Southern literature." See Fulton, *Southern Life in Southern Literature,* v.

37. Carl Holliday, *A History of Southern Literature* (1906; reprint Port Washington, N.Y.: Kennikat, 1969). All parenthetical citations are to the 1969 edition. Born in Ohio in 1879, Holliday moved to the South in 1896, teaching at universities in Virginia and Tennessee. Among his other works are *The Cotton Picker, and Other Poems, Three Centuries of Southern Poetry,* and *The Literature of Colonial Virginia,* the latter receiving a prize from the Colonial Dames of Virginia. For a brief biographical sketch, see Alderman and others, ed., *Library of Southern Literature* 15:205.

38. See William R. Taylor, *Cavalier and Yankee: The Old South and American National Character* (New York: Braziller, 1961).

39. Holliday was not the only scholar to employ organic, even botanical tropes. In their anthology of American short stories, W. P. Trent and John B. Henneman write: "A thoroughly indigenous product of American soil, the short story, having found so many ramifications and divisions and species, and having become so popular in demand and supply, calls for mastery as never before. In its popularity lies its greatest danger—the likelihood that the form will be degraded by too common usage." Trent and Henneman, ed., *The Best*

American Tales (New York: Thomas Y. Crowell, 1907). Of the nine stories included, two were written by Irving, two by Hawthorne, and three by Poe.

40. Alderman and others, ed., *Library of Southern Literature* 12:5462.

41. On the significance of Adams, see Wendell H. Stephenson, "Herbert B. Adams and Southern Historical Scholarship at the Johns Hopkins University," *Maryland Historical Magazine* 42 (March 1947): 1–20.

42. See John McCardell, "Trent's *Simms:* The Making of a Biography," in *A Master's Due: Essays in Honor of David Herbert Donald,* ed. William J. Cooper, Michael F. Holt, and John McCardell (Baton Rouge: Louisiana State University Press, 1985), 179–203; quoted in Edward L. Ayers, *Promise of the New South,* 424.

43. While at Columbia, Trent produced a *History of American Literature* (1903), a *History of the United States* (with C. K. Adams) for use in high schools (1903), and editions of Thackeray and Shakespeare.

44. Wendell Holmes Stephenson, *The South Lives in History: Southern Historians and Their Legacy* (Baton Rouge: Louisiana State University Press, 1955), 4.

45. William P. Trent, "Tendencies of Higher Life in the South," *Atlantic Monthly* 79 (January 1897): 768; quoted in Woodward, *Origins of the New South,* 430.

46. Trent was keenly aware of the diversity present in the South: "A 'Solid South' would seem to presuppose a homogeneous Southern people coextensive with the geographical, or rather political, area thus designated; but to draw this inference would be to make a mistake almost equal to that made by the European who thinks Chicago a three to four hours' ride from New York, and confounds our Eastern and Western populations." Trent, "The Diversity Among Southerners," *Atlantic Monthly* 79 (January 1897): 42–53.

47. William P. Trent, ed., *Southern Writers: Selections in Prose and Verse* (New York: Macmillan, 1905), v.

48. Edwin Mims and Bruce R. Payne, *Southern Prose and Poetry for Schools* (New York: Scribner's, 1910), 18. See Charles Bracelen Flood, *Lee: The Last Years* (Boston: Houghton Mifflin, 1981).

49. Trent, *Southern Writers,* 193, 100.

50. Moses, *Literature of the South,* vii.

51. Ibid., viii–ix, 463.

52. Writers included are Edgar Allan Poe, William Gilmore Simms, John Pendleton Kennedy, John Esten Cooke, Augustus Baldwin Longstreet, William Tappan Thompson, Johnson Jones Hooper, Joseph Glover Baldwin, Joel Chandler Harris, George Washington Cable, Mary Noailles Murfree, Thomas Nelson Page, James Lane Allen, Ellen Glasgow, Mary Johnston, Mrs. Burton Harrison, Grace King, and Frances Little.

53. Mims, quoted in O'Brien, *Idea of the American South,* 11.

54. Almost without exception, the works that I explore in this chapter defined the South as the eleven former Confederate states plus Kentucky, Missouri, and Maryland. West Virginia is also often counted among the southern states. Later works include Oklahoma. See, for instance, J. A. C. Chandler, "Introductory Outline," in Chandler, ed., *The South in*

the Building of the Nation 1:xiv. "Maryland is essentially southern, while West Virginia and Kentucky owe their origin to Virginians. This might also be said of Missouri, which owes its growth to Southerners."

55. Richard Gray, *Writing the South: Ideas of an American Region* (Cambridge, U.K.: Cambridge University Press, 1986), xiii, xii.

56. In this chapter I make no attempt to discuss the historiography of Reconstruction. The work of William Dunning, John Burgess, and their students has long been criticized for the racialist assumptions of their authors. See William A. Dunning, *Essays on the Civil War and Reconstruction* (New York: Macmillan, 1897). For a brief, cogent description of the Dunning School, see Eric Foner, *Reconstruction: America's Unfinished Revolution, 1863–1877* (New York: Harper & Row, 1988), xix–xx.

57. Quoted in Stephenson, "Herbert B. Adams," 3.

58. Chandler, "Introductory Outline," in Chandler, ed., *The South in the Building of the Nation* 1:xiii.

59. Southern History Association, "Historical Sketch of the Association," *Publications of the Southern History Association* (January 1897): 4–5.

60. Founded in New Orleans in 1869 and later transferred to Richmond, the Southern Historical Society aimed to collect and publish "all the documents and facts bearing upon the eventful history of the last few years" (41). In response to a northern study of Gettysburg that grossly overestimated Robert E. Lee's troop strength at that battle: "Ah! if our grand old chieftain had commanded the numbers which Northern generals and Northern writers attribute to him, then the story of Gettysburg and of the war would have been far different" (48). *Southern Historical Society Tracts* 1.

61. James Curtis Ballagh, "Editor's Introduction," in Ballagh, ed., *The South in the Building of the Nation* (Richmond, Va.: Southern Historical Publication Society, 1909), 5:xii.

62. See Bailey, "Free Speech and the Lost Cause in Texas." Also see Foster, *Ghosts of the Confederacy,* especially 115–26. Karen L. Cox, *Dixie's Daughters: The United Daughters of the Confederacy and the Preservation of Confederate Culture* (Gainesville: University Press of Florida, 2003).

63. See August Meier, *Black History and the Historical Profession, 1915–1980* (Urbana: University of Illinois Press, 1986).

64. W. E. B. Du Bois, *The Suppression of the African Slave-Trade to the United States of America, 1638–1870* (New York: Schocken, 1969; orig. ed. 1896), xxxvi.

65. Dunning's mark on early twentieth-century southern historiography was great. A 1914 *Festschrift,* for instance, includes essays by former students such as Walter Lynwood Fleming, Ulrich B. Phillips, Charles W. Ramsdell, J. G. de Roulhac Hamilton, William K. Boyd, and Charles E. Merriam. See *Studies in Southern History and Politics Inscribed to William Archibald Dunning* (New York: Columbia University Press, 1914).

66. Edwin Mims, "Southern Fiction after the War of Secession," in Riley, ed., *The South in the Building of the Nation,* 8:lxiv.

67. Novick, *That Noble Dream,* 76, 80.

68. Julian A. C. Chandler and William Foushee, *Virginia* (New York: Macmillan, 1902), 33.

69. A notable exception to the historiographical era of good feelings is the Agrarian Frank L. Owsley's 1940 Southern Historical Association presidential address, "The Fundamental Cause of the Civil War: Egocentric Sectionalism." Owsley declared that "peace between sections as between nations is placed in jeopardy when one nation or one section fails to respect the self-respect of the people of another section or nation" (89). But overt Yankee baiting was not common at the SHA. More typical were Thomas P. Abernathy's "Democracy and the American Frontier," Fletcher M. Green's "Democracy in the Old South," and Ella Lonn's "Reconciliation Between the North and the South." For these addresses, see George B. Tindall, ed., *The Pursuit of Southern History: Presidential Addresses of the Southern Historical Association, 1935–1963* (Baton Rouge: Louisiana State University Press, 1964).

70. Celebration of the Lost Cause, as Paul Gaston and Gaines Foster have pointed out, certainly did not make one an unrepentant fire-eater. Southerners had little difficulty in celebrating Confederate valor and feats of arms while agreeing that southern defeat had been providential.

71. John Bell Henneman, "Shall Virginians Write Virginian History?" *Hampden-Sidney Magazine* 10 (November 1892): 4.

72. Chandler, "Introductory Outline to the History of the States," in *The South in the Building of the* Nation, 1:xvii.

73. Chandler, "Introductory Outline to the History of the States," in *The South in the Building of the* Nation, 1:xvii. Novick, *That Noble Dream,* 75. Hart wrote: "the danger of sectional divergence seems to have passed away. Almost all the European countries have to deal with irreconcilable regions: England has Ireland, Germany has Posen, Austria has Hungary; no such region exists within the United States." Albert Bushnell Hart, *The American Nation: A History: National Ideals Historically Traced, 1607–1907* (New York: Harper & Bros., 1907), 26:349.

74. Kent, *Revival of Interest in Southern Letters,* 15.

75. Ballagh, "Introduction," in Ballagh, ed., *The South in the Building of the Nation,* 5:xi–xii.

76. Quoted in Arthur S. Link, *Wilson: The Road to the White House* (Princeton, N.J.: Princeton University Press, 1947), 3.

77. Cohn wrote of race relations in the Mississippi Delta: "I felt there was a doom on the land where I was born and raised.... Members of two races lived out their lives on parallel lines, to meet but in infinity, each with a wound in his heart and a torment in his mind.... Living, their ways were separate. Dying, they became a common but not commingled dust. Of these things each spoke only to his own kind." David C. Cohn, *The Mississippi Delta and the World: The Memoirs of David C. Cohn,* ed. James C. Cobb (Baton Rouge: Louisiana State University Press, 1995), 6–7.

78. Chandler and Foushee, *Virginia,* 11.

79. James J. McDonald, *Life in Old Virginia* (Norfolk, Va.: Old Virginia Publishing Co., 1907), 5.

80. Chandler and Foushee, *Virginia,* 14; J. A. C. Chandler, "Preface," in Chandler, ed., *Genesis and Birth of the Federal Constitution* (New York: Macmillan, 1924), vi; Alton B. Parker, "American Constitutional Government," in Chandler, ed., *Genesis and Birth of the Federal Constitution,* 32.

81. Ulrich Bonnell Phillips, "Racial Problems, Adjustments and Disturbances," in Riley, ed., *The South in the Building of the Nation,* 4:194–241; quote at 212.

82. Joyce Appleby, Lynn Hunt, and Margaret Jacob, *Telling the Truth About History* (New York: Oxford University Press, 1994), 295.

83. Chandler and Foushee, *Virginia,* 12.

84. Chandler, "Editor's Preface to the History of the States," in Chandler, ed., *The South in the Building of the Nation,* 1:xix.

85. Franklin L. Riley, "Colonial Origins of New England Senates," in *Johns Hopkins University Studies in Historical and Political Science* 14, no. 3 (March 1896): 5–76; quote at 7; Frederick Robertson Jones, "History of Taxation in Connecticut, 1636–1776," in *Johns Hopkins University Studies in Historical and Political Science* 14, no. 3 (August 1896): 3–71; quote at 7.

86. Woodrow Wilson, *A History of the American People* (New York: Harper's, 1902), 1:25.

87. Harrington Putnam, "The Constitution in the Making," in Chandler, ed., *Genesis and Birth of the Federal Constitution,* 273.

88. Chandler, "Introductory Outline to the History of the States," 1:xvii.

89. Chandler and Foushee, *Virginia,* v.

90. James Curtis Ballagh, ed., *The Letters of Richard Henry Lee* (New York: Macmillan, 1911), vii.

91. E. Merton Coulter, "What the South Has Done About Its History," in Tindall, ed., *The Pursuit of Southern History,* 3. Coulter's address remains a useful overview of nineteenth-century southern historical societies and associations. See also J. G. De Roulhac Hamilton, "History in the South—A Retrospect of Half a Century," *North Carolina Historical Review* 31 (April 1954): 173–81; Wendell H. Stephenson, "A Half Century of Southern Historical Scholarship," *Journal of Southern History* 11 (1945): 4–8; Wendell H. Stephenson, "History of the South in Colleges and Universities, 1925–26," *Historical Outlook* 17 (November 1926): 319–22.

92. Note that Chandler's language is practically identical to that of Margaret Rutherford's, quoted earlier in this chapter.

93. Chandler, "Introductory Outline to the History of the States," 1:xxiii.

94. Thomas Nelson Page, *The Old Dominion* (New York: Scribner's, 1909), vii–viii.

95. Ibid., vii–viii.

96. William P. Trent, *Southern Statesmen of the Old Regime* (New York: Thomas Y. Crowell & Co., 1897), vii–viii. The book's frontispiece is Gilbert Stuart's portrait of George Washington and is dedicated to Theodore Roosevelt.

97. For a discussion of *The Johns Hopkins University Studies in Historical and Political Science,* see John David Smith, *An Old Creed for the New South: Proslavery Ideology and Historiography, 1865–1918* (Westport, Conn.: Greenwood Press, 1985), 137–61. On the more recent historiography of American slavery, see Peter J. Parish, *Slavery: History and Historians* (New York: Harper & Row, 1989).

98. Merton L. Dillon, *Ulrich Bonnell Phillips: Historian of the Old South* (Baton Rouge: Louisiana State University Press, 1985), 104.

99. James Curtis Ballagh, *A History of Slavery in Virginia* (Baltimore: Johns Hopkins University Press, 1902), vii.

100. Other examples of the Johns Hopkins dissertations include Henry Scofield Cooley's "A Study of Slavery in New Jersey" (1896) and Jeffrey R. Brackett's "The Negro In Maryland: A Study of the Institution of Slavery" (1889).

101. Donald Franklin Joyce, ed., *Early Studies of Slavery By States* (Northbrook, Ill.: Metro Books, 1972), 1:foreword, n.p.

102. Quoted in Smith, *Old Creed for the New South*, 141.

103. Stanley M. Elkins, *Slavery: A Problem in American Institutional and Intellectual Life* (Chicago: University of Chicago Press, 1959), 9.

104. Ballagh, *History of Slavery in Virginia*, 107, 108, 109, 113, 115.

105. John Spencer Bassett, "Slavery in the State of North Carolina [orig. ed. 1899]," in Joyce, ed., *Early Studies of Slavery By States*, 80.

106. U. B. Phillips, *American Negro Slavery; Survey of the Supply, Employment and Control of Negro Labor as Determined by the Plantation Régime* (1918; reprint, New York: D. Appleton & Co., 1928), 291. See Dillon, *Ulrich Bonnell Phillips*, and John Herbert Roper, *U. B. Phillips: A Southern Mind* (Macon, Ga.: Mercer University Press, 1984).

107. Dillon, *Ulrich Bonnell Phillips*, 103. See also John David Smith, "The Historiographic Rise, Fall, and Resurrection of Ulrich Bonnell Phillips," *Georgia Historical Quarterly* 66 (1981): 138–53.

108. Phillips, *American Negro Slavery*, 294, 296, 295, 309, 514.

109. Ibid., 292.

110. Roper, *U. B. Phillips*, 41.

111. See U. B. Phillips, "The Plantation as a Civilizing Factor," *Sewanee Review* 12 (July 1904): 257–67.

112. Phillips, *American Negro Slavery*, 514.

113. Ibid., 343.

114. Ibid., 298, 291.

115. Ibid., 291.

116. McDonald, *Life in Old Virginia*, 151, 153.

117. Theodore D. Jervey, "Review of American Negro Slavery," *American Historical Review* 25 (October 1919): 117.

118. Tipton R. Snavely, "Review of American Negro Slavery," *American Economic Review* 10 (1920): 336.

119. W. E. B. Du Bois, "Review of American Negro Slavery," *American Political Science Review* 12 (November 1918): 722.

120. McDonald, *Life in Old Virginia*, 152.

121. Joseph Gregoire de Roulhac Hamilton, "The South in Political Parties, 1789–1860," in Franklin L. Riley, ed., *The South in the Building of the Nation* (Richmond, Va.: Southern

Historical Publication Society, 1909), 4:319–38; quote at 336–37. At the University of North Carolina at Chapel Hill, Hamilton became an influential historian of Reconstruction and as the driving force behind the monumental Southern Historical Collection, shaped research on the region.

122. The concept of "island communities" is drawn from Robert Weibe, *The Search for Order, 1877–1920* (New York: Hill and Wang, 1967), see especially 2–4.

123. Chandler and Foushee, *Virginia,* 16.

124. Thomas Nelson Page, *The Negro: The Southerner's Problem* (New York: Scribner's, 1904).

125. Chandler, "Introductory Outline to the History of the States," in Chandler, ed., *The South in the Building of the Nation,* 1:liv.

126. Williamson, *Crucible of Race,* 318–19.

127. Freeman, *South to Posterity,* ix–x. Freeman studied under James C. Ballagh at John Hopkins, where he received a PhD in 1908 with a study of Virginia's secession convention, and is best known as a one-man Virginia history factory, producing not only multivolume biographies of George Washington and Robert E. Lee, but a three-volume history of Lee's generals in the Army of Northern Virginia, *Lee's Lieutenants.*

128. On the history and contents of the National Statuary Hall, see http://www.aoc.gov/cc/art/nsh/nsh_coll_origin.htm (accessed 16 December 2003).

129. "Acceptance and Unveiling of the Statues of Jefferson Davis and James Z. George," Proceedings in the Congress and in Statuary Hall, United States Capitol, 72d Congress, 1st Session, Senate Document No. 103 (Washington, D.C.: Government Printing Office, 1932), 17, 23, 29, 33.

130. Robert Penn Warren, *Jefferson Davis Gets His Citizenship Back* (Lexington, Ky.: University Press of Kentucky, 1995); orig. ed. 1980.

131. "Statues of Jefferson Davis and James Z. George," 42, 43.

132. Ibid., 43.

133. Frederick Jackson Turner, "Social Forces in American History," *American Historical Review* 16 (January 1911): 217–33; quote at 217.

134. David Donald, *Liberty and Union* (Lexington, Mass.: D. C. Heath, 1978), 26-29. See also Donald, *Lincoln* (New York: Random House, 1995), especially 459–66. As Donald points out, Lincoln's critics disputed his characterization of the Union; the *Chicago Times* called his remarks at Gettysburg "a perversion of history so flagrant that the most extended charity cannot regard it as otherwise than willful," 466. The best study of the Gettysburg Address is Garry Wills, *Lincoln at Gettysburg: The Words that Remade America* (New York: Simon & Schuster, 1992).

135. On building and administering the post–Civil War American state, see Morton Keller, *Affairs of State: Public Life in Late-Nineteenth Century America* (Cambridge, Mass.: Harvard University Press, 1977); Stephen Skowronek, *Building a New American State: The Expansion of National Administrative Capacities, 1877-1920* (Cambridge, U.K.: Cambridge University Press, 1982).

136. Michael O'Brien, "Regionalism," in Wilson and Ferris, ed., *Encyclopedia of Southern Culture,* 1121–22.

137. William Peterfield Trent, "The Diversity Among Southerners," in Fulton, *Southern Life in Southern Literature,* 393.

138. For a definition of the South by reference to climate, see Paul K. Conkin, "Hot, Humid, and Sad," *Journal of Southern History* 64 (February 1998): 3-22.

139. Editors, "Editors' Introduction," in Chandler, ed., *The South in the Building of the Nation,* 1:xv.

140. Gaston, *New South Creed.*

141. Henry Watterson, "Address of Welcome Delivered to the Grand Army of the Republic on Behalf of the City of Louisville by Henry Watterson, at the Great Meeting at Music Hall, Louisville, Ky., [n.p.], 12 September 1895."

142. On literary representations of sectional reconciliation, see Silber, *Romance of Reunion.* See also Dona Brown, *Inventing New England: Regional Tourism in the Nineteenth Century* (Washington, D.C.: Smithsonian Institution Press, 1997).

143. Edward Ayers argues that "[p]eople realize that when they speak of 'Southern culture' they are creating a fiction, a fiction of a geographically bounded and coherent set of attributes to be set off against a mythical non-South. . . . The South feeds the sense of difference and then resents the consequences. Southerners with something to sell traffic in difference, eagerly marketing any distinctiveness they can claim." Ayers, "What We Talk about When We Talk about the South," in Ayers and others, ed., *All Over the Map,* 62-82; quote at 65-66. While I agree with Ayers that there is no essential southernness, it seems clear that many people, at the turn of the twentieth century and today, use the term "southern culture" without a sense that they are merely reifying a construct. Many southerners, especially white southerners, believe that something called southern culture exists. And of course to the degree that they hold that belief and act accordingly, southern culture does exist.

144. The best study of American memories of the Civil War is Blight, *Race and Reunion.* Dominant narratives did not make room for African Americans with the will to make freedom on their own terms. Also, both North and South seemed eager to forget a time when the national government sanctioned the arming of black men against white.

145. *Baltimore American,* 13 June 1902; quoted in Arthur S. Link, "Woodrow Wilson: The American as Southerner," in *The Higher Realism of Woodrow Wilson and Other Essays* (Nashville: Vanderbilt University Press, 1971), 22.

146. Edwin Mims, "Woodrow Wilson: The Happy Warrior," *Methodist Quarterly Review* (April 1924): 9-10. Further stressing Wilson's national, even international stature, Mims continues: "Was he a Burke or a Gladstone, a Jefferson or a Washington, a Webster or a Lincoln?" (4).

147. On Wilson's inauguration, see Tindall, *Emergence of the New South,* 1-5; quote at 2. The classic treatment of North-South reconciliation is Paul H. Buck, *The Road to Reunion, 1865-1900* (Boston: Little, Brown, 1937). Other studies of the era of reconciliation are Foster, *Ghosts of the Confederacy,* and Silber, *Romance of Reunion.*

148. Quoted in Sam G. Riley, *Magazines of the American South* (Westport, Conn.: Greenwood Press, 1986), 214.

149. Painter, *Standing at Armageddon,* 141–69.

150. Chandler, "Introductory Outline to the History of the States," 1:liv.

151. Quoted in Novick, *That Noble Dream*, 76.

152. Blight, *Race and Reunion*, 7-15; quote at 11.

153. See Ivan Musicant, *Empire by Default: The Spanish-American War and the Dawn of the American Century* (New York: Holt, 1998); a fine older study is Frank Freidel, *The Splendid Little War* (Boston: Little, Brown, 1958).

154. Painter, *Standing at Armageddon*, 162.

155. Wilson, *A History of the American People*, 5:300.

156. Page, *The Negro: The Southerner's Problem*, ix. Later, Page fleshed out the nature of the threat posed by black population growth as explicitly as James Vardaman or Ben Tillman: "To say that Negroes furnish the great body of rapists, is not to say that all Negroes are ravishers. To say that they are ignorant and lack the first element of morality, is not to assert that they all are so. The race question, however . . . is caused by the great body of the race, and after forty years in which money and care have been given unstintedly to uplift them, those who possess knowledge and virtue are not sufficient in number and influence to prevent the race question from growing rather than diminishing" (xi–xii).

Conclusion

First epigraph: Florence Mars, *Witness in Philadelphia* (Baton Rouge and London: Louisiana State University Press, 1977), 1.

1. "But is the fair a city?" asked *Scott County (Miss.) Times* editor Sid Salter. "Sho' nuff, neighbor. Complete with streets, neighborhoods, garbage collection, law enforcement, water and sewer systems, a governing body and other vestiges of civilization, the Neshoba County Fair is a microcosm of any number of cities, large or small." *Jackson Clarion-Ledger*, 29 July 1984. On the modern fair, see the Web sites maintained by the fair (www. neshobacountyfair.org) and by Philadelphia, Mississippi, and Neshoba County (www. neshoba.org). The latter promises visitors "the best part of progressive Southern hospitality" and boasts: "If Only Everyone Could Call This Home. . . ." 10 November 1999.

2. Carolyn Bennett Patterson, "Mississippi's Grand Reunion at the Neshoba County Fair," *National Geographic* 157 (June 1980): 854. Historians have given little attention to the Neshoba County Fair. For a folklorist's view, see Ovid Vickers, "Neshoba's Folk Fair," *Mississippi Folklore Register* 11 (Spring 1977): 11–17. "The Neshoba County Fair: It's a Southern Thing." Web site at www.jackkean.com/fair.html. 25 May 2000. On the history of the fair, see Steven H. Stubbs, *Mississippi's Giant Houseparty: The History of the Neshoba County Fair* (Philadelphia, Miss: Dancing Rabbit Press, 2005). See also Trent Watts, "'Mississippi's Giant House Party': Being White at the Neshoba County Fair," *Southern Cultures* 8 (Summer 2002), 38–55.

3. *Jackson Clarion-Ledger*, 5 August 1986; *Jackson Daily News*, 7 August 1986.

4. On white Mississippians' reactions to the social and political currents of the last decades, see Joseph Crespino, *In Search of Another Country: Mississippi and the Conservative Counterrevolution* (Princeton, N.J.: Princeton University Press, 2007). See also Jason Sokol, *There Goes My Everything: White Southerners in the Age of Civil Rights, 1945–1975* (New York: Knopf, 2006).

5. Christopher Lasch took a somewhat different view of nostalgia: "To discuss the complexities of our past under the heading of 'nostalgia' substitutes sloganeering for objective social criticism with which this attitude tries to associate itself. The fashionable sneer that now automatically greets every loving recollection of the past attempts to exploit the prejudices of a pseudoprogressive society on behalf of the status quo." See Lasch, *The Culture of Narcissism: American Life in an Age of Diminishing Expectations* (New York: Norton, 1979), xvii. The Neshoba County Fair seems to me a example of what Svetlana Boym calls "restorative nostalgia," which "puts emphasis on *nostos* [the home] and proposes to rebuild the lost home and patch up the memory gap . . . [restorative nostalgics] do not think of themselves as nostalgic; they believe that their project is about truth." Boym, *The Future of Nostalgia* (New York: Basic Books, 2001), 41.

6. "Brief Historical Data and Preview of Mississippi Fairs, 1940," 14, Mississippi Department of Archives and History [afterward MDAH]. One owner insists: "These cabins are prime collateral at every damn bank in town. . . . You can easily get a $10,000 loan using the cabin for collateral." *Jackson Daily News,* 7 August 1986.

7. In 1907 the Mississippi historian Dunbar Rowland described Neshoba County as "one of the more sparsely populated counties," but noted that "new settlers are rapidly coming in." And although the county's "interests are almost exclusively agricultural . . . [t]he manufactures in the county have increased fully 50 per cent since 1900, and real estate values have increased four-fold during the same period." He continued: "The population in 1900 consisted of whites 9,874; colored 2,852; a total of 12,726 and an increase of 1,580 over the year 1890." In Rowland, *Mississippi; Comprising Sketches,* 2:329–30.

8. Mars, *Witness in Philadelphia,* 2.

9. Clayton Rand, *Ink on My Hands* (New York: Carrick & Evans, 1940), 131; *Jackson Daily News,* 3 August 1979; Mars, *Witness in Philadelphia,* 32.

10. Rand, *Ink On My Hands,* 131; "The Neshoba County Fair"; Web site available at www.rootsweb.com/~msneshob/page2.html (accessed 30 September 2000).

11. *Daily Mississippian,* 22 July 1983; Patterson, "Mississippi's Grand Reunion," 861; Jill Conner Browne, *The Sweet Potato Queens' Book of Love* (New York: Three Rivers Press, 1999), 97 .

12. *Jackson Clarion-Ledger,* 27 July 1976. A decade after the 1964 murders, former Sheriff Lawrence A. Rainey recalled: "If nobody had paid those boys any mind they'd have come and gone and they wouldn't have meant a thing. Nothing, nothing at all." *Jackson Clarion-Ledger/ Jackson Daily News,* 16 June 1974. For an account of black Mississippi in the first half of the twentieth century, see Neil R. McMillen, *Dark Journey: Black Mississippians in the Age of Jim Crow* (Urbana and Chicago: University of Illinois Press, 1989). On the 1964 Philadelphia murders, see Seth Cagin and Philip Dray, *We Are Not Afraid: The Story of Goodman, Schwerner, and Chaney and the Civil Rights Campaign for Mississippi* (New York: Macmillan, 1988); and William Bradford Huie, *Three Lives for Mississippi* (New York: WWC Books, 1965). On the civil rights movement in Mississippi, see John Dittmer, *Local People: The Struggle for Civil Rights in Mississippi* (Urbana and Chicago: University of Illinois Press, 1994).

13. *Neshoba Democrat,* 17 August 1916; Rand, *Ink On My Hands,* 130.

14. Federal Writers' Project of the Works Progress Administration, *Mississippi: The WPA Guide to the Magnolia State* (1938, reprint, Jackson: University Press of Mississippi, 1988), 468.

15. *Neshoba Democrat,* 9 August 1962; quoted in *National Register of Historic Places Inventory—Nomination Form,* 1, in "Neshoba County Fair" Subject File, MDAH.

16. Rand, *Ink On My Hands,* 135.

17. *Jackson Clarion-Ledger,* 29 July 1983.

18. *Jackson Daily News,* 9 August 1974.

19. *Jackson Daily News,* 26 July 1983; *Jackson Clarion-Ledger,* 29 July 1983; *Jackson Clarion-Ledger,* 14 August 1983; *Jackson Clarion-Ledger,* 6 August 1976; *Meridian Star,* 3 August 1994. Note, for instance, the "anecdote-bellowing, guitar-strumming, vaudevillian" ex-governor's characterization of Edward Kennedy: "'A grrrreat ladies' man. . . . A grrreat party-goer. . . . He's a wonderful swimmer. . . . And the only time he went to the right was when he drove off the bridge with Mary Jo (Kopechne),' he said. The crowd exploded." *Jackson Clarion-Ledger,* 5 August 1977; *Jackson Daily News,* 26 July 1984.

20. *Jackson Clarion-Ledger,* 2 August 1979. See longtime Secretary of State Heber Ladner's remarks on the old days, at a fair that witnessed the final public appearance there of Senator James O. Eastland. *Jackson Clarion-Ledger,* 4 August 1978; *Jackson Clarion-Ledger/Jackson Daily News,* 11 August 1974; *Jackson Clarion-Ledger,* 4 August 1978; *Jackson Clarion-Ledger,* 4 August 1978; Quoted in Erle Johnson, *I Rolled With Ross: A Political Portrait* (Baton Rouge, La.: Moran Publishing, 1980), 131.

21. See the Neshoba County Fair's official Web site; available at http://www.neshobacountyfair.org (accessed 6 November 1999).

22. Neshoba County Fair Souvenir Program, in author's possession. *Jackson Clarion-Ledger,* 1 August 2002; 2 August 2002. For biographical data on Shows and Pickering, see *Mississippi Official and Statistical Register, 2000–2004* (n.p., 2001), 184–85. See the American Association of University Women's opposition to the Pickering nomination at http://www.aauw.org/about/newsroom/press_releases/pickering.cfm (accessed 30 December 2003).

23. *Jackson Clarion-Ledger,* 18 June 1989; *Memphis Press-Scimitar,* 2 August 1947; *Jackson Clarion-Ledger,* 8 August 1986.; Browne, *Sweet Potato Queens' Book of Love,* 96.

24. *Jackson Clarion-Ledger,* 3 August 3 1991.

25. *Jackson Clarion-Ledger,* 28 July 1991; *Boston Globe,* 6 August 1995; *Jackson Clarion-Ledger,* 7 August 1981; *Washington Post,* 11 August 1980; *Jackson Clarion-Ledger,* 18 June 1979.

26. Robert Craycroft, *The Neshoba County Fair: Place and Paradox in Mississippi* (Starkville: Center for Small Town Research and Design, Mississippi State University, 1989), 2. Craycroft, a native of Cincinnati, observed that the fair "had one of the strongest senses of place of anywhere I've ever been. . . . This thing has gone on for a hundred years not because it's a giant house party but because there's a true sense of community there." *Jackson (Miss.) Northside Sun,* 3 August 1989.

27. Cleanth Brooks, "Thematic Problems in Southern Literature," in Rubin and Holman, ed., *Southern Literary Study,* 209.

28. *Jackson Clarion-Ledger,* 22 July 1988.

29. For an account of these years written by the former director of Mississippi's State Sovereignty Commission, see Erle Johnston, *Mississippi's Defiant Years, 1953–1973* (Forest,

Miss.: Lake Harbor Publishers, 1990). On the integration of Mississippi's public schools, see Charles C. Bolton, "The Last Stand of Massive Resistance: Mississippi School Integration, 1970," *Journal of Mississippi History* 61 (Winter 1999): 329–50. See also Charles C. Bolton, *The Hardest Deal of All: The Battle Over School Integration in Mississippi, 1870–1980* (Jackson: University Press of Mississippi, 2005).

30. Tom P. Brady, *Black Monday: Segregation or Amalgamation, America Has Its Choice* (Winona, Miss.: Association of Citizens' Councils, 1955), 87, 85. See Daniel Miles Hoehler, "Thomas P. Brady" (master's thesis, University of Mississippi, 1998).

31. Brady, *Black Monday,* 69, 47.

32. Ibid., 47–48, 45.

33. Parents for Segregation, "To All Concerned White Citizens," undated [1968?] typewritten, mimeographed flyer in author's possession. Such fliers were commonly handed out at the State Fair or placed on car windshields. On Americans for the Preservation of the White Race, see Crespino, *In Search of Another Country,* 108, 110–11.

34. Americans for the Preservation of the White Race, Jackson Chapter, *"Emergency!!! Alert!!! Act Now!!!"* 8 January 1968, typewritten, mimeographed flyer in author's possession.

35. Americans for the Preservation of the White Race, untitled, n.d., mimeographed flyer in author's possession.

36. *Jackson Clarion-Ledger,* 1 August 2002. Giles Web site available at http://www.rebelarmy.com (accessed 24 December 2003). On Crooms's hiring, see *Jackson Clarion-Ledger,* 2, 3, 4 December 2003.

37. Charlie Mitchell, "Ugly 'Guest' Reappeared Election Night," *Jackson Clarion-Ledger,* 16 November, 2003.

38. W. Ralph Eubanks, *Ever is a Long Time: A Journey into Mississippi's Dark Past* (New York: Basic Books, 2003), 226–27; Jon Meacham, "A Man Out of Time," *Newsweek* 23 December 2002: 27–28.

39. For an announcement of a major defense contract won by a Mississippi firm, see http://www.sunherald.com/mld/sunherald/7360484.htm (accessed 30 December 2003). Ingalls Shipyard is Mississippi's largest employer.

40. *Jackson Clarion-Ledger,* 1 December 2003.

41. Benedict Anderson, *Imagined Communities: Reflections on the Origins and Spread of Nationalism* (London: Verso, 1983).

42. John Vinson, "Know your mission. . . . What Must We Do?" *Southern Patriot* 3, no. 1 (January/February 1996): 6. The *Southern Patriot* is the newsletter of the League of the South, then called the Southern League. See their Web site at http://www.dixienet.org.

BIBLIOGRAPHY

Primary Sources

Manuscript Collections

Archival and Personal Papers

Author's Personal Collection

Flyer: Americans for the Preservation of the White Race Parents for Segregation

Program: Neshoba County Fair Souvenir Program, 2002

Duke University Library, Durham, North Carolina

Special Collections: Thomas Nelson Page Papers

Mississippi Department of Archives and History, Jackson, Mississippi

"Brief Historical Data and Preview of Mississippi Fairs, 1940"

Governor's Office—Administration of James K. Vardaman, Letterbook

Governor's Office—Administration of James K. Vardaman, Correspondence

George C. Osborn Collection, Accretion

George C. Osborn Collection–John Sharp Williams, Correspondence

John Sharp Williams Papers

"Neshoba County Fair" Subject File

Magazines

Newsweek

Time

U.S. News and World Report

Newspapers

Mississippi

Biloxi Sun Herald

Brandon Free State

Brookhaven Semi-Weekly Leader

Daily Mississippian

Greenwood Commonwealth

Jackson Clarion-Ledger

Jackson Daily News

Jackson Northside Sun

Lincoln County Times

McComb City Enterprise

Meridian Star

Meridian Weekly Star

Neshoba Democrat

Vardaman's Weekly

Vicksburg Golden Rule

Yazoo Herald

Other

Memphis Scimitar

New Orleans Times-Democrat

New Orleans Times-Picayune

New York Times

Published Primary Sources

"Acceptance and Unveiling of the Statues of Jefferson Davis and James Z. George," Proceedings in the Congress and in Statuary Hall, United States Capitol, 72d Congress, 1st Session, Senate Document No. 103. Washington, D.C.: Government Printing Office, 1932.

Alderman, Edwin A., Joel Chandler Harris, and Charles W. Kent, ed. *The Library of Southern Literature*. 17 vols. New Orleans: Martin & Hoyt, 1907–23.

Ballagh, James Curtis. "Editor's Introduction." *The South in the Building of the Nation*. Richmond, Va.: Southern Historical Publication Society, 1909.

———. *A History of Slavery in Virginia*. Baltimore: Johns Hopkins University Press, 1902.

Ballagh, James Curtis, ed. *The Letters of Richard Henry Lee*. New York: Macmillan, 1911.

Baskervill, W. M, and others. *Southern Writers*. 2 vols. Nashville: Church, 1897 and 1902.

Bassett, John Spencer. "Slavery in the State of North Carolina [orig. ed. 1899]." In *Early Studies of Slavery By States*. Edited by Donald Franklin Joyce. Northbrook, Ill.: Metro Books, 1972.

Bledsoe, Albert Taylor. *Is Davis a Traitor, or, Was Secession a Constitutional Right Previous to the War of 1861?* Baltimore: Innes, 1866.

Bowers, Claude. *The Tragic Era: The Revolution After Lincoln*. New York: Blue Ribbon Books, 1929.

Brady, Tom P. *Black Monday: Segregation or Amalgamation, America Has Its Choice*. Winona, Miss.: Association of Citizens' Councils, 1955.

Bureau of Governmental Research. *Inaugural Addresses of the Governors of Mississippi, 1890–1980*. Oxford: University of Mississippi, 1980.

Cable, George Washington. *The Grandissimes: A Story of Creole Life*. New York: Scribner's, 1880.

———. *The Silent South.* New York: Scribner's 1885.

Chandler, J. A. C., Franklin L. Riley, James Curtis Ballagh, John Bell Henneman, Edwin Mims, Thomas E. Watson, Samuel Chiles Mitchell, and Walter Lynwood Fleming, eds. "Editors' Introduction." In *The South in the Building of the Nation.* 12 vols. Richmond, Va.: Southern Historical Publication Society, 1909.

Chandler, Julian A. C. "Introductory Outline to the History of the States." In *The South in the Building of the Nation.* Vol. 4. Edited by Franklin L. Riley. 12 vols. Richmond, Va.: Southern Historical Publication Society, 1909.

———. "Preface." In *Genesis and Birth of the Federal Constitution.* Edited by J. A. C. Chandler. New York: Macmillan, 1924.

Chandler, Julian A. C., and William Foushee. *Virginia.* New York: Macmillan, 1902.

Coody, Archibald S. *Biographical Sketches of James Kimble Vardaman.* Jackson, Miss.: A. S. Coody, 1922.

Dabney, R. L. *A Defense of Virginia and the South.* 1867; reprint, Harrisonburg, Va.: Sprinkle, 1977.

Davis, Jefferson. *The Rise and Fall of the Confederate Government.* New York: Appleton, 1881.

Dickson, Harris. *An Old-Fashioned Senator: A Story-Biography of John Sharp Williams.* New York: Frederick A. Stokes Company, 1925.

Dixon, Thomas W., Jr. *The Clansman: An Historical Romance of the Ku Klux Klan.* 1905. Reprint with an introduction by Thomas D. Clark. Lexington: University Press of Kentucky, 1970.

———. *The Leopard's Spots; A Romance of the White Man's Burden—1865–1900.* New York: Doubleday, Page, 1903.

Du Bois, W. E. B. *The Suppression of the African Slave-Trade to the United States of America, 1638–1870.* New York: Schocken, 1969; orig. ed. 1896.

———. "Review of American Negro Slavery." *American Political Science Review* 12 (November 1918): 722.

Dunning, William A. *Essays on the Civil War and Reconstruction.* New York: Macmillan, 1897.

Fears, Darryl. "Hue and Cry on 'Whiteness Studies.'" *Washington Post,* 20 June 2003.

Federal Writers' Project of the Works Progress Administration. *Mississippi: The WPA Guide to the Magnolia State.* 1938, reprint, Jackson: University Press of Mississippi, 1988.

Fulton, Maurice Garland. *Southern Life in Southern Literature: Selections of Representative Prose and Poetry.* Boston: Ginn and Company, 1917.

Garner, James W. "A Mississippian on Vardaman." *Outlook* 75 (12 September 1903): 139.

Gildersleeve, Basil Lanneau. "The Creed of the Old South." In *Southern Life in Southern Literature: Selections of Representative Prose and Poetry.* Edited by Maurice Garland Fulton. Boston: Ginn and Co., 1917.

Gordon, Armistead. "Thomas Nelson Page: An Appreciation." *Scribner's Magazine* (January 1923): 79–80.

Hamilton, J. G. De Roulhac. "History in the South—A Retrospect of Half a Century." *North Carolina Historical Review* 31 (April 1954): 173–81.

——. "The South in Political Parties, 1789–1860." In *The South in the Building of the Nation*. Edited by Franklin L. Riley. 12 vols. Richmond, Va.: Southern Historical Publication Society, 1909.

Harris, Joel Chandler. Introduction to *Songs of the South*. Edited by Jennie Thornley Clarke. 1896; reprint, Garden City, N.Y., and New York: Doubleday, Page, 1913.

——. *Life of Henry W. Grady*. New York: Cassell Publishing Co., 1890.

Hart, Albert Bushnell. *The American Nation: A History: National Ideals Historically Traced, 1607–1907*. New York: Harper & Bros., 1907.

Henneman, John Bell. "Shall Virginians Write Virginian History?" *Hampden-Sidney Magazine* 10 (November 1892): 4.

Herbert, Hilary A., ed. *Why the Solid South?* New York: Negro Universities Press, 1969; orig. ed. 1890.

Holliday, Carl. *A History of Southern Literature*. New York: Neale Publishing Co., 1906.

Hubner, Charles W. *Representative Southern Poets*. New York: Neale Publishing Co., 1906.

Jelks, William Dorsey. "The Acuteness of the Negro Question." *North American Review* 174 (15 February 1907): 391–94.

Jervey, Theodore D. "Review of American Negro Slavery." *American Historical Review* 25 (October 1919): 117.

Johnston, Joseph E. *Narrative of Military Operations Directed, During the Late War Between the States*. New York: Appleton, 1874.

Jones, Frederick Robertson. "History of Taxation in Connecticut, 1636–1776." *Johns Hopkins University Studies in Historical and Political Science* 14, no. 8 (August 1896): 3–71.

Kent, Charles W. *The Revival of Interest in Southern Letters*. Richmond, Va.: B. F. Johnson Publishing Co., 1900.

King, Grace. *Memories of a Southern Woman of Letters*. New York: MacMillan, 1932.

London, Jack. *The Son of the Wolf*. Boston: Houghton Mifflin, 1900.

——. *South Sea Tales*. New York: Macmillan, 1911.

McDonald, James J. *Life in Old Virginia*. Norfolk, Va.: Old Virginia Publishing Co., 1907.

Manly, Louise. *Southern Literature, from 1579–1895*. Richmond, Va.: B. F. Johnson Publishing Co., 1895.

Mims, Edwin. "Woodrow Wilson: The Happy Warrior." *Methodist Quarterly Review* (April 1924): 9–10

——. "Southern Fiction after the War of Secession." In *The South in the Building of the Nation*. Edited by Franklin L. Riley. 12 vols. Richmond, Va.: Southern Historical Publication Society, 1909.

——. "Thomas Nelson Page." *Southern Writers, Biographical and Critical Studies*. Nashville: Church, 1903.

Mims, Edwin, and Bruce R. Payne. *Southern Prose and Poetry for Schools*. New York: Scribner's, 1910.

Mississippi Code of 1972, As Amended. SEC. 65-3-71.8; available at: http://www.mscode.com/free/statutes/65/003/0071.8.htm. Accessed 1 November 2003.

Moses, Montrose J. *The Literature of the South.* New York: T. Y. Crowell, 1910.

Orgain, Kate. *Southern Authors in Poetry and Prose.* New York: Neale Publishing Co., 1908.

Page, Rosewell. *Thomas Nelson Page: A Memoir of a Virginia Gentleman.* New York: Scribner's, 1923.

Page, Thomas Nelson. "Marse Chan." In *Ole Virginia, Or, Marse Chan and Other Stories,* Southern Classic Series. Edited by M. E. Bradford. Nashville: J. S. Sanders, 1991.

———. "The Gray Jacket of "No. 4." In *The Burial of the Guns and Other Stories.* New York: Scribner's, 1894; available online at http://www.pinkmonkey.com/dl/library1/digi111.pdf. Accessed 18 November 2003.

———. "Uncle Gabe." In *The Novels, Stories, Sketches, and Poems of Thomas Nelson Page,* Plantation Edition. New York: Scribner's, 1906–18.

———. "Marse Chan." *Century* 27 (April 1884): 932–42.

———. "Meh Lady: A Story of the War." *Century* 32 (October 1886): 187–96.

———. *The Negro: The Southerner's Problem.* New York: Scribner's, 1904.

———. *The Old Dominion; Her Making and Her Manners.* New York: Scribner's, 1908.

———. *The Old South: Essays Social and Political.* New York: Scribner's, 1905.

———. *Red Rock; A Chronicle of Reconstruction.* 1898. Reprint, New York: Grosset & Dunlap, 1904.

Painter, F. V. N. *Poets of the South.* New York: American Book Co., 1903.

Palmer, Frederick. "Williams-Vardaman Campaign." *Collier's* 39 (27 July 1907): 11–12.

Parker, Alton B. "American Constitutional Government." In *Genesis and Birth of the Federal Constitution.* Edited by J. A. C. Chandler. New York: Macmillan, 1924.

Payne, L. W., Jr. "Program of the Group-Study Course in Southern Literature." Gonzales, Tex.: Inquirer Print, [1914?].

Payne, Leonidas Warren, Jr., ed. *Southern Literary Readings.* Chicago: Rand McNally, 1913.

Phillips, U. B. *American Negro Slavery; Survey of the Supply, Employment and Control of Negro Labor as Determined by the Plantation Régime.* 1918. Reprint, New York: D. Appleton & Co., 1928.

———. "The Plantation as a Civilizing Factor." *Sewanee Review* 12 (July 1904): 257–67.

Phillips, Ulrich Bonnell. "Racial Problems, Adjustments and Disturbances." In *The South in the Building of the Nation.* Edited by Franklin L. Riley. Vol. 4. Richmond, Va.: Southern Historical Publication Society, 1909.

Putnam, Harrington. "The Constitution in the Making." In *Genesis and Birth of the Federal Constitution.* Edited by J. A. C. Chandler. New York: Macmillan, 1924.

Riley, Franklin L. "Colonial Origins of New England Senates." *Johns Hopkins University Studies in Historical and Political Science* 14, no. 3 (March 1896): 5–76.

Rowland, Dunbar. *History Of Mississippi: The Heart Of The South.* 2 vols. Chicago: S. J. Clarke, 1925.

———. *Mississippi; Comprising Sketches of Counties, Towns, Events, Institutions, and Persons, Arranged in Cyclopedia Form.* 4 vols. 1907. Reprint, Spartanburg, S.C.: Reprint Company, 1976.

Rutherford, Mildred Lewis. *The South in History and Literature. A Handbook of Southern Authors, from the Settlement of Jamestown, 1607, to Living Writers.* Atlanta: Franklin-Turner, 1906.

———. *Truths of History: A Historical Perspective of the Civil War from the Southern Viewpoint.* 1914; reprint, Atlanta: Southern Lion Books, 1998.

Snavely, Tipton R. "Review of American Negro Slavery." *American Economic Review* 10 (1920): 336.

Southern Historical Society. *Southern Historical Society Tracts* 1 (January 1876). Millwood, N.Y.: Kraus Reprint Co., 1977.

Southern History Association. "Historical Sketch of the Association." *Publications of the Southern History Association* (January 1897): 4–5.

Stephens, Alexander. *A Constitutional View of the Late War Between the States; Its Causes, Character, Conduct and Results. Presented in a Series of Colloquies at Liberty Hall.* Philadelphia: National Publishing Co., 1868.

Studies in Southern History and Politics Inscribed to William Archibald Dunning. New York: Columbia University Press, 1914.

Thompson, Holland. *The New South.* New Haven, Conn.: Yale University Press, 1919.

Tourgée, Albion. *A Fool's Errand.* New York: Fords, Howard and Hulbert, 1879.

———. "The South a Field for Fiction." *Forum* 6 (1888–89): 406–8.

Trent, W. P., and John Bell Henneman, ed. *The Best American Tales.* New York: Thomas Y. Crowell, 1907.

Trent, William P. "The Diversity Among Southerners." In *Southern Life in Southern Literature: Selections of Representative Prose and Poetry.* Edited by Maurice Garland Fulton. Boston: Ginn and Co., 1917.

———. "The Diversity Among Southerners." *Atlantic Monthly* 79 (January 1897): 42–53.

———. *Southern Statesmen of the Old Regime.* New York: Thomas Y. Crowell & Co., 1897.

———. "Tendencies of Higher Life in the South." *Atlantic Monthly* 79 (January 1897): 768.

Trent, William P., ed. *Southern Writers: Selections in Prose and Verse.* New York: Macmillan, 1905.

Turner, Frederick Jackson. "Social Forces in American History." *American Historical Review* 16 (January 1911): 217–33.

Watson, James E. *As I Knew Them.* New York: Bobbs-Merrill, 1936.

Watterson, Henry. "Address of Welcome Delivered to the Grand Army of the Republic on Behalf of the City of Louisville by Henry Watterson, at the Great Meeting at Music Hall, Louisville, Ky., [n.p.], 12 September 1895."

Weber, William Lander. *Selections from the Southern Poets.* New York: Macmillan, 1903.

Williams, John Sharp. "Issues of the War Discussed." *Confederate Veteran* 12 (November 1904); available online at: http://members.cox.net/confed/1904/article14.html. Accessed 1 November 2003.

Williams v. Mississippi. 170 US 213 1898.

Wilson, Woodrow. *A History of the American People.* New York: Harper's, 1902.

Woodard, Dudley Weldon, and Charles Banks. *Negro Progress in a Mississippi Town, Being a Study of Conditions in Jackson, Mississippi.* Cheyney, Pa.: Committee of Twelve for the Advancement of the Interests of the Negro Race, 1909.

Secondary Sources

Articles

Arnesen, Eric. "Whiteness and the Historians' Imagination." *International Labor and Working Class History* 60 (Fall 2001): 2–32.

Bailey, Fred A. "Free Speech and the 'Lost Cause' in Texas: A Study of Social Control in the New South." *Southwestern Historical Quarterly* 97 (January 1994): 452–77.

———. "Mildred Lewis Rutherford and the Patrician Cult of the Old South." *Georgia Historical Quarterly* 78 (Fall 1994): 509–35.

Bolton, Charles C. "The Last Stand of Massive Resistance: Mississippi School Integration, 1970." *Journal of Mississippi History* 61 (Winter 1999): 329–50.

Case, Sarah H. "The Historical Ideology of Mildred Lewis Rutherford: A Confederate Historians' New South Creed." *Journal of Southern History* 68 (August 2002): 599–628.

Conkin, Paul K. "Hot, Humid, and Sad." *Journal of Southern History* 64 (February 1998): 3–22.

Dykeman, Wilma. "The Southern Demagogue." *Virginia Quarterly Review* 33 (Autumn 1957): 558–69.

Eagles, Charles W. "'The Fight for Men's Minds': The Aftermath of the Ole Miss Riot of 1962." *Journal of Mississippi History* 71 (Spring 2009): 1–53.

Flusche, Michael. "Thomas Nelson Page: The Quandary of a Literary Gentleman." *Virginia Magazine of History and Biography* 84 (December 1976): 464–85.

Foster, Gaines M. "Mirage in the Sahara of the Bozart: The Library of Southern Literature." *Mississippi Quarterly* 28 (Winter 1974–75): 3–19.

Gilmore, Glenda Elizabeth. "'One of the Meanest Books': Thomas Dixon Jr., and *The Leopard's Spots.*" *North Carolina Literary Review* 2, no. 1 (Spring 1994): 87–101.

Grantham, Dewey. "Review Essay: The Contours of Southern Progressivism." *American Historical Review* 86 (December 1981): 1039–59.

Hall, Jacquelyn Dowd. "'You Must Remember This': Autobiography as Social Critique." *Journal of American History* 85 (September 1998): 439–65.

Holt, Thomas C. "Marking: Race, Race-Making, and the Writing of History." *American Historical Review* 100 (February 1995): 1–20.

Kerber, Linda. "Separate Spheres, Female Worlds, Woman's Place: The Rhetoric of Women's History." *Journal of American History* 75 (June 1988): 9–39.

Kerber, Linda, Nancy F. Cott, Robert Gross, Lynn Hunt, Carroll Smith-Rosenberg, and Christine M. Stansell. "Beyond Roles, Beyond Spheres: Thinking about Gender in the Early Republic" *William and Mary Quarterly* 3, no. 46 (July 1989): 565–85.

Kinney, James. "The Rhetoric of Racism: Thomas Dixon and the 'Damned Black Beast.'" *American Literary Realism, 1870–1910* 15 (Autumn 1982): 145–54.

Kirshenbaum, Andrea Meryl. "'The Vampire that Hovers Over North Carolina': Gender, White Supremacy, and the Wilmington Race Riot of 1898." *Southern Cultures* 4 (Fall 1998): 6–30.

Lago, Barbara. "Path to Power." *UM Lawyer* (Fall–Winter 2002–3); available at: http://www.olemiss.edu/depts/law_school/UM%20LAWYER/UMlaw/pathtopower.html. Accessed 1 November 2003

McLemore, Nannie Pitts. "James K. Vardaman: A Mississippi Progressive." *Journal of Mississippi History* 24 (February 1967): 1–11.

MacKethan, Lucinda H. "Thomas Nelson Page: The Plantation as Arcady." *Virginia Quarterly Review* 54 (1978): 314–32.

Martin, Matthew R. "The Two-Faced New South: The Plantation Tales of Thomas Nelson Page and Charles W. Chesnutt." *Southern Literary Journal* 30 (Spring 1998): 17–36.

Osborn, George C. "Mississippi's Closest Senatorial Contest: John Sharp Williams and James K. Vardaman, 1907." *Journal of Mississippi History* 12 (1950): 192–224.

Ownby, Ted. "'Does the South Still Exist?': A Historian's Critique of the Question." *Crossroads: A Journal of Southern Culture* 5 (Spring 1998): 3–12.

Patterson, Carolyn Bennett. "Mississippi's Grand Reunion at the Neshoba County Fair." *National Geographic* 157 (June 1980): 854–66.

Savage, Kirk. "The Life of Memorials," *Harvard Design Magazine* 9 (Fall 1999): 1–5; available online at http://www.gsd.harvard.edu/research/publications/hdm/back/9savage.pdf. Accessed 3 October 2003.

Smith, John David. "The Historiographic Rise, Fall, and Resurrection of Ulrich Bonnell Phillips." *Georgia Historical Quarterly* 66 (1981): 138–53.

Stephenson, Wendell H. "A Half Century of Southern Historical Scholarship." *Journal of Southern History* 11 (February 1945): 4–8.

——. "Herbert B. Adams and Southern Historical Scholarship at the Johns Hopkins University." *Maryland Historical Magazine* 42 (March 1947): 1–20.

——. "History of the South in Colleges and Universities, 1925–26." *Historical Outlook* 17 (November 1926): 319–22.

Thompson, Wright. "Ghosts of Mississippi." *ESPN Outside the Lines.* Available at http://sports.espn.go.com/espn/eticket/story?page=mississippi62. Accessed 19 March 2009.

Tompkins, Jane. "'Indians': Textualism, Morality, and the Problem of History." *Critical Inquiry* 13 (Autumn 1986): 101–19.

Vicinus, Martha. "'Helpless and Unfriended': Nineteenth-Century Melodrama." *New Literary History* 8, no. 1 (Autumn 1981): 127–43.

Vickers, Ovid. "Neshoba's Folk Fair." *Mississippi Folklore Register* 11 (Spring 1977): 11–17.

Watts, Trent. "'Mississippi's Giant House Party': Being White at the Neshoba County Fair." *Southern Culture* 8 (Summer 2002): 38–55.

Welter, Barbara. "The Cult of True Womanhood: 1820–1860." *American Quarterly* 18 (Summer 1966): 151–74.

Books

Anderson, Benedict. *Imagined Communities: Reflections on the Origins and Spread of Nationalism*. New York: Verso, 1983.

Applebone, Peter. *Dixie Rising: How the South is Shaping American Values, Politics, and Culture*. New York: Harcourt Brace, 1996.

Appleby, Joyce, Lynn Hunt, and Margaret Jacob. *Telling the Truth About History*. New York: Oxford University Press, 1994.

Armstrong, Nancy. *Desire and Domestic Fiction: A Political History of the Novel*. New York: Oxford University Press, 1987.

Arsenault, Raymond. *The Wild Ass of the Ozarks: Jeff Davis and the Social Bases of Southern Politics*. Knoxville: University of Tennessee Press, 1988.

Ayers, Edward L. *The Promise of the New South: Life After Reconstruction*. New York: Oxford University Press, 1992.

———. "What We Talk about When We Talk about the South." In *All Over the Map: Rethinking American Regions*. Edited by Edward L. Ayers, Patricia Nelson Limerick, Stephen Nissenbaum, and Peter Onuf. Baltimore: Johns Hopkins University Press, 1996.

Babb, Valerie. *Whiteness Visible: The Meaning of Whiteness in American Literature and Culture*. New York: New York University Press, 1998.

Bardaglio, Peter W. *Reconstructing the Household: Families, Sex, and the Law in the Nineteenth-Century South*. Chapel Hill: University of North Carolina Press, 1995.

Barrett, Russell H. *Integration at Ole Miss*. Chicago: Quadrangle, 1965.

Bassett, John E., ed. *Defining Southern Literature: Perspectives and Assessments, 1831–1952*. Madison, N.J.: Fairleigh Dickinson University Press, 1997.

Basso, Matthew, Laura McCall, and Dee Garceau, ed. *Across the Great Divide: Cultures of Manhood in the American West*. New York: Routledge, 2001.

Bederman, Gail. *Manliness and Civilization: A Cultural History of Gender and Race in the United States, 1880–1917*. Chicago: University of Chicago Press, 1995.

Bercaw, Nancy D. *Gendered Freedoms: Race, Rights and the Politics of Household in the Delta, 1861–1875*. Gainesville: University Press of Florida, 2003.

Blight, David W. *Race and Reunion: The Civil War in American Memory*. Cambridge, Mass.: Harvard University Press, 2001.

Boym, Svetlana. *The Future of Nostalgia*. New York: Basic Books, 2001.

Boles, John B. *The South Through Time: A History of an American Region*. Englewood Cliffs, N.J.: Prentice Hall, 1995.

Bolton, Charles C. *The Hardest Deal of All: The Battle Over School Integration in Mississippi, 1870–1980*. Jackson: University Press of Mississippi, 2005.

Bond, Bradley G. *Mississippi: A Documentary History*. Jackson: University Press of Mississippi, 2003.

———. *Political Culture in the Nineteenth-Century South: Mississippi, 1830–1900*. Baton Rouge: Louisiana State University Press, 1995.

Brandfon, , Robert L. *Cotton Kingdom of the New South: A History of the Yazoo Mississippi Delta from Reconstruction to the Twentieth Century.* Cambridge, Mass.: Harvard University Press, 1967.

Brear, Holly Beachley. "We Run the Alamo, and You Don't: Alamo Battles of Ethnicity and Gender." In *Where These Memories Grow: History, Memory, and Southern Identity.* Edited by W. Fitzhugh Brundage. Chapel Hill: University of North Carolina Press, 2000.

Brooks, Cleanth. "Thematic Problems in Southern Literature." In *Southern Literary Study: Problems and Possibilities.* Edited by Louis D. Rubin and C. Hugh Holman. Chapel Hill: University of North Carolina Press, 1975.

Brooks, Peter. *The Melodramatic Imagination.* New Haven, Conn.: Yale University Press, 1976.

———. *Reading for the Plot: Design and Intention in Narrative.* Cambridge, Mass.: Harvard University Press, 1984.

Brown, Dona. *Inventing New England: Regional Tourism in the Nineteenth Century.* Washington, D.C.: Smithsonian Institution Press, 1997.

Browne, Jill Conner. *The Sweet Potato Queens' Book of Love.* New York: Three Rivers Press, 1999.

Brundage, W. Fitzhugh. *The Southern Past: A Clash of Race and Memory.* Cambridge, Mass.: Harvard University Press, 2005.

Brundage, W. Fitzhugh, ed. *Where These Memories Grow: History, Memory and Southern Identity.* Chapel Hill: University of North Carolina Press, 2000.

———. "White Women and the Politics of Historical Memory in the New South, 1880–1920." In *Jumpin' Jim Crow: Southern Politics from Civil War to Civil Rights.* Edited by Jane Dailey, Glenda E. Gilmore, and Bryant Simon. Princeton, N.J.: Princeton University Press, 2000.

Buck, Paul H. *The Road to Reunion, 1865–1900.* Boston: Little, Brown, 1937.

Burns, Wayne. *Charles Reade: A Study in Victorian Authorship.* New York: Bookman Associates, 1961.

Bynum, Victoria E. *Unruly Women: The Politics of Social and Sexual Control in the Old South.* Chapel Hill: University of North Carolina Press, 1992.

Cagin, Seth, and Philip Dray. *We Are Not Afraid: The Story of Goodman, Schwerner, and Chaney and the Civil Rights Campaign for Mississippi.* New York: Macmillan, 1988.

Cash, W. J. *The Mind of the South.* New York: Random House, 1941.

Cecelski, David, and Timothy Tyson, ed. *Democracy Betrayed: The Wilmington Race Riot of 1898 and Its Legacy.* Chapel Hill: University of North Carolina Press, 1998.

Censer, Jane Turner. *The Reconstruction of White Southern Womanhood, 1865–1895.* Baton Rouge: Louisiana State University Press, 2003.

Chalmers, David M. *Hooded Americanism: The History of the Ku Klux Klan.* Durham, N.C.: Duke University Press, 1987.

Clare, Virginia Pettigrew. *Thunder and Stars: The Life of Mildred Rutherford.* Oglethorpe, Ga.: Oglethorpe University Press, 1941.

Clark, Thomas D. *The Southern Country Editor.* Indianapolis: Bobbs-Merrill, 1948.

Clayton, Bruce. *The Savage Ideal: Intolerance and Intellectual Leadership in the South, 1890–1914.* Baltimore: Johns Hopkins University Press, 1972.

Cmiel, Kenneth. *Democratic Eloquence: The Fight over Popular Speech in Nineteenth-Century America.* New York: William Morrow, 1990.

Cobb, James C. *Away Down South: A History of Southern Identity.* New York: Oxford University Press, 2005.

———. *The Most Southern Place on Earth: The Mississippi Delta and the Roots of Regional Identity.* New York: Oxford University Press, 1992.

Cohodas, Nadine. *The Band Played Dixie: Race and the Liberal Conscience at Ole Miss.* New York: Free Press, 1997.

Cohn, David C. *The Mississippi Delta and the World: The Memoirs of David C. Cohn.* Edited by James C. Cobb. Baton Rouge: Louisiana State University Press, 1995.

Coleman, George C. *James Kimble Vardaman: Southern Commoner.* Jackson, Miss.: Hederman Brothers, 1981.

Coleman, James P. "The Mississippi Constitution of 1890 and the Final Decade of the Nineteenth Century." In *A History of Mississippi.* Edited by Richard A. McLemore. Jackson: University and College Press of Mississippi, 1973.

Cook, Raymond A. *Fire from the Flint: The Amazing Careers of Thomas Dixon.* Winston-Salem, N.C.: John F. Blair, 1968.

———. *Thomas Dixon.* New York: Twayne, 1974.

Cott, Nancy F. *The Bonds of Womanhood: "Woman's Sphere" in New England, 1780–1835.* New Haven, Conn.: Yale University Press, 1977.

Courtwright, David T. "Alcohol and Alcoholism." In *Encyclopedia of Southern Culture.* Edited by William Ferris and Charles Reagan Wilson. Chapel Hill: University of North Carolina Press, 1989.

Cox, Karen L. *Dixie's Daughters: The United Daughters of the Confederacy and the Preservation of Confederate Culture.* Gainesville: University Press of Florida, 2003.

Craycroft, Robert. *The Neshoba County Fair: Place and Paradox in Mississippi.* Starkville: Center for Small Town Research and Design, Mississippi State University, 1989.

Crespino, Joseph. *In Search of Another Country: Mississippi and the Conservative Counterrevolution.* Princeton, N.J.: Princeton University Press, 2007.

Cresswell, Stephen. *Multiparty Politics in Mississippi, 1877–1902.* Jackson: University Press of Mississippi, 1995.

———. *Rednecks, Redeemers, and Race: Mississippi After Reconstruction, 1877–1917.* Jackson: University Press of Mississippi, 2006.

Cullen, Jim. "'I's a Man Now': Gender and African American Men." In *A Question of Manhood: A Reader in U.S. Black Men's History and Masculinity.* Edited by Darlene Clark Hine and Earnestine Jenkins. Bloomington: Indiana University Press, 1999.

Daniel, Pete. *Breaking the Land: The Transformation of Cotton, Rice, and Tobacco Cultures since 1880.* Urbana: University of Illinois Press, 1985.

———. "Cotton Culture." In *Encyclopedia of Southern Culture*. Edited by William Ferris and Charles Reagan Wilson. Chapel Hill: University of North Carolina Press, 1989.

Davidson, Cathy N., and Jessamyn Hatcher, ed. *No More Separate Spheres!* Durham, N.C.: Duke University Press, 2002.

Delgado, Richard, and Jean Stefancic, ed. *Critical White Studies: Looking Beyond the Mirror*. Philadelphia: Temple University Press, 1997.

Dickson, Sam G. "Introduction." *The Reconstruction Trilogy: The Clansman, The Leopard's Spots, The Traitor*. By Thomas Dixon. Newport Beach, Calif.: Noontide Press, 1994.

Dillon, Merton L. *Ulrich Bonnell Phillips: Historian of the Old South*. Baton Rouge: Louisiana State University Press, 1985.

Dittmer, John. *Local People: The Struggle for Civil Rights in Mississippi*. Urbana and Chicago: University of Illinois Press, 1994.

Donald, David. *Liberty and Union*. Lexington, Mass.: D.C. Heath, 1978.

———. *Lincoln*. New York: Random House, 1995.

Doyle, Don H. *Nations Divided: America, Italy, and the Southern Question*. Athens: University of Georgia Press, 2002.

Doyle, William. *An American Insurrection: The Battle of Oxford, Mississippi, 1962*. New York: Doubleday, 2001.

Draaisma, Douwe. *Metaphors of Memory: A History of Ideas about the Mind*. Trans. Paul Vincent. Cambridge, U.K.: Cambridge University Press, 2000.

Dyer, Richard. *White*. London: Routledge, 1997.

Eagles, Charles W. *The Price of Defiance: James Meredith and the Integration of Ole Miss*. Chapel Hill: University of North Carolina Press, 2009.

Edwards, Laura. *Gendered Strife and Confusion: The Political Culture of Reconstruction*. Urbana and Chicago: University of Illinois Press, 1997.

———. "Law, Domestic Violence, and the Limits of Patriarchal Authority in the Antebellum South." In *Gender and the Southern Body Politic*. Edited by Nancy Bercaw. Jackson: University Press of Mississippi, 2000.

Egerton, John. *The Americanization of Dixie: The Southernization of America*. New York: Harper's Magazine Press, 1974.

Elkins, Stanley M. *Slavery: A Problem in American Institutional and Intellectual Life*. Chicago: University of Chicago Press, 1959.

Ellison, Ralph. *Shadow and Act*. London: Secker and Warburg, 1964; reprint, New York: Vintage, 1972.

Eubanks, W. Ralph. *Ever is a Long Time: A Journey Into Mississippi's Dark Past: A Memoir*. New York: Basic Books, 2003.

Fairley, Laura Nan, and James T. Dawson. *Paths to the Past: An Overview History of Lauderdale County, Mississippi*. Meridian, Miss.: Lauderdale County Department of Archives and History, 1988.

Fields, Barbara J. "Race and Ideology in American History." *Region, Race, and Reconstruction Essays in Honor of C. Vann Woodward*. Edited by J. Morgan Kousser and James M. McPherson. Oxford, U.K.: Oxford University Press, 1982.

Flood, Charles Bracelen. *Lee: The Last Years.* Boston: Houghton Mifflin, 1981.

Foner, Eric. *Reconstruction: America's Unfinished Revolution, 1863–1877.* New York: Harper & Row, 1988.

Fossett, Judith Jackson. "(K)night Riders in (K)night Gowns: The Ku Klux Klan and Constructions of Masculinity." In *Race Consciousness: African-American Studies for the New Century.* Edited by Judith Jackson Fossett and Jeffrey A. Tucker; foreword by Nell I. Painter and Arnold Rampersand; introduction by Robin D. G. Kelley. New York: New York University Press, 1997.

Foster, Gaines M. *Ghosts of the Confederacy: Defeat, the Lost Cause, and the Emergence of the New South.* New York: Oxford University Press, 1987.

Fox-Genovese, Elizabeth. *Within the Plantation Household: Black and White Women of the Old South.* Chapel Hill: University of North Carolina Press, 1988.

Frederickson, George M. *The Black Image in the White Mind: The Debate on Afro-American Character and Destiny, 1817–1914.* New York: Harper and Row, 1971.

——. *White Supremacy: A Comparative Study in American and South African History.* New York: Oxford University Press, 1981.

Freeman, Douglas Southall. *The South to Posterity: An Introduction to the Writing of Confederate History.* 1939; reprint, New York: Scribner's, 1983.

Freidel, Frank. *The Splendid Little War.* Boston: Little, Brown, 1958.

Gaston, Paul M. *The New South Creed: A Study in Southern Mythmaking.* New York: Knopf, 1970.

Gebhard, Caroline. "Reconstructing Southern Manhood: Race, Sentimentality, and Camp in the Plantation Myth." In *Haunted Bodies: Gender and Southern Texts.* Edited by Anne Goodwyn Jones and Susan V. Donaldson. Charlottesville: University Press of Virginia, 1997.

Geertz, Clifford. "Thick Description: Toward an Interpretive Theory of Culture." In *The Interpretation of Cultures: Selected Essays.* 1973. Reprint, New York: Basic Books, 2000.

Gellner, Ernest. *Nations and Nationalism.* Ithaca, N.Y.: Cornell University Press, 1983.

Genovese, Eugene D. *Roll, Jordan, Roll: The World the Slaves Made.* New York: Random House, 1972.

Gillespie, Michele K., and Randal L. Hall, ed. *Thomas Dixon Jr., and the Birth of Modern America.* Baton Rouge: Louisiana State University Press, 2006.

Gilmore, Glenda E. *Gender and Jim Crow: Women and the Politics of White Supremacy in North Carolina, 1896–1920.* Chapel Hill: University of North Carolina Press, 1996.

Goldfield, David. *Still Fighting the Civil War: The American South and Southern History.* Baton Rouge: Louisiana State University Press, 2002.

Graff, Gerald. *Professing Literature: An Institutional History.* Chicago: University of Chicago Press, 1987.

Grantham, Dewey W. *The Life and Death of the Solid South: A Political History.* Lexington: University Press of Kentucky, 1988.

——. *Southern Progressivism: The Reconciliation of Progress and Tradition.* Knoxville: University of Tennessee Press, 1983.

———. *The South in Modern America: A Region at Odds*. New York: HarperPerennial, 1994.

Gray, Richard. "Foreword: Inventing Communities, Imagining Places: Some Thoughts on Southern Self-Fashioning." In *South to a New Place: Region, Literature, Culture*. Edited by Suzanne W. Jones and Sharon Monteith. Baton Rouge: Louisiana State University Press, 2002.

———. *Writing the South: Ideas of an American Region*. Cambridge, U.K.: Cambridge University Press, 1986.

Greenblatt, Stephen. "Culture." In *Critical Terms for Literary Study*. Edited by Frank Lentricchia and Thomas McLaughlin. Chicago: University of Chicago Press, 1990.

Gross, Theodore L. *Thomas Nelson Page*. New York: Twayne Publishers, 1967.

Gunning, Sandra. *Race, Rape, and Lynching: The Red Record of American Literature, 1890–1912*. New York: Oxford University Press, 1996.

Hale, Grace Elizabeth. *Making Whiteness: The Culture of Segregation in the South, 1890–1940*. New York: Pantheon, 1998.

———. "'Some Women Have Never Been Reconstructed': Mildred Lewis Rutherford, Lucy M. Stanton, and the Racial Politics of White Southern Womanhood 1900–1930." In *Georgia in Black and White: Explorations in the Race Relations of a Southern State, 1865–1950*. Edited by John C. Inscoe. Athens: University of Georgia Press, 1994.

Hall, Jacquelyn Dowd, James Leloudis, Robert Korstad, Mary Murphy, Lu Ann Jones, and Christopher B. Daly. *Like a Family: The Making of a Southern Cotton Mill World*. New York: Norton, 1987.

Hamilton, Charles Granville. *Progressive Mississippi*. Aberdeen, Miss.: n. p., 1978.

Hiers, John T. "John Bell Henneman." In *Southern Writers: A Biographical Dictionary*. Edited by Robert Bain, Joseph M. Flora, and Louis D. Rubin. Baton Rouge: Louisiana State University Press, 1979.

Higham, John. *History: The Development of Historical Studies in the United States*. Princeton, N.J.: Princeton University Press, 1965.

Hobsbawn, Eric, and Terence Ranger, ed. *The Invention of Tradition*. Cambridge, U.K.: Cambridge University Press, 1983.

Hobson, Fred. *But Now I See: The White Southern Racial Conversion Narrative*. Baton Rouge: Louisiana State University Press, 1999.

———. *Tell About the South: The Southern Rage to Explain*. Baton Rouge: Louisiana State University Press, 1983.

Hoffman, Gilbert M. *Dummy Lines Through the Longleaf: A History of the Sawmills and Logging Railroads of Southwest Mississippi*. Oxford: Center for the Study of Southern Culture, University of Mississippi, 1992.

Holmes, William F. "James Kimble Vardaman." In *The Encyclopedia of Southern History*. Edited by David C. Roller and Robert W. Twyman. Baton Rouge: Louisiana State University Press, 1979.

———. *The White Chief: James Kimble Vardaman*. Baton Rouge: Louisiana State University Press, 1970.

Holt, Michael F. *The Rise and Fall of the American Whig Party: Jacksonian Politics and the Onset of the Civil War*. New York: Oxford University Press, 1999.

Holt, Thomas C. *The Problem of Race in the Twenty-First Century*. Cambridge, Mass.: Harvard University Press, 2000.

Horwitz, Tony. *Confederates in the Attic: Dispatches from the Unfinished Civil War*. New York: Pantheon, 1998.

Huie, William Bradford. *Three Lives for Mississippi*. New York: WWC Books, 1965.

Ignatiev, Noel. *How the Irish Became White*. New York: Routledge, 1995.

Inge, M. Thomas. "The Study of Southern Literature." In *The History of Southern Literature*. Edited by Louis D. Rubin Jr., Blyden Jackson, Rayburn S. Moore, Lewis P. Simpson, and Thomas Daniel Young. Baton Rouge: Louisiana State University Press, 1983.

Jacobson, Matthew Frye. *Whiteness of a Different Color: European Immigrants and the Alchemy of Race*. Cambridge, Mass.: Harvard University Press, 1998.

Johnston, Erle. *I Rolled with Ross: A Political Portrait*. Baton Rouge, La.: Moran, 1980.

———. *Mississippi's Defiant Years, 1953–1973*. Forest, Miss.: Lake Harbor, 1990.

Jordan, Winthrop. *White Over Black: American Attitudes Toward the Negro, 1550–1812*. Chapel Hill: University of North Carolina Press, 1968.

Jones, Anne Goodwyn, and Susan V. Donaldson, ed. *Haunted Bodies: Gender and Southern Texts*. Charlottesville: University Press of Virginia, 1997.

Joyce, Donald Franklin, ed. *Early Studies of Slavery By States*. Northbrook, Ill.: Metro Books, 1972.

Kammen, Michael. *Mystic Chords of Memory: The Transformation of Tradition in American Culture*. New York: Vintage: 1991.

Kantrowitz, Stephen. *Ben Tillman and the Reconstruction of White Supremacy*. Chapel Hill: University of North Carolina Press, 2000.

Kasson, John F. *Houdini, Tarzan, and the Perfect Man: The White Male Body and the Challenge of Modernity in American*. New York: Hill and Wang, 2001.

Katagiri, Yasuhiro. *The Mississippi State Sovereignty Commission: Civil Rights and States' Rights*. Jackson: University Press of Mississippi, 2001.

Keller, Morton. *Affairs of State: Public Life in Late-Nineteenth Century America*. Cambridge, Mass.: Harvard University Press, 1977.

Keener, Joseph B. *Shakespeare and Masculinity in Southern Fiction: Faulkner, Simms, Page, and Dixon*. New York: Palgrave McMillan, 2008.

Key, V. O. *Southern Politics in State and Nation* Orig. ed. 1949; reprint, Knoxville: University of Tennessee Press, 1984.

Kirby, Jack Temple. *Darkness at the Dawning: Race and Reform in the Progressive South*. Philadelphia: Lippincott, 1972.

Kirwan, Albert D. *The Revolt of the Rednecks: Mississippi Politics, 1876–1925*. Lexington: University of Kentucky Press, 1951.

Kousser, J. Morgan. *The Shaping of Southern Politics: Suffrage Restriction and the Establishment of the One-Party South, 1880–1910*. New Haven, Conn.: Yale University Press, 1974.

———. "Williams v. Mississippi." In *The Encyclopedia of Southern History*. Edited by David C. Roller and Robert W. Twyman. Baton Rouge: Louisiana State University Press, 1979.

Kovecses, Zoltan. *Metaphor: A Practical Introduction.* New York: Oxford University Press, 2002.

Lambert, Frank. *The Battle of Ole Miss: Civil Rights v. States' Rights.* New York: Oxford University Press, 2010.

Lasch, Christopher. *The Culture of Narcissism: American Life in an Age of Diminishing Expectations.* New York: Norton, 1979.

Levine, Lawrence W. *The Opening of the American Mind: Canons, Culture, and History.* Boston: Beacon, 1996.

Link, Arthur S. *Wilson: The Road to the White House.* Princeton, N.J.: Princeton University Press, 1947.

———. "Woodrow Wilson: The American as Southerner." In *The Higher Realism of Woodrow Wilson and Other Essays.* Edited by Arthur S. Link. Nashville: Vanderbilt University Press, 1971.

Link, William A. *The Paradox of Southern Progressivism, 1880–1930.* Chapel Hill: University of North Carolina Press, 1992.

Link, William A., ed. *The Rebuilding of Old Commonwealths and Other Documents of Social Reform in the Progressive Era South.* Boston and New York: Bedford, 1996.

Litwack, Leon F. *Trouble in Mind: Black Southerners in the Age of Jim Crow.* New York: Knopf, 1998.

Loewen, James W., and Charles Sallis, ed. *Mississippi: Conflict and Change.* New York: Pantheon, 1974.

Logan, Rayford W. *The Betrayal of the Negro: From Rutherford B. Hayes to Woodrow Wilson.* 1954; reprint, New York: Collier Books, 1965.

Logue, Cal M., and Howard Dorgan. "The Demagogue." In *The Oratory of Southern Demagogues.* Edited by Cal M. Logue and Howard Dorgan. Baton Rouge: Louisiana State University Press, 1981.

McCardell, John. "Trent's *Simms:* The Making of a Biography." In *A Master's Due: Essays in Honor of David Herbert Donald.* Edited by William J. Cooper, Michael F. Holt, and John McCardell. Baton Rouge: Louisiana State University Press, 1985.

McCloskey, Donald N. *If You're So Smart: The Narrative of Economic Expertise.* Chicago: University of Chicago Press, 1992.

McCurry, Stephanie. *Masters of Small Worlds: Yeoman Households, Gender Relations and the Political Culture of Antebellum South Carolina.* New York: Oxford University Press, 1995.

McGerr, Michael. *A Fierce Discontent: The Rise and Fall of the Progressive Movement in America, 1870–1920.* New York: Free Press, 2003.

McLemore, Nannie Pitts. "The Progressive Era." In *A History of Mississippi.* Edited by Richard A. McLemore. Jackson: University Press of Mississippi, 1973.

McMillen, Neil R. *Dark Journey: Black Mississippians in the Age of Jim Crow.* Urbana: University of Illinois Press, 1989.

McPherson, Tara. *Reconstructing Dixie: Race, Gender, and Nostalgia in the Imagined South.* Durham, N.C.: Duke University Press, 2003.

Manring, M. M. *Slave in a Box: The Strange Career of Aunt Jemimah*. Charlottesville: University Press of Virginia, 1998.

Mars, Florence. *Witness in Philadelphia*. Baton Rouge: Louisiana State University Press, 1977.

Meier, August. *Black History and the Historical Profession, 1915–1980*. Urbana: University of Illinois Press, 1986.

Michie, Allan, and Frank Rhylic. *Dixie Demagogues*. New York: Vanguard Press, 1939.

Mississippi Official and Statistical Register, 2000–2004. n.p., 2001.

Morris, Willie. *North Toward Home*. Boston: Houghton Mifflin, 1967.

Morrison, Toni. *Playing in the Dark: Whiteness and the Literary Imagination*. Cambridge, Mass.: Harvard University Press, 1992.

Musicant, Ivan. *Empire by Default: The Spanish-American War and the Dawn of the American Century*. New York: Holt, 1998.

Nelson, Dana D. *National Manhood: Capitalist Citizenship and the Imagined Fraternity of White Men*. Durham, N.C.: Duke University Press, 1998.

Nelson, John S., Allan Megill, and Donald McCloskey. *The Rhetoric of the Human Sciences: Language and Argument in Scholarship and Public Affairs*. Madison: University of Wisconsin Press, 1991.

Newby, I. A. *Jim Crow's Defense: Anti-Negro Thought in America, 1900–1930*. Baton Rouge: Louisiana State University Press, 1965.

Novick, Peter. *That Noble Dream: The "Objectivity Question" and the American Historical Profession*. Cambridge, U.K.: Cambridge University Press, 1988.

O'Brien, Michael, ed. *All Clever Men, Who Make Their Way: Critical Discourse in the Old South*. Fayetteville: University of Arkansas Press, 1982.

——. *The Idea of the American South, 1920–1941*. Baltimore: Johns Hopkins University Press, 1979.

——. "Regionalism." In *Encyclopedia of Southern Culture*. Edited by Charles Reagan Wilson and William Ferris. Chapel Hill: University of North Carolina Press, 1989.

——. *Rethinking the American South: Essays in Intellectual History*. Baltimore: Johns Hopkins University Press, 1988.

Osborn, George C. *John Sharp Williams: Planter-Statesman of the Deep South*. Baton Rouge: Louisiana State University Press, 1943.

Oshinsky, David M. *"Worse Than Slavery": Parchman Farm and the Ordeal of Jim Crow Justice*. New York: The Free Press, 1996.

Ownby, Ted. *American Dreams in Mississippi: Consumers, Poverty, and Culture, 1830–1998*. Chapel Hill: University of North Carolina Press, 1999.

——. *Subduing Satan: Religion, Recreation and Manhood in the Rural South, 1865–1920*. Chapel Hill: University of North Carolina Press, 1990.

Painter, Nell Irvin. *Standing at Armageddon: The United States, 1877–1919*. New York: Norton, 1987.

Parish, Peter J. *Slavery: History and Historians*. New York: Harper & Row, 1989.

Parker, Joseph B., ed. *Politics in Mississippi*. 2nd ed. Salem, Wisc.: Sheffield, 2001.

Patterson, Randall G. "Edwin Mims." In *Southern Writers: A Biographical Dictionary*. Edited by Robert Bain, Joseph M. Flora, and Louis D. Rubin Jr. Baton Rouge: Louisiana State University Press, 1979.

Percy, William Alexander. *Lanterns on the Levee: Recollections of a Planter's Son*. 1941; reprint, Baton Rouge: Louisiana State University Press, 1973.

Perman, Michael. *Struggle for Mastery: Disfranchisement in the South, 1888–1908*. Chapel Hill: University of North Carolina Press, 2001.

Pope, Robert Dean. "Of the Man at the Center: Biographies of Southern Politicians from the Age of Segregation." In *Region, Race, and Reconstruction: Essays in Honor of C. Vann Woodward*. Edited by J. Morgan Kousser and James M. McPherson. Oxford, U.K.: Oxford University Press, 1982.

Potter, Stephen. *The Muse in Chains: A Study in Education*. London: Jonathan Cape, 1937.

Rabinowitz, Howard. *The First New South, 1865–1920*. Arlington Heights, Ill.: Harlan Davidson, 1992.

Rable, George. *Civil Wars: Women and the Crisis of Southern Nationalism*. Urbana: University of Illinois Press, 1989.

Rand, Clayton. *Ink On My Hands*. New York: Carrick & Evans, 1940.

Rasmussen, Birgit Brander, Eric Klinenberg, Irene J. Nexica, and Matt Wray, ed. *The Making and Unmaking of Whiteness*. Durham, N.C.: Duke University Press, 2001.

Reed, John Shelton. *The Enduring South: Subcultural Persistence in Mass Society*. Chapel Hill: University of North Carolina Press, 1974.

Riley, Sam G. *Magazines of the American South*. Westport, Conn.: Greenwood Press, 1986.

Roberts, Diane. *The Myth of Aunt Jemima: Representations of Race and Region*. London: Routledge, 1994.

Roediger, David R. *The Wages of Whiteness: Race and the Making of the American Working Class*. London: Verso, 1991.

———. *Toward the Abolition of Whiteness: Essays on Race, Politics and Working Class History*. London: Verso, 1994.

Romine, Scott. *The Narrative Forms of Southern Community*. Baton Rouge: Louisiana State University Press, 1999.

Roper, John Herbert. *U. B. Phillips: A Southern Mind*. Macon, Ga.: Mercer University Press, 1984.

Sacks, Sheldon, ed. *On Metaphor*. Chicago: University of Chicago Press, 1979.

Saxton, Alexander. *The Rise and Fall of the White Republic: Class Politics and Mass Culture in Nineteenth-Century America*. New York: Verso, 2003; orig. ed. 1990.

Scarborough, William K. *Masters of the Big House: Elite Slaveholders of the Mid-Nineteenth-Century South*. Baton Rouge: Louisiana State University Press, 2003.

Schivelbusch, Wolfgang. *The Culture of Defeat: On National Trauma, Mourning, and Recovery*. New York: Metropolitan Books, 2003.

Schwartz, Lawrence H. *Creating Faulkner's Reputation: The Politics of Modern Literary Criticism*. Knoxville: University of Tennessee Press, 1988.

Scott, Anne Firor. *The Southern Lady: From Pedestal to Politics, 1830–1930*. Chicago: University of Chicago Press, 1970.

Showalter, Elaine. *Sexual Anarchy*. New York: Penguin, 1990.

Shumway, David R. *Creating American Civilization: A Genealogy of American Literature as an Academic Discipline*. Minneapolis: University of Minnesota Press, 1994.

Silber, Nina *The Romance of Reunion: Northerners and the South, 1865–1900*. Chapel Hill: University of North Carolina Press, 1993.

Silver, James W. *Mississippi: The Closed Society*. New York: Harcourt, Brace, 1964.

Simkins, Francis Butler. *Pitchfork Ben Tillman: South Carolinian*. Baton Rouge: Louisiana State University Press, 1944.

Skates, John Ray. *Mississippi: A Bicentennial History*. New York: W. W. Norton, 1979.

Skowronek, Stephen. *Building a New American State: The Expansion of National Administrative Capacities, 1877–1920*. Cambridge, U.K.: Cambridge University Press, 1982.

Smith, John David. *An Old Creed for the New South: Proslavery Ideology and Historiography, 1865–1918*. Westport, Conn.: Greenwood Press, 1985.

Sokol, Jason. *There Goes My Everything: White Southerners in the Age of Civil Rights, 1945–1975*. New York: Knopf, 2006.

Sollors, Werner. *The Invention of Ethnicity*. New York: Oxford University Press, 1989.

Stephenson, Wendell Holmes. *The South Lives in History: Southern Historians and Their Legacy*. Baton Rouge: Louisiana State University Press, 1955.

Stokes, Mason. *The Color of Sex: Whiteness, Heterosexuality, and the Fictions of White Supremacy*. Durham, N.C.: Duke University Press, 2001.

Strickland, William M. "James Kimble Vardaman: Manipulation Through Myths in Mississippi." In *The Oratory of Southern Demagogues*. Edited by Cal M. Logue and Howard Dorgan. Baton Rouge: Louisiana State University Press, 1981.

Stubbs, Steven H. *Mississippi's Giant Houseparty: The History of the Neshoba County Fair*. Philadelphia, Miss.: Dancing Rabbit Press, 2005.

Sundquist, Eric J. *To Wake the Nations: Race in the Making of American Literature*. Cambridge, Mass.: Harvard University Press, 1993.

Taylor, William R. *Cavalier and Yankee: The Old South and American National Character*. New York: Braziller, 1961.

Thompson, Julius E. *The Black Press in Mississippi, 1865–1985: A Directory*. West Cornwall, Conn.: Locust Hill Press, 1988.

Tindall, George B. *The Emergence of the New South, 1913–1945*. Baton Rouge: Louisiana State University Press, 1967.

Tindall, George B., ed. *The Pursuit of Southern History: Presidential Addresses of the Southern Historical Association, 1935–1963*. Baton Rouge: Louisiana State University Press, 1964.

Tompkins, Jane. *Sensational Designs: The Cultural Work of American Fiction, 1790–1860*. New York: Oxford University Press, 1985.

Trachtenberg, Alan. *The Incorporation of America: Culture and Society in the Gilded Age*. New York: Hill and Wang, 1982.

Turner, Arlin. "Dim Pages in Literary History." In *Southern Literary Study: Problems and Possibilities*. Edited by Louis D. Rubin Jr. and C. Hugh Holman. Chapel Hill: University of North Carolina Press, 1975.

Urofsky, Melvin. "Josephus Daniels." In *The Encyclopedia of Southern History*. Edited by David C. Roller and Robert W. Twyman. Baton Rouge: Louisiana State University Press, 1979.

Vanderbilt, Kermit. *American Literature and the Academy: The Roots, Growth, and Maturity of a Profession*. Philadelphia: University of Pennsylvania Press, 1986.

Walkowitz, Judith R. *City of Dreadful Delight: Narratives of Sexual Danger in Late-Victorian London*. Chicago: University of Chicago Press, 1992.

Warren, Robert Penn. *Jefferson Davis Gets His Citizenship Back*. Lexington: University Press of Kentucky, 1995; orig. ed. 1980.

Watson, Richard L., Jr. "Furnifold McLendel Simmons." In *Encyclopedia of Southern History*. Edited by David C. Roller and Robert W. Twyman. Baton Rouge: Louisiana State University Press, 1979.

Watts, Sarah. *Rough Rider in the White House: Theodore Roosevelt and the Politics of Desire*. Chicago: University of Chicago Press, 2003.

Weibe, Robert. *The Search for Order, 1877–1920*. New York: Hill and Wang, 1967.

Wheeler, Marjorie Spruill. *New Women of the New South: The Leaders of the Woman Suffrage Movement in the Southern States*. New York: Oxford University Press, 1993.

Whites, LeeAnn. *The Civil War as a Crisis in Gender: Augusta, Georgia, 1860–1890*. Athens: University of Georgia Press, 1995.

Williams, Linda. *Playing the Race Card: Melodramas of Black and White from Uncle Tom to O. J. Simpson*. Princeton, N.J.: Princeton University Press, 2001.

Williamson, Joel. *The Crucible of Race: Black-White Relations in the American South Since Emancipation*. New York: Oxford University Press, 1984.

Willis, John C. *Forgotten Time: The Yazoo-Mississippi Delta After the Civil War*. Charlottesville: University Press of Virginia, 2000.

Wills, Garry. *Lincoln at Gettysburg: The Words that Remade America*. New York: Simon & Schuster, 1992.

Wilson, Charles Reagan. *Baptized in Blood: The Religion of the Lost Cause*. Athens: University of Georgia Press, 1980.

Wilson, Edmund. *Patriotic Gore: Studies in the Literature of the American Civil War*. New York: Oxford University Press, 1962.

Woodruff, Nan Elizabeth. *American Congo: The African American Freedom Struggle in the Delta*. Cambridge, Mass.: Harvard University Press, 2003.

Woodward, C. Vann. *Origins of the New South, 1877–1913*. Baton Rouge: Louisiana State University Press, 1951.

———. *Thinking Back: The Perils of Writing History*. Baton Rouge: Louisiana State University Press, 1986.

———. "The Search for Southern Identity." In *The Burden of Southern History*. Baton Rouge: Louisiana State University Press, 1968.

———. *Tom Watson: Agrarian Rebel*. New York: Macmillan, 1938.

Wray, Matt, and Annalee Newitz, ed. *White Trash: Race and Class in America*. New York: Routledge, 1997.

Wright, Richard. *White Man, Listen!* New York: Doubleday, 1957.

Wyatt-Brown, Bertram. *The House of Percy: Honor, Melancholy, and Imagination in a Southern Family*. New York: Oxford University Press, 1994.

Theses and Dissertations

Bolian, Orleane Pope. "The Meaning of James K. Vardaman." Master's thesis, Tulane University, 1933.

Boschert, Thomas N. "A Family Affair: Mississippi Politics, 1882–1932." PhD diss., University of Mississippi, 1995.

Brackett, Jeffrey R. "The Negro In Maryland: A Study of the Institution of Slavery." PhD diss., Johns Hopkins University, 1889.

Catsam, Derek C. "The Jackass Brays: Massive White Resistance to the Integration of Ole Miss." Master's thesis, University of North Carolina at Charlotte, 1996.

Cooley, Henry Scofield. "A Study of Slavery in New Jersey." PhD diss., Johns Hopkins University, 1896.

Hoehler, Daniel Miles. "Thomas P. Brady." Master's thesis, University of Mississippi, 1998.

Holman, Harriet. "The Literary Career of Thomas Nelson Page, 1884–1910." PhD diss., Duke University, 1947.

Johnson, Bethany Leigh. "Regionalism, Race, and the Meaning of the Southern Past: Professional History in the American South, 1896–1961." PhD diss., Rice University, 2001.

Larson, Allan Louis. "Southern Demagogues: A Study in Charismatic Leadership." PhD diss., Northwestern University, 1964.

Web sites

American Association of University Women's opposition to the nomination of Charles Pickering; available at http://www.aauw.org/about/newsroom/press_releases/pickering.cfm. Accessed 30 December 2003.

Council of Conservative Citizens Web site; available at http://www.cofcc.org/ourwar2.htm. Accessed 10 February 2003.

Essays, articles, and court decisions on recent Confederate flag controversies in the South, including the 2001 Mississippi state flag referendum. See the archive maintained by the University of Mississippi School of Law; available at http://library.law.olemiss.edu/library/news/flag.shtml. Accessed 11 May 2003.

Jim Giles Web site; available at http://www.rebelarmy.com. Accessed 24 December 2003.

National Statuary Hall; available at http://www.aoc.gov/cc/art/nsh/nsh_coll_origin.htm. Accessed 16 December 2003.

Neshoba County Fair's official Web site, available at http://www.neshobacountyfair.org/countyfair.htm. Accessed 24 September 2009.

"The Neshoba County Fair: It's a Southern Thing." Available at www.jackkean.com/fair.html. Accessed 25 May 2000.

"Philadelphia, Mississippi and Neshoba County." Available at www.neshoba.org. Accessed 24 September 2009.

Southern League Web site. Available at http://www.dixienet.org. Accessed 20 May 2001.

INDEX

xxxi, 11, 18, 19, 61, 70, 120, 135, 153, 155;
alcohol related to, 69–70; in Dixon's
work, 62, 66; political, 53–54
divisions: tropes of, 65; white denial of,
xv–xvi, xxv, 32, 57, 166n37. *See also* racial
differences
Dixon, Thomas W., Jr., xxx, 41–44, 172n35,
180n32, 181n44, 181n47, 181n48, 182n50;
The Leopard's Spots, xxx, 38, 58–82,
84, 182n49, 187n35; literary criticism
of, 59–60, 66, 86; model of African
Americans, 82, 84; Page compared to,
62–63; portrayals of white men, 55, 154;
racialized narratives of, 85, 124–25, 136;
rhetoric of, xx, xxxi–xxxii; Vardaman
compared to, 43, 44, 61, 83, 84, 136,
172n35
Dodd, William E., 106, 108
domesticity, white, xxxii, 8, 54, 63, 66, 141;
African-American threats to, xxi, 14, 72,
83; literary explorations of, 47, 51, 61;
narratives of, xxi, xxx, 9, 32, 44; political
uses of, 10–11; rhetoric of, xvii, 163n7;
Victorian notions of, xvi, xxii, 31, 65.
See also family, white southern; homes,
white southern
Donald, David, 193n134
Doyle, Don H., 89
Du Bois, W. E. B., xx, 93, 106, 108, 112, 124,
181n47
Dunning, William A., 106, 108, 119, 122,
190n65

Early, Jubal, 107–8
economic status, divisions according to, 11,
44, 66, 144. *See also* symbolic economy
education, Vardaman's efforts to deny African
Americans, 5, 13–15, 175n86
Edwards, Laura, 162n6
egalitarianism, 8, 9, 42, 43, 68, 143
elections, 8, 71–72, 180n33. *See also*
Mississippi, primary elections
Elkins, Stanley M., 119
Ellison, Ralph, 177n128
emancipation, xx–xxi, 59, 61, 109, 133

equality, 78, 134; language of, 142–43; racial,
24, 64, 80, 127; social, 68, 72, 84, 141,
181n48
ethnicity, xv, xvi, xxiii
Eubanks, W. Ralph, 157
eugenics, 19, 178n2, 181n47

family, metaphor of, xviii, xxiii, xxviii, 5,
166n38
family, white southern, 152; African-
American men seen as threat to, 19,
32, 63, 64, 65, 72; literary explorations
of, 44, 60, 62; narratives of, 54, 159; at
Neshoba County Fair, 141, 143, 146, 151;
sanctity of, 9, 27, 40; white man's duty to
defend, 6, 36, 40, 61, 83. *See also* white
southern identity, as family
family values, xxxi, 83
Faulkner, William, 96
fiction: British, 172n36; local-color, 49, 97,
185n15; political uses of, 10–11, 30;
romance, 45, 48–49, 59, 60, 77, 181n38;
southern, 42–44, 85, 86, 106, 178n2. *See
also* Dixon, Thomas W., Jr.; novels; Page,
Thomas Nelson; plantations, tales of;
short stories
Field, Florence Lathrop, 48
Fields, Barbara J., 166n37
Fifteenth Amendment, U.S. Constitution,
Vardaman's efforts to repeal, 5, 10, 12,
26, 27, 28, 29, 32, 37
Flusche, Michael, 46
Fordice, Kirk, at Neshoba County Fair, 150,
157
Foster, Gaines M., 93, 190n70
Fox-Genovese, Elizabeth, xix
Frederickson, George M., 161n3, 166n35
Freedman's Bureau, 69
Freeman, Douglas Southall, 128–29, 184n5,
193n127
Fusion political tickets, 126

Garner, James W., 15
Gaston, Paul, 190n70
Gebhard, Caroline, 43, 52, 54–55

Johns Hopkins University, 108; slavery studies, 118–21; southern studies, 106–7

"Johnson's English Classics," 92

Johnston, Erle, 168n5

Johnston, Joseph E., 88

Kantrowitz, Stephen, xxv, 167n39

Kemper County, Mississippi, violence in, 22–23

Kennedy, Edward, 197n19

Kennedy, John F., 3

Kennedy, John Pendleton, 105

Kent, Charles W., xxiii, 93, 112

Kentucky, 189n54; Wildcats football team, 1–2

Key, V. O., xxi

King, Grace, 45

Kinney, James, 60

Kirksey, Henry, 148

Ku Klux Klan, 59, 75, 181n44

laborers: African-American, 19–20, 31; field, 32; white, xxv

Ladner, Buck, 147

Lamar, L. Q. C., xxvi

Lanier, Sidney, 185n15

Lasch, Christopher, 196n5

League of the South, 159

Lee, Richard Henry, 116

Lee, Robert E., 128; at Battle of Gettysburg, 189n60; biography of, 101, 102, 193n127; monuments to, 83, 130; surrender of, 65–66

Lee, Stephen D., 186n26

Leopard's Spots, The (Dixon), xxx, 38, 58–82, 84, 182n49, 187n35

Library of Southern Literature, 93–98, 104, 186n26

Lincoln, Abraham, 125, 131, 146, 193n134

Link, William A., 166n38

literary criticism, xxviii, 59–60, 99, 101

literary realism, 49, 51, 77, 185n15

literature, 95, 96–97; British, 98, 99, 100; French, 99, 100; German, 100. *See also* fiction; melodrama

literature, southern: anthologies of, xxx, 88–106; canon of, 93–98, 104, 105, 106, 107, 128–29; geographical distinctiveness of, 99, 185n15; Old South, 44–58, 84, 86, 101, 109; studies of, 100, 131, 134, 185n14, 186n23. *See also* writers, southern

Literature of the South, The (Moses), 103

Lodge, Henry Cabot, 17, 79

Logan, Rayford, 35

Long, Huey, 7, 8, 173n59

Longino, Andrew, 14, 38

Lost Cause, 16, 111, 121; guardians of, xix, 101, 108; memorializations of, xxvi, 190n70

Lott, Trent, 157–58; at Neshoba County Fair, 148, 150

lumber camps, 31

lynching, 38, 65, 70, 83, 134; in Mississippi, 22, 23, 24, 156; symbolic means of, 128–29

Making Whiteness (Hale), xxviii

mammy myth, 12, 120, 124, 154, 187n35

management, 134; of African Americans, 89, 118, 136, 181n47; household, 54, 55

manhood, meanings of, 10, 61, 72, 167n39, 183n62. *See also* masculinity, white southern; men, African-American; men, white southern

marriage plot novels, 77–78, 79, 80, 81–82

Mars, Florence, 139

"Marse Chan" (Page), xxx, 48, 49–58, 67, 179n20

Marx, Karl, 160

Maryland, 115, 189n54

masculinity, white southern, 42, 44, 75; Christian, 43, 63, 78; Dixon's model of, 59, 60–61, 62, 65, 67–69, 72, 74, 76–77, 81; literary representations of, 4, 58, 64, 85; narratives of, 155; in plantation tales, 54–55. *See also* men, African-American; men, white southern

Mayes, Edward, xxvi

McCurry, Stephanie, xx

McLaurin, Anselm: death of, 37; at Neshoba County Fair, 145

McLemore, Leslie, 157

Medgar Evers Homecoming Parade, 147

ONE HOMOGENEOUS PEOPLE was designed and typeset on a Macintosh computer system using InDesign software. The body text is set in 10/15 Mercury and display type is set in Trade Gothic. This book was designed and typeset by Chad Pelton, and manufactured by Thomson-Shore, Inc.